The Vegetable Passion

The Vegetable Passion

Janet Barkas

CHARLES SCRIBNER'S SONS
New York

Library of Congress Cataloging in Publication Data

Barkas, Janet.
   The vegetable passion.

   Bibliography: p.
   1. Vegetarianism.   I. Title.
TX392.B33   641.5′636   74–10983
ISBN 0–684–13925–1

1 3 5 7 9 11 13 15 17 19 C/C 20 18 16 14 12 10 8 6 4 2

Printed in the United States of America

To my Mother, Father, Eileen,
and our brother Seth's memory

Author's Note

Last summer I returned to Greenwood Lake, New York, my childhood summer retreat where this book really began. I ambled down the steep concrete to stare at the olive-colored lake. Though the long wooden dock was gone, I easily envisioned my sister Eileen, who was then eleven, bending over it.

"I've got a bite, Dad!"

My father set aside his tackle and helped Eileen pull in a shiny catfish that she had hooked through one gazing eye. Transfixed by that tug of life and death, I shared the slimy creature's anguish as I squirmed while my father removed the metal catch.

"That one's too small," he said, tossing it back into the lake.

I retained those vivid images and never again was able to see flesh food as separate from the original sea or land mammal. Then, while a junior-high-school student, I learned from a brief reference in William Shirer's *The Rise and Fall of the Third Reich* that Adolf Hitler was a vegetarian. At that point, I was still a carnivore, though a guilty one. But I pondered the implications if Hitler did in fact eschew meat: What were *his* reasons? What did that say about a meatless diet or about me? Who were other notable abstainers?

It was as a sixteen-year-old college freshman hundreds of miles from my familial roots that I enacted my ethical convictions. In addition to the practical difficulties in the dormitory cafeteria, I was constantly the focus of inquisitions and defensive reprisals. But I was too busy with academic studies to provide a more literate retort than, "I just feel it's something I *have* to do."

About three years later, in 1968, I had to prepare a five-minute discourse for a public speaking class. A historical survey of vegetarianism seemed an intriguing subject, but I failed to locate one comprehensive or up-to-date volume that treated the meatless diet in an objective or thorough way; certainly not as a distinct philosophical movement. I was also dissatisfied by the unsubstantiated claims for well-known disciples that were advanced by one-sided organizations. This seemed to me a historical distortion.

In my spare time, I continued reading original sources. Then in February of 1971, while a graduate student, I published an author's query in *The New York Times Book Review* requesting information about any famous vegetarians as well as personal testimonials. The variety, enthusiasm, and unexpected suggestions for further research in hundreds of replies convinced me of the need for a literate and scholarly book on the subject. My search began in libraries, but led me around the world.

This is *not* a book about food: it is a selective history of those notable persons and organized groups who have raised philosophical objections to a diet that includes any slaughtered creatures—persons distinguished by a culinary practice based on ideological convictions rather than taste, tradition, or poverty. In significant contrast to the meat eater, who automatically consumes animal and fish products because of flavor or custom, the vegetarian is motivated by an intricate web of beliefs. Indeed, except for certain parts of India, vegetarians are considered the societal deviants, rather than the norm.

Filet mignon is a delicacy to most Americans, just as fried termites are relished by the Congolese. If economic conditions are favorable, men are generally omnivorous—eating available plant and animal foods. Yet in spite of the presence of meat-eating since man's earliest days, it is a practice that is constantly criticized, analyzed, and modified.

Most omnivores group vegetarians into a unified faction. In fact, their meatless diets are as diversified as their theories. The word "vegetarian" was not even used until 1847, when the members of the newly formed British Vegetarian Society coined the term to describe their followers who lived on a diet of vegetables, fruits, and grains with or without the inclusion of eggs and dairy products. The Latin root of "vegetarian," however, is *vigitore*, meaning "giving strength and health" rather than "vegetable"—*arian*. The former implies a doctrine; the latter merely a diet.

Vegetarians may be divided by what they eat as well as by what they believe. Although the actual diet is far less noteworthy than the doctrines, even that is complicated by a plethora of categories. All the following vegetarians do *not* eat fish, flesh, or fowl, but there are further specifications: *lactarians* include dairy products; *ovo-lactarians* also add eggs; *vegans* refrain from eating or using *any* animal products; *fruitarians* consume just fruits; *herbivores* only plants; and *granivores* solely seeds and grains.

Those terms elucidate the dietary subdivisions of vegetarianism, but once a meatless regimen leaves the dinner plate and enters the mind, it is far from simple. To discount vegetarianism as merely a diet for radicals and fanatics is an unfair generalization. Rather, vegetarianism is a distinct philosophy, adopted by groups as dissimilar as the Pythagoreans in Greece, the Jains in India, the Doukhobors in Russia and Canada, or Seventh Day Adventists throughout the world; and by persons as contradictory as King Asoka, Leonardo da Vinci, Shelley, Hitler, or Gandhi. This book probes the extensive history and personalities submerged under the misunderstood label "vegetarian."

Contents

1

Roots

Evolutionary Trends

Just a hundred years ago, many persons still believed in the theories of Archbishop James Ussher, who affixed the creation of the earth at the year 4004 B.P.* Now, however, there is little trace of the shocks absorbed by the once radical evolutionary principles of Charles Darwin and Alfred Wallace. With each new unearthing of a fossilized human skull, animal bone, or plant, their theories of natural selection and evolution are only verified. There is no returning to an era when men believed that they were created on a particular day or women conceived from a rib. In time, those postulates will universally appear as mythological as the Hellenistic depictions of two-headed gods responsible for human failings and virtues.

Until new archeological finds can further eradicate the vast gaps in our knowledge, the collective evidence must serve as a guide to chiefly theoretical reconstructions of evolution. Now we realize that the first

---

* Before Present. This abbreviation will be consistently used in place of *B.C.* since I fail to believe that the chronology of the world should be a constant reminder of the life of one man. Because it is impractical to recalculate all dates, *B.P.* and *C.E.* (Current Era) will replace the corresponding terms *B.C.* and *A.D.*

creatures were probably insectivores which slowly, over a period of millions of years, evolved into distinct groups, such as the primates.

Of all the primates, man most closely resembles the great apes—chimpanzees and gorillas. Of course man did not descend *from* the apes. Instead, about 20 million years ago, during the Miocene Epoch, the apes and man branched off and followed unique evolutionary developments. There was probably not just one ancestral stock, but many. Yet we may only hypothesize what those creatures were like or precisely when the diversification occurred.

It is easier to point out the similarities between the *Pongid* (chimpanzees, gorillas, orangutans) and the *Hominid* (prehistory through modern man) than the differences. In skeletal structure, alimentary system, protein chemistry, and central nervous system, the apes and man are brothers. Behavioral distinctions, such as toolmaking, are differentiated only by degree since chimpanzees create and use simple tools, such as a grass stem utilized almost like a fork to extract termites from below ground.

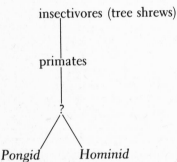

insectivores (tree shrews)

primates

?

Pongid   Hominid

Yet apes became quite specialized and characteristically display mobility by swinging. They also have large canine teeth, used mostly for ripping the outer bark of plants rather than for defense, although these discernible teeth are sometimes used in tearing apart smaller animals. Man lacks defensive teeth; eventually, he developed a far more elaborate and effective means of attack—weapons. Apes also demonstrate shrinkage or atrophy of the thumb and a comparatively limited brain capacity, although chimpanzees are now learning to "talk" with computers, through renewed efforts during the past five years.

How then did man evolve? Originally a tree dweller, for some still undetermined reason he descended and became uniquely bipedal, traveling on two legs in contrast to the rest of the quadripedal, four-legged, animal world. As a cause or an effect of this arboreal descent, his brain capacity increased to a size which, in proportion to his body weight, is unequaled by all other animals including the large-brained whale and elephant. As the brain capacity expanded, the size of the face decreased and the more obvious physical and behavioral distinctions, such as hairlessness, efficient grasping, an omnivorous diet, and warfare, gradually evolved.

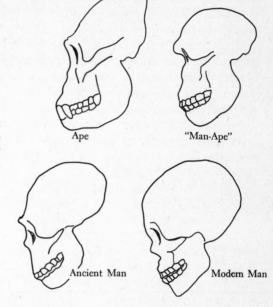

Comparison of skulls demonstrating the difference in brain area and number of canine teeth.

Ape

"Man-Ape"

Ancient Man

Modern Man

An examination of the eating habits of our closest animal relatives, chimpanzees and gorillas, is neither a justification nor an explanation for the patterns of man. But the undeniable similarities in physical structure make such an exploration a more relevant point of departure than the vegetarian cow or elephant.

Until the 1960's, chimpanzees were classified as complete vegetarians. It was then that the first-hand observations of Jane van Lawick-Goodall revealed that chimpanzees of the Gombe Stream Reserve in Tanganyika were occasional meat eaters. Chimpanzees, however, are primarily frugivorous, consuming about fifty species of fruit, as well as herbivorous, devouring over ninety species of plants and trees, leaf and leaf buds, blossoms, stems, seeds, barks, piths, and resin from tree trunks. They also chew on chunks of dead wood fiber.

At the Gombe Stream Reserve, chimpanzees averaged twelve kills each year, resulting from attacks on bay pigs, baboons, bushpigs, young and adult red Colobus monkeys, and an occasional redtail or blue monkey. They chew the meat with leaves, almost like a sandwich.

To obtain animal flesh, the chimpanzees organize into hunting parties of about thirty-five males, who attack and kill their prey, tearing their victims apart. Only twice did female chimpanzees accompany the hunters, although they always shared in eating the spoils. Chimpanzees also ate ants, termites, caterpillars, and a variety of larvae of beetles and wasps.

A consequence of meat-eating is an increase in aggressive behavior. The chimpanzees become possessive and defensive about their share of the meat, although the precise cause-and-effect relationship between meat and hostile interaction is unclear. The rarity of a carnivorous feast might enhance the greed for meat.

The Budongo Forest in Uganda, a typical rain forest, contrasts strongly with the narrow mountainous strip of Gombe Stream which stretches for ten miles along the east shore of Lake Tanganyika. It was in Uganda in 1962 that Vernon and Frances Reynolds also observed chimpanzees, but *failed* to find any evidence of meat-eating or toolmaking. Instead, the diet of the Uganda chimpanzees consisted of 90 per cent fruits, 5 per cent leaves, 4 per cent bark and stems, and 1 per cent insects. These findings are as important as those of Dr. Goodall, for they point out that we should not offer the opposite generalization in saying that *all* chimpanzees are omnivorous, like man, eating flesh as well as plants and fruits. Nor should the extent of chimpanzee meat-eating be exaggerated; they still thrive on a largely vegetarian diet.

Direct observations of gorillas in the wild to date have only reconfirmed their vegetarianism. Both Dian Fossey, studying mountain gorillas in a forest in Mount Visoke in Rwanda, and George Schaller, living among gorillas in East and Central Africa, failed to see one gorilla eat meat. Furthermore, in over 2,000 hours of direct observation, Ms. Fossey witnessed only five minutes of behavior that could possibly be termed aggressive and even that was motivated by a misconceived fear. In fact, Ms. Fossey observed that mountain gorillas will ignore animal carcasses, whether fresh or in various stages of decay when passing by them.

Gorillas are shy, gentle, ground-living creatures. Primarily herbivorous, they dine 80 percent of the time on *Galium* vines, as well as wild celery, thistles, nettles, and bamboo shoots during the rainy season. *Rubus* is the only fruit eaten throughout the year, although the blue fruits of *Pygeum* are eaten extensively after ripening in April. These large creatures do not drink water from a lake or stream, ·but absorb it indirectly from moist leaves.

Gorillas fail to share food in the wild, although this happens in captivity. In Rwanda, their last snack is consumed after they build their night nest, and experimentation with new foods seems to be left only to the juvenile gorillas.

It is significant that observed gorillas are completely vegetarian in their natural habitat, but they will eat meat if provided for them when caged in zoos. Some theorize that there is an actual change in the flora and fauna of the intestines, a chemical alteration that serves to enhance the desire for meat. Rather than a physiological explanation, however, it is more probable that the man-made environment of bars and sneering spectators inspires psychological reactions in the gorilla. Thus meat-eating in captivity is probably a manifestation of aggression due to a stressful and unnatural habitat.

Obviously the diverse eating habits of gorillas and chimpanzees fail to provide a clear-cut case for what the "natural" diet of man should be, since apes, like humans, are affected by environmental changes. Furthermore, particular apes may be as selective in their diet as various members of the same human family. Detailed studies in the wild have helped man to gain respect for the unique personality traits of each ape, which enable observers to tell them apart even after a year's separation.

Climate, of course, had an effect on the evolution of the diet of the first ape-man. The completely carnivorous menu of the ice-bound Eskimos is contemporary proof of the relationship between weather and food habits. Yet in spite of the dozens of excellent books about the earliest periods of the earth's history, most concepts that are discussed today are largely theory. In truth, our concrete knowledge of what happened 600 million years ago is infinitesimal. That in part accounts for an over-reliance on more recent history—there is simply more evidence.

The Ice Age is often considered a monumental climatic event. Yet there was not just one cold period, but a continuous vacillation between cold and warm. Documentation is available for at least four major ice ages and numerous minor ones. Nevertheless, for some hidden reason, between 12 to 7 million years ago prehominids came down from the trees. That descent was the first major step in the evolution of man and one we know very little about.

The classical explanation for the arboreal descent is that a drying up of the forests occurred which forced ground exploration for new potential food sources. Evidence, however, fails to denote a specific temperature and climate change radical enough to foster such a drastic step. There is a second theory: if you could not swing to a distant fruit-bearing tree, why not try traveling greater distances on the ground?

Or a third conjecture: perhaps the prehominids reached a progressive stage when a viable mode of life was available on the ground that would be at least as good as what they had been accustomed to in the trees. Was the descent because of curiosity, hunger, or just an accident?

Whatever the cause, prehominids became ground-living, two-legged carnivores just as baboons became ground-living, four-legged herbivores. That first step onto land was for the evolution of mankind on earth as paramount as the more recent first step on the moon will prove in the development of our exploration of the universe.

Arboreal descent was the first of five phases in the growth of man from his anthropoid origins to his position as ruler of the earth. The primary stage spanned the longest proportionate time; the next stages followed in rather quick succession. Stage two was the progressive growth of a terrestrial hunting mode of life from primarily vegetarian beginnings. Because of the success of this second stage, the population was able to diversify and disperse during the third period. Consequently came the fourth stage: the domestication of plants and animals, beginning about 10,000 B.P. We are now on the periphery of a fifth stage: man's technological mastery over all his physical needs. Scientific discoveries, now unimaginable, will enable a complete control over environment, food production, and therefore hunger, within the next few hundred years—unless destructive behavioral traits persist and interfere.

The first stage during the Pliocene Epoch, man's descent from the trees, coincides with the appearance of *Ramapithecus*, who is believed to have been the first primate who is more man than ape. Anthropologists have unintentionally intensified the difficulties in grasping the evolution of man by their habit of dubbing each anthropological find with a completely new name rather than collecting similar types under a general category. For instance, in 1961 Dr. L. S. B. Leakey found an ape-man believed to be of the same period as *Ramapithecus*, but he called it *Kenyanthropus wickeri*, after Kenya and Fred Wicker, on whose farm Leakey discovered the fossil. For convenience, *Ramapithecus*, originally discovered in 1934, will here serve as the evolutionary type that marks the ascendency of a man-ape.

Ramapithecus, mostly tree-living and probably quadrupedal, had a diet of fruits, nuts, berries, insects, grubs, eggs, young birds, and other small animals. He was probably diverging toward tougher foods, such as seeds and hard roots. Meat was typically included in his diet through scavenging since he lacked the weapons to actively hunt and kill animals. However, *Ramapithecus* was alert to the abandoned carcasses of larger animals whether they had been killed by carnivores or died of natural causes.

Various anthropologists have overemphasized the importance of the addition of meat into man's diet. Those writers dramatize the intellectual challenges of the hunt as a major force that led to adaptability, a bipedal posture, an enlarged brain capacity, and the need for toolmaking as a more efficient method of obtaining meat. Meat-eating is also suggested as a dietary change that intensified the need for community cooperation and thus a necessary ingredient to the eventual establishment of "civilization."

Yet substantial evidence for a carnivorous view of civilization is lacking. On the contrary, field observations of contemporary hunting and gathering societies around the world invalidate such a proposition. Except for Eskimos, present-day groups that still acquire food by primitive means are 80 per cent vegetarian. For example, in aboriginal Australia, even where game and fish are abundant on the northern coast, vegetables comprise 70–80 per cent of the diet.

Among the !Kung Bushmen of the Kalahari Desert, a semi-arid northwestern region in Botswana, the mongongo nut provides by weight 50 per cent of the vegetable diet. To the !Kung Bushman, mongongo nuts are as basic as staple crops, such as rice or maize, in agricultural societies. The average daily consumption per person of three hundred nuts equals about 1,260 calories and 56 grams of protein. Seven and one half ounces of mongongo nuts provide as much protein as 14 ounces of lean beef or 2½ pounds of cooked rice. These nuts are far more reliable than cultivated crops since the hard outer shell protects the inner kernel from rotting for up to twelve months after the nuts have fallen to the ground. It is, therefore, clear why the !Kung Bushmen fail to see the advantages of farming. In addition to the mongongo nut, the Bushmen have available for gathering eighty-four species of edible plants, including twenty-nine varieties of fruits, berries, and melons, and thirty types of roots and bulbs.

Anthropologist Richard B. Lee did not see one case of nutritional deficiency when he lived among the !Kung Bushmen for a two-year period in the 1960's. In fact, Lee found that two to three days of gathering each week was enough to provide a more than adequate diet for the !Kung Bushmen with an *excess* of 165 calories and 33 grams of protein. For these people, meat is a treat, rather than a staple food; protein-rich plant substitutes are available when meat is sparse. Gathering is also about two and a half times more productive than hunting. Thus if meat were as vital to hunting and gathering societies as was once believed, there would be mass starvation and nutritional deficiencies. These findings have major bearing on understanding the dietary patterns of similar communities in the remote past.

Hunting is often cited as the point in evolutionary history when men and women diverged and accepted distinct roles: the men became the more worthwhile hunters; the women stayed home, bore children, and did the more meager work of gathering seeds and vegetables. A survey of present-day hunting societies, such as the Pygmies of the African Congo, the Indians of Tierra del Fuego in South America, and so forth, demonstrates just the opposite. For among the !Kung Bushmen, the men are conscientious hunters but not particularly successful ones. The women, however, provide two or three times as much food by weight as the men. Even among the carnivorous Eskimos, it is the women who contribute the most food since they are the ones who fish; again the men are the less profitable hunters.

Returning to a survey of the establishment of the human race, or anthropogenesis, there is a void in our knowledge from the estimated appearance of *Ramapithecus* about 13 million years ago until the next link in the puzzle, *Australopithecus*, about 2 million years ago. We do know that the time of *Australopithecus*, the Pleistocene Epoch, was an unstable one, with fluctuating cold and moderating warm climate periods. There were at least four primary glaciations, or advances of the ice sheets, and numerous intermediate ones.

Raymond Dart discovered the first fossilized example of *Australopithecus* in 1924 and he named it *Australopithecus africanus*, South African ape. By this period there is a distinct change in dentition, due to a shift in diet from fruit and grass stems to seed-eating. Dr. Clifford Jolly concludes that the reduction in the canine teeth was caused by the requirements of seed-eating: front teeth capable of separating the seeds from their stems, and back teeth able to grind.

Australopithecus is divided into two definite types: *africanus* and *robustus*, which includes those specimens discovered by Leakey and Robert Broom. *Africanus*, who lived in a dry environment and was more advanced phylogenetically, is thought to have been a small-game hunter and a seed-and-vegetable gatherer. He also used tools made of bones and was agile as well as petite, weighing from 50 to 90 pounds.

Robustus, on the other hand, is believed to have been a vegetarian, who lived on roots, berries, seeds, and fruits in a stream and lake environment. Both types probably lived from about 5.5 million to 700,000 years ago. Although *robustus* was almost twice the size of *africanus*, it appears that the vegetarian-type ancient man became

Papago woman gathering cactus fruit. These North American Indians, who formerly occupied southern Arizona and North Sonora, Mexico, are a semi-sedentary tribe who farm beans, corn, and cotton and gather wild vegetable products, such as the fruit of the giant cactus and beans of the mesquite tree.

extinct whereas the meat-eating and hunting one continued to evolve and, eventually, to become a full-fledged carnivore, *Homo erectus*.

With *Homo erectus*, dated at about 500,000 B.P., geologically speaking we enter modern times. Eugene Dubois, a Dutchman, discovered the first specimen in Java in 1890–94. Dubois thought he had found an ape; three decades later Henry Fairfield Osborn, an American evolutionist, rectified Dubois's classification. Java man and other specimens of *Homo erectus*, such as Pekin man found near the capital of

Simplified Evolutionary History During the Cenozoic Era
Denoting Introduction Point of Newest Life Forms

Epoch	Years Before Present	Newest Life Form
Recent	15,000	
Pleistocene	100,000	*Homo sapiens* (modern)
	500,000	*Homo erectus* (Java, Pekin)
	2–3 million	*Australopithecus*
Pliocene	13 million	*Ramapithecus*
Miocene	25 million	Apes
Oligocene	35 million	Monkeys
Eocene	60 million	Small mammals (including first primates)
Paleocene	65 million	Placental mammals

China, depict the third ecological epoch of differentiation and population expansion in a time of geological upheaval with volcanic activity, drastic drops in temperature, and periodic expansion of ice sheets across the northern continents.

Homo erectus is clearly a member of the human race, denoted by *Homo* (man) and *erectus* (bipedal posture). However, he cannot be admitted to the classification of *Homo sapiens* because his brain capacity fails to meet the minimum accepted volume. But in his standing posture he used tools and belongs to cultures that demonstrate definite growth and sophistication from earlier stages.

There is evidence that Pekin man was a head hunter who consumed the brains and bone marrow of fellow men, as well as animals. Whether this cannibalism was an act of aggression or merely a sensible way of utilizing all the flesh of those who had died naturally is unknown, since it is presently difficult to determine if dents in the found skulls are caused by intentional blows or the fossilization process. Thus their cannibalism might have been any of three kinds: ritualistic; gustatory, because of the tastiness of human flesh; or for survival because of hunger.

Pekin man dined mostly on venison, although the remains of sheep, antelope, roebuck, small horses, and camels are also known. He was apparently a proficient hunter, yet all indications are that at this stage hunting was simply an act of necessity: there was no sport or glory attached to the kill.

Thus by no later than 100,000 B.P., *Homo sapiens* thrived and at least a hundred examples have been found in Europe—for instance, Neanderthal man in 1848 in Gibraltar, and 1856 in the Neander Valley near Dusseldorf, Germany—as well as in North Africa and Palestine. But the fossil evidence for anthropogenesis shifted from purely African origins for the first hominids to Europe, where rather abundant evidence of early cultures is provided by cave drawings and preserved artifacts.

Neanderthal man, who became extinct as a clearly recognizable type by 35,000 B.P., is the most familiar. He used fire, probably not only for cooking but also for warmth, and to drive away dangerous carnivores. He buried his dead within or just outside his caves, and there is evidence of a well-developed devotional system. For example, the careful way of burying the dead indicates a concern with immortality. In the cavern of La Ferrassie in France, newborn infants were buried in a careful pattern; another Neanderthal person was buried in Shanidar Cave, Iran, over an area covered with pine branches and flowers. Ample and varied evidence also exists for the practice of bear cults throughout Neanderthal cultures. Part of the jaws of carnivores with extending canines were used as ripping tools; and antlers, leg bones of woolly rhinoceroses, jawbones of reindeer were employed as hammers and splitting wedges. Those animals were butchered where they were killed and various parts brought back to the caves.

Unfortunately, only a few meager facts may be deduced with any certainty about the lives of Neanderthal men and women. They seem to have organized into hunting bands; however, specifics of their hunting activities or details of their family lives are lacking. We do know that they probably practiced cannibalism but what the motivation was is unknown. Although it was originally believed that Neanderthal man was exterminated by his fellow men, now it seems he simply became absorbed into later types.

However, the straight-line view of evolution as a progressive step from less primitive to more sophisticated, cultural types is no longer acceptable. There was certainly a great deal of crisscrossing; more advanced forms became extinct; other less developed types continued to advance slowly. In fact, "less intelligent" groups may have thrived in near Utopian communities, only to become evolutionary dead ends and so forever lost to our historical gleanings.

Thus from 35,000 to 8,000 B.P., the first monumental cultural revolution of human history began. That period marks the beginning of the agricultural or Neolithic revolution; hunting and gathering need never again provide the only means for nutritional survival. Although this later period of cultivation represents only 1 per cent of cultural man's history on earth, it was during this time that civilization prospered, accelerating in the artistic, scientific, and philosophical areas that are worshiped today.

The development of meat-eating therefore evolved over millions of years in several identifiable stages before the next primarily vegetarian, or agricultural, phase occurred. Those stages may be summarized as:

1. Ape-man descends from the trees where he had lived on a vegetarian diet. Gradually, meat is added by scavenging, then by eating creatures that are slow-moving and easily caught, such as tortoises, lizards, porcupines, catfish, aquatic birds, and small mammals like ground squirrels.
2. Some species continue to thrive on a purely vegetarian diet, but they become extinct—perhaps because they have no need to develop weapons and therefore cannot defend themselves against carnivorous predators.
3. The taste of meat becomes more natural and desirable. Advanced toolmaking leads to obtaining and devouring the young of larger animals. Cannibalism is practiced by certain cultures.
4. Actual hunting of larger animals becomes a natural way of life, although fruits and vegetables still form a large part of the diet during winter months, when game is harder to find. Man is now truly omnivorous, eating all types of food, although his nutritional dependency on plant foods in this pre-domestication period is usually underestimated.

Tilling the Soil

The fourth ecological stage is marked by man's control over the production of an increasing variety of plants and animals. The Middle East evidenced the development of agriculture and farming settlements and villages by 9500 B.P., North Africa by 5500 B.P., and East Africa and Burma by 3000 B.P.—obviously it was far from a "revolution." Agriculture developed during the last deglaciation, as did the domestication of various animals, such as sheep (10,800 B.P.), dogs (9500 B.P.), and cattle (8500 B.P.).

Why did man finally realize that a seed would sprout and bear food if planted and sown? Obviously the gathering of seeds had been practiced for hundreds of thousands of years, so hunger could not have been the reason for this eventual discovery or men would have pursued planting earlier. Furthermore, starving people are rarely inclined to experiment or develop new methods—all their energies are absorbed in struggling to survive. Agriculture evolved because of a combination of factors: a favorable climate with a well-diversified terrain, sedentary people, and a more highly developed brain capacity.

But within a relatively short time, agronomy became a mixed blessing. Once persons settled down to cultivate their land, problems of ownership arose. Obvious material gain from larger land holdings encouraged selfishness and hoarding. In a hunting and gathering economy, storage is impossible because of primitive methods and imminent spoilage. Sharing is not just expected but enjoyed, as among the Bushmen of Africa. Yet with the developed methods of agriculture and reliable storage, vast differences in wealth among community members arose, along with rivalry. Those with greater resources could hire others to do the less desirable work, so that social and economic classes began to emerge.

As the dependency on agriculture increased, so did the over-reliance on uncontrollable environmental factors and natural climatic events. Thus, persons were in even greater danger of mass starvation if crops failed, insects devoured harvests, or unforeseen natural disasters occurred. Group cooperation also became less important since individual family units could develop an isolated self-sufficiency. Any closeness in the evolving urban life was an illusion; the extended community family was reduced to a smaller group based on direct blood relationships.

With the domestication of plants, the population multiplied at an alarming rate and has continued to explode in almost the same geometric proportions as Thomas Malthus's nineteenth-century predictions. For example, the total world population of the early hominids about 1 million years ago was probably less than half a million. Within two or three thousand years, after the development of village farming and urban life, the population was over 100 million.

By 5000 B.P., village life flourished in Southwest Asia, with wheat, barley, lentils, peas, onions, and cucumbers as principal crops; beer was available by 4000 B.P. Other inventions came in quick succession that continued to promote village life, such as the plow, wheel, and loom. Iron was a revolutionary discovery because the ore was abundant and cheap, and easily transformed into tools and agricultural implements, as well as effective weapons. The arms once used only against carnivorous animals became equally effective against fellow men, one of the distinctions between man and other animals: warfare within its own species.

At first, domestic animals were not eaten because they were precious and scarce. These tamed creatures also fulfilled an emotional need in primitive man, a longing which has certainly persisted over the centuries. But once the knowledge of effective breeding became well known, ensuring a continual supply of these controllable animals, they became food. As with plants, how or why animals were originally domesticated is a mystery, but there are some clues in primitive contemporary cultures. For example, a Papuan woman will suckle a small pig with one breast and her own infant with the other. Perhaps in ancient times a wild pig might wander into a Neolithic village, be nurtured by a lactating mother, and then stay on to multiply.

Modern Papuan woman suckling an infant and a small pig. (After a photograph by A. A. Vogel)

At first the new and unique domestic animals were worshiped. Later they were killed as part of ritualistic ceremonies as supreme sacrifices to the gods. However, someone ate the sacred offerings, probably the priests. It has always been difficult to comprehend the rationale of sacrificing what is most highly prized. But in contemporary times we see a similar love-hate relationship between wildlife and diet: often it is the hunter who expresses the deepest concern and admiration for the beauty of his prey.

As a controllable vegetarian way of life evolved, hunting decreased in dietary importance. Furthermore, ferocious carnivorous animals were following their own evolutionary roads. Yet the hunting instinct, once established, was hard to extinguish. One theory is that men turned their weapons against each other when the challenge of the hunt was decreased by the advancement of domestication. However, war is at least 30,000 years earlier than domestication.

Human aggression did indeed accelerate at an alarming rate after the introduction of farming. Self-sufficiency might have been a logical point for killing to cease. But agriculture itself brought unforeseen social changes. Before the development of agriculture, hunting cannot be considered an example of violence. In areas where natural resources did not support a gathered diet of nuts, seeds, and roots, killing animals was a necessity.

"Lions eat zebras, but that is not aggression," says Dr. Leakey. "That is hunting food."

After the development of agriculture, however, any form of violence against man or animal is unnecessary killing in areas where the land may support adequate nutritional growth. Thus unnecessary and premeditated slaughter begins with the domestication of plants and animals.

One of the basic causes of increased violence was the amplified population—an agricultural consequence. The Danubians exemplify an early culture that began peacefully but became violent. These pioneers from the Mediterranean brought farming to northern Europe. From 5000 to 4000 B.P., they entered the region from the Balkans by the valley of the Danube and eventually spread across Europe as far as Belgium. The Danubians followed a definite pattern: first they cleared an area of land, then they cultivated wheat and barley for about ten to twenty-five years until the loess soil was depleted. They would travel further and returned only after the soil had been replenished. Such a cultivation process necessitated lots of land and a small population.

Eventually, the Danubians expanded in numbers. They pressed even further west into the forest and by 4200 B.P. they reached Magdeburg. The supply of loess land, the only type that they could cultivate with their primitive stone-bladed hoes, was no longer adequate. Food became scarce.

The earlier villages of the Danubians were unfortified, and graves dated to that period contain only tools for farming and hunting. Later, after the increasing density in population, the villages had fortification and war weapons remain. Thus there seems to be a direct relationship between hunger, population pressures, and violence.

If Darwin's theory of natural selection continues to be valid, it will be those men and women who are best at adapting to new environmental changes who will survive and flourish. Though millions of years were necessary for the evolutionary history of the earth, we seem shortsighted in our view of contemporary and future man. Most persons act as if man as we know him today is assured of a continued similar existence. It is far easier to gaze backwards than to stare at the present or even the next hundred years.

Yet the fifth ecological epoch—that of technological advances—has the potential both to free man from the physical sufferings of starvation and to bring about instant destruction of the entire species. Anthropological evidence demonstrates that species have become extinct before, without any apparent explanations, and easily could again. *Homo sapiens* is just another rung in the evolutionary ladder, although his increased brain capacity enables judgment of other creatures and grander schemes.

The trend toward urbanization that began with plant domestication unhaltingly expands. By providing enough food and simultaneously decreasing population, increased violence *may* be avoided. The contemporary focus on a "natural" diet is, in some cases, the desperate effort of many advanced and prophetic persons to get to that next ecological stage when the hunting of animals and men replaces the Neolithic revolution with an ethical one based on nutritional self-sufficiency.

2

Land of the Sacred Cow

Hinduism

Mahendra sat in a lotus position on his bed—a mattress extending between the walls of his spacious bedroom in an upper-class house outside the congested Indian city of Benares. A Hindu of the Brahman caste, he had just completed his daily sunrise meditation. Mahendra, a sari merchant, is a lactarian and, being very religious, prays several times each day.

"How important is the sacred cow?" I asked.

Mahendra preferred to retell a story to answer my question.

"I was driving my car along the main road of Benares," he said, "when all of a sudden a cow got in the way. It happened so quickly that my driver hit it. He stepped on the gas, but still the villagers ran after us. I could feel them pounding their fists against the car, screaming names at me. Finally we had to stop because the crowd encircled us. They rocked the car back and forth. We locked all the windows and just had to sit there until a policeman arrived. They actually would have killed us for hitting a sacred cow."

Mahendra explained that in most parts of India, sacred cows, vegetarianism, and Hinduism are synonymous. Yet liberal Hindus, who defiantly eat meat, quickly point out that the sacred cow is a later development in Hinduism—originally, the cow was sacrificed and eaten.

Bombay woman anointing a sacred cow with water.

It is difficult to trace the development of vegetarianism in India, since even Hinduism is arduous to explain; unlike Christianity or Islam, it does not have one sacred text or a distinct founding father. Instead, Hinduism developed over thousands of years as the result of a fusion of non-Aryan and Aryan doctrines and cultural patterns.

The excavations at Mohenjo-Daro and Harappa provide some insight into the pre-Aryan culture of about 2800 B.P. Ancient seals reveal the importance of sacred animals in the religion of the Indus people. This animal worship, particularly of the bull, is probably related to the primitive idea of the totem. The totem became a symbol of fertility. Taboos were associated with it: to destroy it might lead to the ruin of a harvest, either by drought or locusts, and could foster disease or floods.

Then the Aryans invaded India through the northwestern passage and settled in the upper region of the Indus Valley. Later, in about 1200 B.P., they moved to the central Ganges River region known as Madhadesa where the Vedic developments occurred, the first major literary doctrines of the Hindu religion, and the *Upanishads* were written. Some of the Aryan contributions were the introduction of the Sanskrit language and animal sacrifices. These elements merged with the non-Aryan attitudes of extreme asceticism, a world-negating and suffering belief, and image worship.

Humped bull seal indicative of
the thousands found in the
ruins of the Harrappa Culture.

The dynamic history of Hinduism can be simplified by dividing it
into several distinct periods: the Vedic period, during which the Vedic
hymns were composed and collected, which lasted from 2000 to 800 B.P.;
the *Upanishads* phase, which lasted until 400 B.P., when beliefs such as
karma and rebirth were incorporated into a more monastic image-
worshiping religion; the classical phase that lasted until 500 C.E., when
Hinduism acquired its typical form; the fourth, or medieval period,
important for the further evolution of bhaktic cults, especially in the
Dravidian south, and for the elaboration of major theological and
philosophical positions within the orthodox tradition; and the modern
period resulting from the impact of Western colonization.

During the Vedic period, Hindus were extremely liberal in their diet,
eating not just fish and cattle but sheep, horses, and the entrails of dogs
as well. A guest was called *goghna*, one for whom a cow is killed. Oxen
were also slaughtered for food at weddings. Indra, a Vedic god, is
described as a relisher of beef. He is also master of lightning and thunder
and often depicted as being drunk with the fermented drink offered to
him in sacrifice.

However, the cow was beginning to acquire a special sanctity because
of its value for purposes other than flesh food, and was called
aghnya—"not to be slain." In *Rig-Veda*, still considered the most sacred
of the numerous religious texts of the Hindus, offerings of milk, ghi,
grain, and the intoxicating liquor known as *soma* are of equal importance to the animal sacrifices. However, these offerings as the best food
man had to offer were replaced by the blood sacrifice as the most
honored.

The Aryans lived in a society that was both agricultural and pastoral.
Cattle was vitally important, even serving as a form of currency. It was
the reward to a priest for his sacrificial activities and payment for a
warrior. Clearly, however, oxen and cattle are also food during the
historical period of the *Rig-Veda*, written from about 1500 to 1000 B.P.

From that time to the age of Buddha, a period of four or five hundred years elapsed. These important years of change are eclipsed in written history, except for texts written from a literary and religious point of view—the later *Vedas, Brahmanas,* and *Upanishads.*

The Battle of Kuruksetra, which is situated close to modern Delhi, is the basis for the epic poem, the *Mahabharata.* This poem, said to be the longest poem in the world, consists of 24,000 verses. It describes a war that enveloped all India, and there are already references to sparing animals. Some examples are: "Who can be more cruel and selfish than he who increases the flesh of his body by eating the flesh of innocent animals?"; "All that kill and eat and permit the slaughter of cows rot in hell for as many years as there are hairs on the body of the cow slain"; and "Those who desire to possess good memory, beauty, long life with perfect health, and physical, moral and spiritual strength, should abstain from animal food."

This later period of Aryan culture is marked by excesses in drinking, gambling, and the development of the sacrificial cult. Although not mentioned in the *Rig-Veda,* much of the *Brahmana* literature is embellished with instructions for the careful performance of new sacrifices, such as the *rajasuya,* or royal consecration, the *vajapeya,* a strength-drinking rejuvenation ceremony, and the *asvamedha,* or horse sacrifice, the ambition of each king. A horse was chosen to roam free for a year and a band of warriors would follow. Wherever the horse went, chieftains and kings were forced to pay homage or to fight. If, at the end of the year, the horse was not captured by a neighboring king, it was returned to the capital and sacrificed. Because each king wanted to perform a horse sacrifice, this custom had a definite effect on relations between states.

India was already divided into castes by the time of the *Rig-Veda:* the priest, *brahmana;* warrior, *kshatriya;* peasant, *vaisya;* and serf, *sudra.* Priests set the standard for the society and they were actively involved in animal sacrifices, which supposedly reached 2,000 cattle each day. In this phase of Hindu history, the importance of the Brahman caste is demonstrated by the name for that period: Brahmanism. However, after the spiritual and cultural forces transformed religious teachings—by 200 C.E.—the main religion of India is known as Hinduism.

Hinduism would have remained a typical meat-eating way of life if not for the broad and sweeping moral reforms inspired by Jainism and Buddhism. The effect of those influences is pointed out by the later *Laws of Manu,* composed about the year 200 B.P., where there is still ambivalence regarding the slaughter of cows and meat-eating. However, those contradictions are proof of the new ideas that were emerging as a result of Buddhism and Jainism, which had been introduced three hundred years before and were to have a lasting cultural impact.

Jainism

Although Jainism had a crucial influence in transforming Hinduism from a cow-sacrificing to a cow-sanctifying religion, there are only about 2 million followers in India today. Yet the number of Jains is disproportionate to the impact of this unique religion on both Hinduism and the cultural development of India. Jains are followers of Jinas, persons who attain immortality and happiness by righteous thoughts and deeds. A Jina is someone who preaches Jainism and is known as a *Tirthankara*. There were twenty-four Tirthankaras: the first was Shri Adinath, who supposedly lived about 800 B.P. and attained nirvana in 772 B.P., when he was renamed Parsva.

Contemporary Jains are followers of the twenty-fourth Tirthankara, Mahavira, who flourished about the same time as Buddha, around 500 B.P. Mahavira is often credited with the founding of Jainism, but the religion extended many centuries earlier than Buddhism. Mahavira, however, was a definite historical figure. He was born of the *kshatriya* or warrior caste; his parents strictly worshipped Parsva. Mahavira married and bore a daughter, but in his thirtieth year, when his parents died, he asked his guardian and older brother, Nandavirdhana, to allow him to become a monk. After receiving his permission, Mahavira spent the next twelve years wandering through the forests, practicing denial, and becoming a nudist. Because at seventy-two he obtained release from the dreaded Hindu fate of constant reincarnations, Mahavira proved that such release was possible for men and women who were not Brahmans. Mahavira died by a method that became an example for later ascetics: self-starvation, a symbol of his oneness with all life, including plants.

Ahimsa, or non-violence, is not just the foundation of Jainism but a daily principle for every thought and deed. Jains do not actively seek converts, but anyone who wishes to follow their road to self-awareness is free to do so, regardless of caste or nationality.

"How many American Jains are there?" I asked the president of the Jain Society in New York.

"We have four."

There was a long pause. "No," he added, "there are only three. One member died last year."

Yet Jainism is more of a philosophy than a religion—it is an ideology of non-violence. There are five strict principles that a Jain monk must follow, which are also guidelines for the lay Jains:

ahimsa—to avoid all killing; thus a Jain must walk carefully to
  prevent destroying unseen creatures
asatya tyaga—never to lie, be greedy, or lose one's temper
asetya vrata—never to accept what is not given
brachmacarva—to practice celibacy and chastity
aparigraha vrata—to avoid attachments to any living or dead
  objects

Jain ascetics wear masks to avoid breathing in microscopic organisms and the same principle forces the avoidance of beverages that are fermented. There are further taboos against gambling, hunting, adultery, thieving, debauchery, fur or feathers, silk, and woolen garments. In addition to a strict avoidance of fish, flesh, or fowl, a principle that is adhered to even in contemporary times, Jains will not eat *kandamulas*—underground vegetables such as potatoes, garlic, radish, turnip, carrot, beetroot, or anything similar that has to be uprooted.

Until the year 300, Jains were a unified group, but then a rift resulted in two factions: the *Shutambaras*, or "white-robed," a liberal sect that included women in the priesthood and encouraged typical dress; and the *Digambaras*, or "sky-robed," a stricter branch that considered women evil and practiced nudism as a symbol of freedom from worldly possessions.

Because of their deep belief in *ahimsa*, lay Jains for centuries have consistently made their living in certain professions since they are unable to have any connection with agriculture, butchery, fishing, or brewing. As a result, their careers have been limited to business and therefore the Jains in India are on the whole far more successful and prosperous than the Hindu majority. Jains have also contributed hospitals for birds and animals as well as rest homes, operated for free, for travelers.

Jainism is considered a heretic religion because it does not recognize the authority of the *Vedas* scriptures. Furthermore, Jains do not believe in one god but that god is within each man. Strict asceticism is recommended as a means to finding the god within.

A Jain layman must go through two preliminary stages if he is to follow Jain principles. They are:

1. Having faith in Jainism by studying the doctrines and believing in them.

2. Becoming a *Pakshika Sravaka*, a layman intent on following the path to salvation. There are twelve duties involved, as described by Pandit Asadhara in the *Sagara-Dharmarita*, written in the thirteenth century:

To have faith in Jainism.
To abstain from intoxicants.

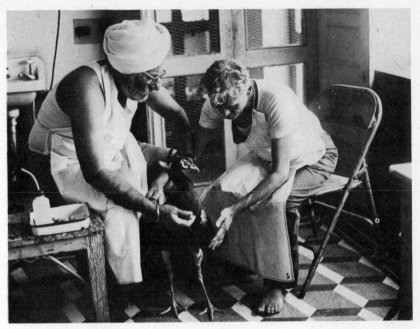

Jains carry their belief in the rights of animals and birds into the treatment of their wounds in special hospitals throughout India.

To abstain from flesh foods.
To abstain from fruits which contain or are likely to contain insects; to abstain from honey.
To abstain from taking four kinds of food at night: eatable, tastable, lickable, drinkable.
To drink clean, filtered water.
To abstain from gambling.
To follow the five small vows such as that related to killing.
To abstain from hunting.
To abstain from adultery or lasciviousness.
To perform daily religious exercises.
To abstain from making a living by any of these means: agriculture, trade, military, crafts, singing, and music.

Munishree Chandraprabh Sagar, known as "Chitrabhanu," was the first Jain ascetic, or sadhu, to leave India in the religion's thousands of years of history. This was a radical step since Jainism expressly forbids travel for priests because of the fear of hurting a living creature in the locomotive process. However, Munishree left India in spite of riots that occurred at the airport. In addition to his unconventional departure from the rule against travel, he also took a wife.

Now, the word of Jainism is beginning to spread outside India. Munishree, who is fifty years old but appears no more than forty, attributes his youth to three principles: good will with all, ill will to none, and his philosophy that Karma determines what will happen so there is no reason to fear tomorrow. Although conversion has never been an active goal of Jainism, there is a growing inclination to spread its basic principles. The proposed Jain temple to be built in Queens, New York, symbolizes this trend toward worldwide practice of Jain attitudes. However, the basic difference between Jainism and most other religions is the extreme to which the sadhus actually practice the two principles which are supposedly part of every religion—"Love thy neighbor" and "Thou shalt not kill."

Buddhism

In contrast to Jainism, which began in India, maintained a firm foothold there, but until recently did not expand outside its birthplace, Buddhism originated in India but within a few hundred years showed influence there only in the changes it provoked in Hinduism. In fact Buddhism exerted a far greater historical effect on the religious developments of Ceylon, Burma, Cambodia, Siam, China, Japan, Korea, Tibet, and Mongolia.

Gautama Buddha lived about the same time as Mahavira and was also a member of the warrior caste. He too was disgusted with the excesses of the Brahman priests and the doctrine that only they might find nirvana. Buddha set out at the age of twenty-nine to discover his own path to salvation. For several years he practiced severe asceticism and starvation, but unlike Mahavira, he did not feel self-denial would lead to nirvana. Instead, Buddha found a middle path based on complete awareness of himself and his environment. That middle path had eight turns: right views, right aspirations, right speech, right conduct, right livelihood, right efforts, right mindfulness, and right contemplation.

Buddha was overwhelmed by the suffering he saw to be an unavoidable part of life. Kindness toward all creatures was one of his fundamental principles and he spoke two maxims that relate to vegetarianism: "Do not butcher the ox that plows thy field," and "Do not indulge a voracity that involves the slaughter of animals."

Although Buddha stressed the importance of compassion and

ahimsa, neither he nor his followers had any firm objections to the use of meat. Buddha himself ate boar's flesh and it is even alleged that he died from some rancid pork. Buddhist monks took many vows, such as to accept nothing unless given willingly, to live in absolute moral purity, to speak only the truth, to kill no living thing, to eat no animal and drink no alcohol, to eat only at prescribed times, to abstain from all unnecessary contacts with the world, to use no ornament, to have no luxuries, and to live in voluntary poverty. However, the injunction against meat was a complex one based upon how the meat was obtained. For example, they were not allowed to eat the flesh of any animal they had actually seen put to death or that they knew, or even suspected, had been slaughtered just for their benefit. But where these circumstances did not apply, meat-eating was generally practiced.

Even if vegetarianism was not a basic tenet of Buddhism, as it was for Jainism, Buddhism did introduce a strong wave of asceticism and heightened morality which made a permanent impression on a country with cross-cultural roots in the Harappa and Aryan cultures.

King Asoka

Before Buddhism left India in the twelfth century, it made one major convert—King Asoka. That conversion is as important to Buddhism in the East as the persuasion of Emperor Constantine to Christianity in the West.

Asoka, who reigned from about 264 to 232 B.P., seemed to have reached a turning point in his life after the conquest of Kalinga, a victory gained only after the slaughter of tens of thousands of Indians. According to Buddhist sources, Asoka's own rise to power was equally bloody: he killed all possible rivals in order to begin his despotic reign. Asoka's own words inscribed in various edicts, the first written Indian documents of historical consequence, describe the actions that led to his conversion. He relates how he took 150,000 people captive and killed 100,000 although many more died. At that point, "Righteousness" enveloped him. Of course, Asoka's account is just one of many colorful tales, but instantaneous conversions are not uncommon. Through legislation and persuasion, Asoka proclaimed that certain species of animals were to be spared. He tells how hundreds of thousands of living animals have been slaughtered, but now: "At the time of writing this inscription . . . only three animals are killed, two peacocks and a deer, and the deer not invariably. Even these three animals will not be killed in the future. . . ."

Not only was Asoka a vegetarian, but he refrained from hunting and banned it for his subjects. Forests which might injure living creatures were burned. Medical care became available for animals as well as people; trees were planted to provide shade and to ease travel for creatures and men. Yet Asoka remained a benevolent dictator, employing Buddhism chiefly so that he might be a better king. Although the Asoka experiment with Buddhism was not entirely successful, since it did not replace Hinduism with Buddhism, his example was a powerful influence on the evolving Hindu ideology which gradually adopted non-violence toward animals as a unifying principle.

As we have seen, Buddhism left India to become far more influential in other countries, such as China, Tibet, Japan, and Korea. Whether vegetarianism is a contemporary practice of laymen or priests depends on the particular Buddhist sect. Thus in the three major areas of Mahayan Buddhism—China; Tibet, including Mongolia, Sikkim, Nepal, Bhutan; and Japan—only the Chinese monks abstain from animal flesh. The Jodo Shin school of Japanese Pure Land Buddhism does permit the consumption of flesh. On the other hand, Theravada Buddhism, the faith of the majority of the people in Burma, Laos, Cambodia, Thailand, and Ceylon, encourages vegetarianism among those who live in a *wat*, or religious compound, as well as silence, meditation, and fasting from noon until the following day. Vows are taken that also require avoiding sexual activity, sleeping on a soft bed, alcohol or drugs that would clutter the mind, or accepting anything that is not freely given.

Vegetarianism Develops in India

Probably because of Asoka's high position in Indian society, in an extraordinary about-face, the very priests who were the avid practitioners of ceremonial animal sacrifices became the strictest vegetarians. Even in contemporary India, it is the Brahmans who are consistently vegetarians, whereas in the other castes eschewing meat is less imperative; in the flesh-eating castes, only *Sanyasis*, or holy men, and widows abstain.

Thus Jainism and Buddhism were slowly absorbed; the *Laws of Manu* have contradictory advice: "Meat may never be obtained without injury to living creatures and injury to sentient beings is detrimental to the attainment of heavenly bliss. A twice-born man must therefore shun the use of meat." "He who permits the slaughter of an animal, he who cuts it up, he who kills it, he who buys or sells meat, he who cooks it, he who serves it up and he who eats it must all be considered slayers of the animal." Yet in the same chapter, there are several statements that recognize the acceptability of animal food without any attempt at reconciliation with the earlier conflicting moral decrees. The *Laws of*

Manu are a good example of the state of flux of the growing national identity of India. As late as the fifth century C.E., the orthodox did not eat meat but most other Indians did. The *kshatriya* class enjoyed not only hunting but eating what they caught. Although oxen, cows, elephants, horses, pigs, dogs, foxes, lions, frogs, and monkeys were not generally part of the diet, they did eat goats, tortoises, deer, parrots, peacocks, porcupines, alligators, and giant lizards.

Yet most Hindus today who adhere to vegetarianism fail to explore the historical development of a meatless diet and attribute their practice to the "will of God." Others feel that the sacred cow developed because of a high regard for milk as a food for babies: forbidding the killing of cows ensured the continuation of a milk supply. Today, cow manure and urine are also believed to be purifying. "I feel that vegetarianism probably originated as our saints felt that this was the ideal diet for a sound mind," says a college-educated Brahman girl. "It helps in concentration and meditation, besides being good for one's physical welfare."

Hindus divide food into three categories: *satvik, rajsik,* and *tamsik. Satvik* should provide peace of mind and therefore all foods which excite the senses and contain spices are forbidden. This kind of food is for Brahmans, sages, and old people. *Rajsik* is also essentially vegetarian, but includes onions and garlic, various spices, as well as light wine; it is intended for the average family. The third type of food, *tamsik,* is meant for the *kshatrivas* and the lowest caste; meats and liquors are allowed.

Food has as much symbolic meaning in a Hindu household as in any other part of the world. While in Benares, I decided to fast for two days as a means of undoing the drastic effect of weeks of spicy, rich foods. Of course, to refuse food would displease a host in any country.

"You must eat," Mahendra said.

"Tomorrow, Mahendra."

"You do not understand," he continued. "My wife will not eat until you do. You are her guest. If you do not eat, she will not either."

It was useless to argue with such sincere hospitality. Mahendra and his family were pleased that I shared their vegetarian habits, but rather confused. They *had* to be vegetarians because they were Brahmans, but I was not forced to follow such a custom. In India today, numerous younger persons are turning away from a meatless diet. Their rebellion is against a custom they see as part of the old tradition. They are confused by the growing Western emulation. In Delhi, parents who were members of vegetarian societies were eager for a Westerner to speak to their children who had forgotten that *ahimsa* is a timeless belief and not necessarily another reactionary custom.

Mahatma Gandhi

The worldwide focus on vegetarianism in India was accomplished through the efforts of one man: Mohandas Karamchand Gandhi. To Gandhi, a meatless diet was not just a religious principle but an obsession that consumed a great portion of his energies: his writings on the subject alone fill five volumes. But it was through self-analysis, struggle, and sacrifice that Gandhi reaffirmed his Hindu-derived ritual of vegetarianism, developing the idea of a meatless diet from a simple dietary taboo to an overall philosophy of non-violence toward men as well as animals.

Born in 1869 to a middle-class Bania family of a father who became the *dewan* or prime minister of Kathiawar and married four times, Gandhi grew up in Porbandar—a seaport trading center in Ahmedabad where Jainism exercised a strong influence. In his *Autobiography*, subtitled *The Story of My Experiments with Truth*, Gandhi describes his father Karamchand as "a lover of his clan, truthful, brave and generous, but short-tempered. To a certain extent he might have been given to carnal pleasures." It was to his deeply religious mother, Putlibai, who always prayed with her meals and often kept two or three consecutive fasts, that the thin, awkward boy gave his increasing devotion. Sometimes Putlibai would vow to fast until she saw the sun set. Her children would run outside, stare at the sky, and catching a glimpse of the blazing disc, would hurry inside to assure her that she might then eat. But when Putlibai came outside to check, the sun would be hidden behind a cloud.

"God did not intend for me to eat today," she would calmly say.

Gandhi was the youngest of four children, all born during a period of seven years. He was the pampered baby, extremely close to his mother and fond of imitating her. Throughout Gandhi's *Autobiography*, his intense guilt feelings and rigid superego are apparent. However, it is not unusual that a son would have such a severe sense of righteousness with a mother of such intense, uncompromising piety.

One year, under the influence of an older friend, Sheikh Mehtab, Gandhi experimented with meat-eating. At that time Indian youths were questioning whether the British were able to dominate their country because they ate strength-giving meat. Gandhi actually violated vegetarianism only six times, but he suffered deeply from the shame of keeping such a dreaded secret from his parents and from his dramatic deceptions to avoid outright lies. Although his memoirs were written decades after the events, Gandhi was able vividly to recall the nightmare he had during the meat-eating phase of his life.

"Every time I dropped off to sleep," he wrote, "it would seem as though a live goat were bleating inside me, and I would jump up full of remorse. . . ."

To tempt Gandhi further into meat-eating, his friend disguised the flesh. But still Gandhi vowed never to eat meat again, until his parents were no more and he had found his "freedom." "This decision I communicated to my friend," writes Gandhi, "and I have never since gone back to meat."

As was customary in those days, Gandhi married at thirteen; he writes that he was a lustful and jealous husband. "I was passionately fond of her. . . . Separation was unbearable. . . ." Shortly thereafter came the circumstances surrounding his father's death which were to leave indelible scars on Gandhi's adolescent psychosexual development. As his father lay dying, Gandhi was in his own room in bed with his young wife. When he learned the next day that his father had died while Gandhi was enjoying hedonistic sensual pleasures, he suffered intense remorse and self-hatred. Sex and guilt were eternally bonded in his mind and no doubt had a direct bearing on his later renunciation of sexual intercourse.

To pursue his law studies, Gandhi at eighteen decided to travel to England, despite the angry protests of the leaders of his caste, who forbade crossing the ocean. Putlibai insisted her son take vows against women, wine, and meat. When Gandhi took those vows, he gave more of a commitment than just a promise. To an Indian, a vow is intended to increase one's willpower. A punishment, such as fasting, is enforced for breaking a vow to enhance self-discipline. But to break a vow and demonstrate lack of self-control is severely condemned by Indians, since restraint is a highly treasured virtue.

The long boat trip was a hardship for Gandhi since little vegetarian food was available. He had to rely on the meager fruits and nuts his family had provided him for the voyage.

After arriving in London, Gandhi tried outwardly to imitate the British but appeared ridiculous in morning coat, double-breasted vest, dark-striped trousers, leather gloves, boots, spats, and a silver-mounted cane. It was not long before he realized his comic garb was pointless and his expensive living habits draining his small funds. Abandoning his European affectations, he found a room in West Kensington where he cooked his own breakfasts and suppers of oatmeal porridge and cocoa.

Numerous influences in England reasserted Gandhi's traditional beliefs in vegetarianism, for it was a new and radical philosophy there that had become part of several movements, including the Theosophists. In 1889, Gandhi met Madame Helena Petrovna Blavatsky, the founder of the Theosophical Society, but he was unimpressed by her. Annie

Besant, however, was a vegetarian Theosophist whom he admired; he would later cross her path when she lived and organized in India. Gandhi also met a Christian vegetarian who convinced him that neither drinking nor meat-eating were advocated in the Bible.

London was a difficult testing ground for Gandhi's vows since the atmosphere was far more liberal than his native Porbandar. But he managed to keep his vow against women, wine, and meat. He lived very simply on lentils, boiled rice, and raisins, studying hard, taking long walks, associating with people who lived quietly, and constantly reminding himself of his vows.

"I launched out in search of a vegetarian restaurant," Gandhi writes.

> . . . I would trot ten or twelve miles each day, go into a cheap restaurant and eat my fill of bread, but would never be satisfied. During these wanderings I once hit a vegetarian restaurant in Farringdon Street. The sight of it filled me with the same joy that a child feels on getting a thing after its own heart. I saw among them Salt's *Plea for Vegetarianism*. This I purchased for a shilling and went straight to the dining room. This was my first hearty meal since my arrival in England. . . . From the date of reading this book, I may claim to have become a vegetarian by choice. I blessed the day on which I had taken the vow before my mother. I had all along abstained from meat in the interests of truth and of the vow I had taken, but had wished at the same time that every Indian should be a meat-eater, and had looked forward to being one myself freely and openly some day, and to enlisting others in the cause. The choice was now made in favour of vegetarianism, the spread of which henceforward became my mission. . . .

Gandhi, a rebel against vegetarianism in his own country where it was an expected duty, took up the unpopular cause in London and became very active in the vegetarian movements. He even founded his own Vegetarian Club in Bayswater with Dr. Josiah Oldfield as president, Sir Edwin Arnold the poet as vice-president, and himself as secretary. Dr. Oldfield was vital to the British vegetarian movement as editor of *The Vegetarian* and author of most of its articles. Gandhi and Oldfield developed a strong friendship, rooming together and spending their spare time lecturing at clubs and public meetings. Thus Gandhi, a vegetarian by birth, became reconverted to a meatless diet on new ethical and nutritional grounds.

Upon returning to India in 1891, Gandhi was met by his brother Laxmidas.

"Mother is dead," Laxmidas told the grieving lawyer. The family had decided to save the news until Gandhi had passed his examinations.

Within a short time after his return, Gandhi met Shrimad Rajchandra, a young Jain completely involved in pure Hindu doctrine. Although a jeweler by profession, Rajchandra was equally renowned as a poet and a *Shatavadhani*, one who can accomplish numerous tasks at once. Because of superior concentration, he was able to play musical instruments, recite from a book or play, and excel in mathematics and chess. Here was someone, like his recently deceased mother, whom Gandhi could respect. Later Gandhi would cite Rajchandra as one of the three most influential persons on the formation of his ideas. The other two were Leo Tolstoy, through his book *The Kingdom of God Is Within You*, which Gandhi read in 1893, and John Ruskin through *Unto This Last*, which he read in 1904.

Gandhi tried unsuccessfully to be a barrister in Bombay. His first two court cases ended in disaster and humiliation. Then Abdul Karim Jhaveri, a partner in a firm with important interests in South Africa, asked Gandhi to go to Durban to advise the firm in a lawsuit against another merchant from Kathiawar. Assured that he would have to stay "not more than a year" Gandhi went at once in April 1893, leaving his young family behind once more.

South Africa was a time of trials and tribulations. However, it is probable that that chance to prove himself to the Indian community of Durban, a far easier task than in competitive Bombay, allowed Gandhi to develop and test his unorthodox views of righteousness and his revolutionary political methods. In South Africa Gandhi encountered Michael Caotes, a young man who tried to convert him to Christianity. Perturbed, Gandhi wrote to Rajchandra, asking twenty-seven questions, such as: What is God? What is the soul? What is salvation? What is duty? Who wrote the *Vedas* and the *Bhagavad-gita*? What will finally happen to the world? Who were Brahma, Vishnu, and Siva? Is there any merit to be gained by sacrificing animals to the gods? Can we obtain salvation through faith in Rama and Krishna? Can a man be reborn as an animal, a tree, a stone? Were all the Old Testament prophesies fulfilled in Christ and was He an incarnation of God? If a snake were about to bite me, should I allow myself to be bitten or should I kill it?

Gandhi was disappointed in Rajchandra's replies because they were not absolute statements providing the clear-cut answers he had desired. For instance, to Gandhi's question about the snake, Rajchandra wrote: "The question is not what I would wish you do, but what you wish your choice to be. That choice will depend on the degree of your illumination and enlightenment."

Rajchandra died a few years later in his early thirties. A true ascetic, he perished as a mere skeleton, still devoting himself to contemplation and the hope of seeing God face to face. Rajchandra lived his Jain beliefs; the outward signs of compassion, such as sweeping a floor to avoid injuring any living creatures, did not impress him. Instead he viewed every lie, each act of hypocrisy, every oppression and injury inflicted on another human being as an act of violence. It was this deepest and more subtle type of non-violence that later became part of Gandhi's major contribution to the materialistic twentieth century, the age of the mass war machine—his concept of *ahimsa*. Though Gandhi did not immediately employ Rajchandra's views, the ideals of his philosophical mentor would remain in his collective conscience to be revived when Gandhi's intellectual development had progressed to the point where he could utilize them.

Practicing law was just one of Gandhi's numerous activities during those twenty South African years, from 1893 to 1914, except for brief intervals abroad. He became executive director of the Natal Indian Congress, and of the colonial-born Indian Educational Association, an agent for the Esoteric Christian Union, and a representative for the London Vegetarian Society. His zealous need to save souls was apparent in his club affiliations and the leadership he commanded in his own home. There were then twelve people on his staff and one employee was Sheikh Mehtab, the school friend who had once taken him to a brothel and tempted him with meat-eating. Gandhi had invited Mehtab to South Africa for he had an unusually intense concern for the activities of his former playmate. But Mehtab was still a rebel. First Gandhi wrongly dismissed a law clerk because Mehtab, who was employed as a handyman, had pinned the guilt on him. Gandhi would have continued to tolerate Mehtab's abuses if he had not discovered him at home with a prostitute and been forced to dismiss him. But his concern for Mehtab lingered and he was pleased when Mehtab later married, settled down, and fathered a daughter; still later Mehtab became a champion of *Satyagraha*, or truth-force, Gandhi's method of releasing India from Britain.

Once again, Gandhi started a law practice in Bombay in 1901, determined to be a successful lawyer on the homeland. But a second brief, one-year stay in India since law school again proved frustrating and unsatisfying. Gandhi's second son Manilal came down with a severe attack of typhoid, but Gandhi refused to allow him to be fed meat or given drugs. Using naturopathic techniques, Gandhi managed to save his son's life and so became even more committed to a natural diet without the use of drugs. Throughout his life, Gandhi would wrestle with doctors over the necessity for providing one of his sick relatives, either his wife Kasturbai or his sons, with beef tea. It now seems illogical that the medical profession would make an issue of beef tea, such a pointless cure, and all the more credit to Gandhi that he would protest violating his principles for so trivial a point.

"It is necessary to correct the error that vegetarianism has made us weak in the mind," wrote Gandhi, "or passive or inert in action . . . I do not regard flesh-food as necessary for us at any stage . . . I hold flesh-food to be unsuited to our species. . . ."

Gandhi soon returned to Johannesburg, South Africa, intent on improving the conditions of the lower classes, which had regressed since the Boer War. It was at vegetarian restaurants, where he enjoyed having his morning and evening meals, and at meetings of the South African Theosophical Society, that Gandhi met persons who would give up their chosen professions to follow his uncompromising ways. One such person was Albert West, who ran a printing shop but cast aside his salaried job to take charge of the *Indian Opinion* press at Durban at petty wages. Gandhi met another European, twenty-two-year-old Henry Polak. Their mutual vegetarianism bound them closer as they discussed the principles of Adolf Just's *Return to Nature*, a treatise advocating a diet of fruit and nuts, mudpacks, and regular bowel evacuation. Constipation was one of Gandhi's problems and he took Eno's fruit salts each morning. He was also addicted to onions; Polak humorously began the Amalgamated Society of Onion Eaters, a membership of two, with Gandhi as president and Polak as treasurer.

The next step in Gandhi's asceticism was his decision in 1904 to become a celibate, *brahmacharya*, enacted in 1906, during the Zulu Revolution when he was a sergeant major working as a medic for the British. His reasons for giving up sexual pleasure were that a public figure should be devoted to the people, rather than to his personal pleasures or his own family. By remaining chaste, he also retained the seminal fluids which were otherwise lost, along with mental vigor, during sexual intercourse. This is not an uncommon belief among old-fashioned Indians; now many will seek the help of psychiatrists who use diagrams and sex education to eradicate an age-old superstition. However, Gandhi held firmly to his conviction and felt that *brahmacharya* would have only good effects. That celibacy was a struggle for Gandhi is apparent in the amount of writing he devotes to trying to advise others as to the best food to eat to reduce sexual passion.

"Six years of experiment," Gandhi later wrote, "have shown me that the *brahmachari*'s ideal food is fresh fruit and nuts." Milk and milk products, he concluded, aroused the sexual passions and therefore were to be avoided.

In becoming a celibate, Gandhi further severed his cultural ties with

Europe as he merged the harsh restrictions for ascetics or sadhus of Hinduism and Jainism. Yet Gandhi was the product of so many religious and philosophical influences that he was not really a prophet of any specific one. "All religions are like different roads leading to the same goal," he wrote. "All religions are founded on the same moral laws. My ethical religion is made up of laws which bind men all over the world."

The next major step was the implementation of *ahimsa*, or non-violence, as a political weapon. The first time Gandhi employed it was in the Empire Theatre in Johannesburg on September 11, 1906. After several speakers had been cheered at the mention of going to jail on behalf of the cause, Gandhi rose and said that all Indians in South Africa should take a pledge that they would refuse under any conditions to submit to fingerprinting or to carrying registration cards. A name had to be coined for their defiance because it was more drastic than civil disobedience or even passive resistance. It was an active movement, and they gave it the name *satyagraha*.

After the first campaign, Gandhi compromised with the British; his countrymen accused him of being a traitor and he was even physically assaulted. Gandhi tried to get other concessions for the Indians, but even a trip to England in 1909 proved futile.

Upon returning to South Africa, Gandhi was presented with two important gifts: money for the families of the *satyagrahas* who were in prison, and a track of land outside of Johannesburg.

Naming it Tolstoy Farm, Gandhi set out to model this farm into an ideal community. Everyone would eat the same simple vegetarian food from a single kitchen at a group table. Hindus had to observe *pradosha*, fasting till evening, whenever there was an appropriate religious occasion. "Fasting can help to curb animal passion only if it is undertaken with a view to self-restraint," Gandhi wrote.

It was no coincidence that Gandhi named the farm in honor of his political mentor. He had even started a correspondence with the elderly Tolstoy and sent him a copy of his first biography, written by Reverend Doke. Tolstoy replied by agreeing to allow Gandhi to reprint his explosive "Letter to a Hindu" and by praising his views on passive resistance. However, Tolstoy's failing health prohibited a more extensive contact between the two kindred spirits.

With the beginning of World War I, Gandhi left South Africa forever. He arrived in England and was unable to shake off an attack of pleurisy; still he was determined to maintain his dietary experiments and his meals now consisted of ground nuts, ripe and unripe bananas, lemons, tomatoes, grapes, and olive oil. He refused the advice of his doctor to include milk and cereal in his régime. Milk was as severe a violation of *ahimsa* as meat-eating.

Gandhi consulted a well-known vegetarian doctor who had been forced out of the London Vegetarian Society for advocating birth control. Dr. Allison agreed that milk was unnecessary for good health and he suggested raw vegetables and fresh fruit. Though Gandhi agreed to the fruit, he found the grated raw vegetables disagreeable to his system. He did agree that fresh air was essential and since none was possible in his London boardinghouse room, which had French windows, he broke one pane of glass to let in some air.

However Gandhi had to admit his dietary experiments were failing: "Just now my own health seems to have been completely shattered," he wrote, "I feel that I hopelessly mismanaged my constitution. . . ."

Gandhi returned to India and soon settled down at his ashram at Sabarmati. He was unable to interest even one Indian in being a recruit for the medical corps of the British Army, a participation which Gandhi did not feel was in violation of *satyagraha*. After a month of walking from village to village delivering numerous discourses while subsisting on an inadequate diet of groundnut butter and lemons, he contracted dysentery and was ill for seven weeks. This was his most severe illness so far and Gandhi, though ashamed that he broke his vow never to drink milk, began ravenously to drink goat's milk: a necessary step for which he was to chastise himself until he died. He called for a new doctor and submitted to a treatment using ice packs, massage, and deep breathing. Another doctor injected him with arsenic, strychnine, and iron, while a third ordered an operation to remove his piles. Gandhi was bedridden for the rest of the year.

For the remainder of his life, Gandhi used fasting as a means of punishing the world and himself for the injustices he witnessed, as well as those for which he felt personally responsible. The reasons for his starvation periods ranged from political to moral to personal. In 1919, there was a massacre in Amritsar when Brigadier-General Reginald Dyer decided to teach the Indians a lesson for their disobedience and ordered the Gurkhas and Baluchi soldiers to fire for ten minutes on men, women, and children. About 400 died and at least 800 were injured in that blood bath. Gandhi fasted for three days and vowed to fast for twenty-four hours on the massacre anniversary for the rest of his life.

His next fast, lasting only two days, followed the riots and murders in Bombay caused by the hostility between Hindus, Muslims, Parsis, Christians, and Jews. Then, early in the morning of September 17, 1924, he began his longest fast to date in response to another Muslim and

Hindu blood bath. Gandhi reaffirmed his belief in the power of fasting as a weapon as all India waited for the fast to end; Hindu and Muslim leaders assured Gandhi of peace, although it was to prove short-lived.

The seven-day fast in November 1925 had a different purpose: some boys had been caught practicing homosexuality and Gandhi accepted full responsibility for their moral shortcomings. Though a shorter fast than those in the previous year, it proved a painful and exhausting one. A year of silence and meditation followed; Gandhi contemplated his next actions and reassessed his goals for India. By now a loin cloth was all he wore: his material poverty a symbol of his moral strength.

At the end of January 1928, an incident occurred at the ashram that caused a commotion throughout India. An injured calf lay in agony. What should be done? Should they kill the calf? Vallabhai Patel, a lawyer who joined Gandhi at Sabarmati, explained that since the calf would be dead in a day or two anyway, nature should take its course.

"We cannot sit still and do nothing while the calf writhes away its last moments in agony," Gandhi said. "I believe that it would be sheer wickedness to deny to a fellow-creature the last and most solemn service we can render it."

Gandhi's will prevailed, in spite of its superficial contradiction to his solemn doctrine of *ahimsa*. However, rather than shoot the calf, a Parsi doctor came and instantly killed it by injecting poison into its veins. Significantly, Gandhi was becoming more flexible about *ahimsa* and permitting exceptions to his moral condemnation of all killing. In an article entitled "The Fiery Ordeal," he dealt with the entire controversy surrounding the killing of the calf and his loyal followers responded to his thesis with outraged cries that Gandhi had abandoned *ahimsa*. It seemed he was finally answering for himself the questions he had posed years before to Rajchandra: Gandhi now believed in killing snakes that could not be rendered harmless by any other method, or destroying mosquitoes with kerosene.

He returned to Europe intent on solving the Indian question through legislative means. While in London, Gandhi addressed the London Vegetarian Society on November 20, 1931; in his speech, he outlined his ethical conversion to vegetarianism during his student days. Then, "What I want to bring to your notice," he continued, "is that vegetarians need to be tolerant if they want to convert others to vegetarianism. Adopt a little humility. We should appeal to the moral sense of the people who do not see eye to eye with us. If a vegetarian became ill, and a doctor prescribed beef tea, then I would not call him a vegetarian. A vegetarian is made of sterner stuff. Why? Because it is for the building of the spirit and not of the body. Man is more than meat. . . ."

Gandhi explained the reason he limited his daily number of foods to only five was not because of vegetarianism but as a means of combating a pampered childhood. All his eating was completed by sunset because this was healthier. ". . . I discovered that in order to keep health," he said, "no matter what you ate, it was necessary to cut down the quantity of food, and reduce the number of meals. Become moderate; err on the side of less, rather than on the side of more. When I invite friends to share their meals with me I never press them to take anything except only what they require. On the contrary, I tell them not to take a thing if they do not want it. . . ."

He left England, disappointed by the indifference of the British government to the real issues at hand and the seriousness of the pleas of the Indians, and traveled to France. There he met Romain Rolland, writer, humanitarian, and a vegetarian, although Rolland does not seem to have impressed Gandhi as much as the Frenchman was moved by that shriveled, curious Indian. Gandhi was also able to catch a glimpse of Benito Mussolini; afterwards he described the Italian leader in the most condemning words that a Hindu can utter: "He looked like a butcher."

Gandhi, in typical loincloth, distributes fruit after a prayer meeting.

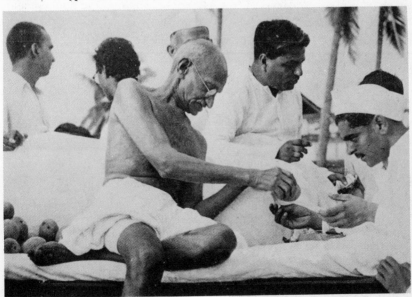

The years from 1932 until Gandhi's death in 1948 were filled for the controversial leader with discussions of fasts, actual fasts, long marches, and experiments in dietetics. The reasons for his fasts ranged from the horrid conditions of the untouchables to violence in Calcutta to the moral failings of others to fasts as prayer. But he was weakening from his severe deprivations and once tried to alter his program of total abstinence.

"Why are you adding the lime juice, when you say you are putting yourself entirely in God's hands?" asked Rajagopalachari, who was then governor of Bengal.

Gandhi agreed that he should continue drinking *only* water during his fasts; any record of that suggested change was deleted from the public announcement of his fast. Like numerous public figures, Gandhi was locked in by the expectations of his followers.

What were some of Gandhi's other habits? He went to bed about nine o'clock and awoke about four in the morning. He regularly took a brisk walk before bed and early the next morning. Gandhi was a disciplinarian in most aspects of his life: he regulated his reading habits, avoiding passion-breeding novels and magazines, denounced cigarettes, and praised the soybean, unpolished rice, and skimmed milk. Gandhi's strength was so awe-inspiring that Vincent Sheean, the noted journalist, abstained from smoking when in Gandhi's presence. I experienced a similar sense of reverence when I sat before Vinoba Bhave, known as Gandhi's "fifth son" and present leader of the land reform movement in India, and felt that I would not do anything to offend that thin, righteous, ascetic man.

Cleanliness was one of Gandhi's firm principles. These are his toilet and bathing facilities preserved at his Sabaramati ashram outside Nagpur.

Much has been written about Gandhi's harsh parental methods and it is true that one of his sons denounced Gandhi and drank excessively. Gandhi was rigid and resentful of any remembrance of his own sexual guilt. Throughout his almost fifty years of celibacy, Gandhi tried to repress his guilt by devoting all his passion to mother India. Scientific methods of birth control were not acceptable as means of controlling a multiplying people—to Gandhi only abstention and self-discipline were permissible. Therefore, at a crucial period in the population explosion of India, the advice of the revered leader hampered progress. By contrast, Gandhi was instrumental in improving the social status of women by advocating the end of child marriages and the development of equal education.

Of course, the austere controls in Gandhi's life were unattainable to the average Indian. In a letter to *Young India* in 1929, Gandhi listed his daily diet:

8 tolas of germinating wheat
8 tolas of sweet almonds reduced to a paste
8 tolas of green leaves pounded
6 sour lemons
2 ounces of honey

Gandhi was called "Mahatma" or "great soul" because to the people of India he was a saint. Yet he was the first to acknowledge the inconsistencies in his ideas:

"In my search after Truth," he wrote, "I have discarded many ideas and learnt many new things. . . . What I am concerned with is my readiness to obey the call of Truth, my God, from moment to moment, and, therefore, when anybody finds any inconsistency between any two writings of mine, if he has still faith in my sanity, he would do well to choose the later of the two on the same subject."

Though Gandhi disliked the label of "Mahatma," he could not avoid it. Right before his death, he said that he would be qualified to be called Mahatma only if he remembered to say the name of God and blessed his murderer should he die at the hands of an assassin. That was exactly what happened. He was shot by a Hindu fanatic, a vegetarian named Nathuram Godse. Godse believed he was doing a service to India by eliminating Gandhi, who stubbornly insisted that Hindus and Muslims could live in harmony. Gandhi died calling "Ram" with a smile on his face, which indicated to many that he bore no ill will toward his executioner.

Gandhi's fasts were far from peaceful: he used his physical deprivations to manipulate the minds of men and the affairs of state. His suffering and torment became a symbol of the suppression of his people. His ability to channel men toward non-violent actions is as inexplicable as the reverse talents of Hitler. Merely to label both qualities as "charisma" minimizes the monumental effect of these two men. Gandhi's example in fact reaffirmed faith in vegetarianism in a people who were beginning to see it as an outdated and regressive way of life and a possible cause for their oppression by the British. Many Indians readopted a meatless diet in admiration of their spiritual mentor and leader. It is regrettable that the very people that he fought for, the lowest castes and the uneducated, today wonder who this man might have been.

So ingrained was Gandhi's concept of *ahimsa* that he expected the Jews to pray for Hitler to help him realize the error of his ways. On December 24, 1941, Gandhi wrote an open letter to the Führer, reprinted in *The Life and Death of Mahatma Gandhi.* The communication begins:

Dear Friend,
That I address you as a friend is no formality. I own no foes. . . .
During this season when the hearts of the peoples of Europe yearn for peace, we have suspended even our own peaceful struggle. Is it not too much to ask you to make an effort for peace during a time which may mean nothing to you personally, but which must mean much to the millions of Europeans whose dumb cry for peace I hear, for my ears are attuned to hearing the dumb millions. . . .

Although Gandhi's applications of *satygraha* were often shortsighted and childishly imagined, as in this letter to Hitler, he did institute realistic measures that demonstrated humane alternatives to satisfying material needs. Perhaps the most original was the establishment of the Kora Kendra slaying works outside Bombay, which flourishes even today. This is the only place in the world devoted to the production of leather goods, such as sandals, shoes, and pocket books, made from the carcasses of animals that died of natural causes, proof that leather may be rendered useful without painful slaughter and premature death.

In Gandhi's writings on health and nutrition, he tried to re-educate Indians who had long blamed their malnutrition and poverty on the absence of meat from their diet rather than poor education. He tried to demonstrate how comfortably and healthfully anyone might live on simple foods, such as nuts and pulses. That his dietary theories were unsuccessful in reaching the masses is clear in the current situation in India. In fact, even the wealthy in India who can afford all the food they need and want are symbols of the very excesses Gandhi preached against, enjoying diets of carbohydrates and starches rather than high-protein, uncooked foods. If Gandhi's dietary theories were truly heeded today, most of the nutritional diseases caused by sheer ignorance would be eradicated.

Gandhi deeply regretted that Rabindranath Tagore, the Pulitzer Prize-winning poet of India, gave up vegetarianism. However, Tagore acknowledged the moral issues involved. "As I was looking out on the river," Tagore wrote,

> I saw all of a sudden an odd-looking bird making its way through the water to the opposite bank, followed by a great commotion. I found it was a domestic fowl which had managed to escape impending doom in the valley by jumping over-board and was now trying frantically to swim across. It had almost gained the bank when the clutches of its relentless pursuers closed on it, and it was brought back in triumph, gripped by the neck.
> I told the cook I would not have any meat for dinner. I really must give up animal food. We manage to swallow flesh, only because we do not think of the cruel and sinful thing we do.

Krishna Consciousness

Today the strict asceticism of Gandhi is being carried on by the ridiculed and misunderstood followers of A. C. Bhaktivedanta Swami Prabhupada, the spiritual master of the Hare Krishna Movement, who came to the United States from India in 1965. The Hindu Movement, based on the doctrines of love of God, *ahimsa*, and the *Bhagavad-gita*, has been growing steadily and setting up centers throughout the Western world. Hare Krishna followers do not eat meat or wear leather products. In fact, vegetarianism is essential to Krishna Consciousness, a philosophy according to which man must live strictly in cooperation with the laws of god Krishna in order to be peaceful and prosperous. All unnecessary violence must be avoided.

Food has further religious overtones since nourishment is offered to Krishna and is another way of bringing a disciple back to Godhead, the spiritual goal after death. Hare Krishnas base their vegetarianism on the *Bhagavad-gita*, the sacred Vedic text of Krishna, where it is written that only four foods are to be offered to him: a leaf, a flower, fruit, or water. These gifts are interpreted as vegetables, grains, fruits, milk, and water.

Followers of Prabhupada are generally middle-class youths who forego comfort and material gains to lead simple, often celibate, lives. They eat Indian food with their hands and use a minimum of spices. Small *puris* substitute for bread; green vegetables (*bhaji*) and *halivah*, consisting of farina and raisins, are other offerings. There is an abundant supply of milk since it is considered a complete food that also constitutes a major part of the Hare Krishna diet.

A former Catholic newspaper journalist who has been a member of the movement for five years explains why garlic and onions are forbidden. "These foods excite the animal passions," he says passion-

A married Hare Krishna follower who was a commercial photographer before joining the movement five years ago.

ately. "We also prohibit all stimulants, such as coffee, tea, alcohol, drugs, meat, fish, and eggs. Gambling and illicit sex are also taboo."

Krishna Consciousness divides life into three modes: goodness, passion, and ignorance. Foods of goodness, such as milk, increase the duration of life. Passionate foods are hot and spicy. Foods of ignorance include old and decayed food as well as meat.

The married devotees of the movement wear white robes; those in saffron are bachelors. "Marriage has a different meaning to us," a married devotee explained. "We see it as a duty to be fulfilled when we are ready. Our marriages are not based on passion or romance; therefore there are few divorces. My wife decided she wanted to marry at the same time that I did. We went to the Master and he agreed to our betrothal."

There is little sex in the Hare Krishna Movement; most are allowed to indulge about once a month. "But we have a higher passion," the youth continued, "God."

Cleanliness is another basic principle for these followers, as it was for Gandhi, since the body is a statement of their spirituality. "I shower every time I go to the bathroom, although many devotees are not as rigid and only shower or bathe twice a day."

Finances for the Hare Krishna Movement come from their incense business, the largest in the world and one that grosses several million dollars annually. They are also taking over churches throughout the United States. The building in Los Angeles where the Master lives during the three months he is away from India was a former Methodist church.

The devotees carry symbolic beads which they fondle with the same intensity that a nun manipulates her rosary. "Hearing begins spiritual life," a visiting Swami explains in a gentle tone. "If you are inattentive during the chanting, that is an offense. The goal is to become completely absorbed in the Krishna *mantra*. There are sixteen words and each word has two syllables. You should listen very carefully to every syllable."

The Swami pauses for a moment and asks, "Are there any questions? If there are no questions, you all must agree that the goal of human life is chanting 'Hare Krishna.' Good. Then I'll continue.

"What do the beads mean? There are one hundred and eight beads. The beads help you to achieve some regulation in your life. Each day, you should chant and meditate for one complete round. Those who live in the temples meditate for two hours a day or about sixteen rounds. But if you are only beginning, five minutes a day is a good amount of time. If you regulate your life, Krishna will reciprocate and your whole life will change."

This thin, quiet man is capable of potent words. He describes a concert he attended at Madison Square Garden as an example of the false gods of American worship. "There was a rock singer sitting on a stool steeped in urine and sweat. He is worshipped, but when you die, will that rock singer or that movie star help you? No! But Krishna will treat you nicely, the more you surrender to him."

Altar of the Hare Krishna house in Brooklyn, New York, where daily meditation and chanting is practiced on a barren wood floor.

There has to be an ingredient in the Krishna movement that enables its members to be almost one hundred per cent effective in their drug rehabilitation programs. They share a passion for their beliefs and an abhorrence of materialism. They also have unusual energy because of

43

their asceticism. Why are there only a few thousand followers now? "When a rare jewel is for sale," says a leader in Boston, "not everyone is prepared to pay the price. So similarly not everyone can take a bona fide spiritual life which involves some sacrifice of sense gratification."

Unlike Gandhi, who rejected and despised the Hindu caste system, followers of Prabhupada accept the four castes as the law of god and they yearn to reach the level of *Brahmana*—the intellectual—in this life or the next as the soul transmigrates. The goal is an eternal reunion with Krishna in a spiritual corner of the universe known as *Viakunta*.

Unlike the Macrobiotic Movement, which is based on the teachings of Japanese-born George Ohsawa, Hare Krishnas incorporate vegetarianism as a non-violent way of living. It is an upcoming, worldwide community of doing for others and denying your own passions. Macrobiotics, which does include fish, is more of an "I am the center of a universe" movement, with the use of a systematic method of diet, based on the Yin-Yang principle, to increase one's efficiency and health in *this* life. There is little concern in the Macrobiotic Movement for the next one. Ohsawa, author of more than 300 books, even advocated sex. "If a man or woman has no appetite for sex and experiences no pleasure," Ohsawa writes, "he or she is estranged from the dialectical law of life, Yin-Yang. Violation of this law through ignorance can only lead to sickness and insanity." He warns against even attempting celibacy.

Although the dietary principles of macrobiotics do not necessarily advocate abstention from meat, many followers do not eat it. Some even avoid fish, although raw fish is allowed. Ohsawa recommended that at least 60 per cent of the diet be cereals, which he considered a principal food. There are ten grades of diet, with number seven consisting of 100 per cent cereals. On the list of forbidden foods are chemicalized and canned ones, soft drinks, potato, tomato, and eggplant; but fertile eggs, fish, shellfish, and "wild birds" are permissible. However, Ohsawa encouraged the avoidance of any and all animal products because of a subsequent increase in violence and cruelty. Excessive and incorrect eating was his explanation for all diseases, including schizophrenia and cancer.

3

Orpheus Ascending

Greek Thinkers

Although there are some early allusions to a simple, meatless diet in ancient Greece, it does not emerge as a viable philosophy until Pythagoras, who was contemporaneous with Buddha and Mahavira. Some believe that in old age Hesiod, who lived two centuries earlier, retreated from city life to live in the mountains on grains, berries, and fruits. Specific biographical details supporting that vegetarian retirement are lacking. All we know are the few facts gleaned from *The Works and Days*, Hesiod's abrasive yet delightful poem and major work. It seems his hardworking father died and left his farmland to be divided between his two sons, Hesiod and Perses. Hesiod believes his brother seized the better share. *The Works and Days* is an advisory guide to farming and righteous living.

Hesiod chides his fellow men who never learned that the half is better than the whole, and that a good living is possible on such vegetables as "mallow and asphodel." If those truths were learned, men would be able to hang up their "steering oar in the smoke of the fireplace" and the work of the oxen and the "patient mule" would be unnecessary. Hesiod also speaks of giving a "loaf" to a hired man and of eating cheese and drinking wine. He glorifies working; it is not working that is the sin. Get a woman—not for marriage, but for plowing. Later he describes the importance of knowing the value of each day: the fourth day of the month is recommended for opening a jar of wine, and the ninth day is always good since "a man or a woman may be beget or be born."

However in *Theogony*, another verse work ascribed to Hesiod, he speaks of animal sacrifices practiced in ancient Greece: men got "the better portion" while the gods received the less edible parts. Hesiod's depiction of the simple diet contrasts with those banquets during earlier Homeric times when meat was roasted on spits. In those days, after singeing the animal hair, the skin was removed and the body pierced through with a spit so it would turn over in the fire. Flour and salt seasoned bits of ox, sheep, or pig. Brains were considered acceptable food and highly praised for their softness. Beans, chick peas, cabbage, cheese mixed with honey and wine, and milk from cows, sheeps, or goats completed the festive meal.

The diet of classical Greece was far simpler and consisted of fish, vegetables, and fruits. During the sixth century, when Mahavira and Buddha were spiritually revolutionizing India, the mystical, vegetarian cults of Orpheus were similarly laying the foundations for the philosophies of Pythagoras and Plato. To understand the Orphic communities is to appreciate what it was they were reacting against: the hedonistic cult of Bacchus.

Bacchus, or Dionysus, depicted as a man or a bull, originated as a fertility god to the Thracians, a primitive agricultural society in an area occupying the southeastern tip of the Balkan Peninsula. As with all the colorful Greek gods, there are numerous contradictory legends about the birth and parentage of Bacchus. With the discovery of beer, Bacchus became the god of intoxication to which the inebriated Thracian paid homage. When wine was added to the liquid fare, Bacchus grew in importance. Then, at some unknown date, Bacchus cults migrated to Greece where they clashed with a more tempered society. Wild orgiastic festivals complete with music, dancing, drinking, and eating the flesh and blood of sacrificial animals contrasted to a culture that was being transformed into a more stable agricultural economy based on planned actions and delayed impulses.

Orpheus is another semi-legendary figure who also hails from Thrace. Some Greek myths describe him as the son of Caliope by Apollo; in others he is fathered by Oeagrus, a king of Thrace. Yet his magnificent ability at playing the lyre was so renowned that it was said rivers ceased flowing and wild animals stopped in their tracks.

In the legend of Orpheus, he married Eurydice, a nymph. When

Aristaeus attempted to rape her, she fled, was bitten by a snake, and died. Orpheus descended to Hades, where he was told that if he would avoid looking at Eurydice until he brought her into the sunlight, she would again be his. But Orpheus succumbed to temptation, losing his nymph forever. Grief-stricken and desperate, he became a recluse and wandered aimlessly for years. Other versions of the legend describe Orpheus as a follower of Bacchus who was torn to pieces by the women of Thrace because of his inattentiveness. Another variation declares that Dionysus forced the Thracian wives to murder their husbands and mutilate Orpheus. His head was tossed into the Hebrus River, but he continued singing as it floated into the sea to the island of Lesbos, where an oracle of Orpheus was established.

Euripedes was aware of the ascetic principles of the Orphic cults. In his powerful drama *Hippolytus*, the hero, Hippolytus, is a follower of Orpheus. Phaedra, wife of Theseus, king of Athens, commits suicide because of her love for Hippolytus, her illegitimate stepson by Theseus' previous union with the Amazon Hippolyta. Theseus, outraged and stricken with grief, immediately accepts his wife's death as proof of her incest. He condemns Hippolytus to exile—a worse punishment than death—and then chides his radical offspring:

> THESEUS: Look at this man. My own son, yet he tried to seduce my wife. He is manifestly proven more base by the hand of her who is dead. Show your face here to your father: your company has already polluted me. *You* are that superior creature that associates with gods? *You* are temperate and uncontaminated by evil? Your high claims will never convince me; I won't be such a fool as to attribute to the gods such a lack of discernment. Go then and brag, cry up your vegetarian diet like a quack. Hold Orpheus your master, rant away, revere the vaporing of your many creeds. But you are caught. I charge you all, shun such men as this. [Translated by Moses Hadas and John Harvey McClean]

Hippolytus pleads his innocence since he is a sincere friend, reverent to the gods, and knowledgeable about sexual intercourse only from pictures and hearsay, since celibacy was another principle of the Orphic cults. Artemis, chaste goddess of the hunt to whom he owed allegiance, rather than the hedonistic Aphrodite, defends the youth and reveals his innocence. But, as Artemis declares, Hippolytus was destroyed by his own noble heart. Theseus learns too late that his son is indeed virtuous for Hippolytus, thrown against rocks by his own horses, has his flesh ripped to shreds in an "Orphic" manner. As he lies dying, Hippolytus releases his father from all guilt.

Thus the meatless diet that Hippolytus followed served to purify his soul—a relationship intrinsic to the Orphic communities. They also believed in transmigration of the soul or that the fate of the soul depended on how one acted on earth. In contrast to the Bacchae, who sought a tangible intoxication with wine, the Orphics aspired to a mental and spiritual inebriation by union with god. Life was painful and tragic to the Orphics. Only an ascetic life might help in attaining the ecstasy of the ultimate consummation with god. The Orphics, though outwardly quiet and contemplative men, directed all their energies toward intense mental probings and introspection.

It is possible that if the development of science had not interceded, Greek religious and philosophical leanings would have continued to progress from Orphic beliefs to purely Oriental cults. There are undeniable similarities between the Orphic communities and those religions arising in the East, although proof of substantial contact between these distant cultures is still doubtful.

Pythagorean Serum

The next Western advocate of a meatless diet was Pythagoras, a reformer of Orphism. It is difficult to differentiate between the beliefs of the real Pythagoras and those of the Pythagoreans, who followed and probably embellished his theories. Pythagoras is said to have been the son of a wealthy citizen named Mnesarchos, who was perhaps a jeweler, and a woman named Parthenis. Pythagoras was a native of the island of Samos and he flourished about 532 B.P. Unhappy with the government of the militaristic Polycrates, Pythagoras left Samos and probably visited Egypt and Babylon. Ultimately he established himself at Croton, a rich and prosperous Greek city in southern Italy famous for medicine.

In Croton, Pythagoras founded a religious community which for a time exerted considerable influence. Eventually, however, the citizens turned against him and he moved to Metapontion, another southern Italian city, where he died. Soon Pythagoras became a legend; it was even said he was the son of Apollo.

To some, Pythagoras is known as the "father of vegetarianism"; to others, as the discoverer of the Pythagorean theorem that the sum of the squares on the sides adjoining the right angle of a triangle is equal to the square of the remaining side, the hypotenuse. The combination of religious mystic and mathematician has enhanced Pythagoras' impact on Western culture and philosophy.

One of the more revolutionary aspects of the Pythagorean community was the equal admission of men and women. Indeed, the association of vegetarian sects with male and female equality is as common as the association of a meatless diet with pacifism.* Property was also held communally by the Pythagoreans. The Orphic belief in transmigration of the soul, or metempsychosis, was accepted and developed further. Thus, if a man may reappear as an animal, flesh-eating is little better than cannibalism. A story is often told that Pythagoras, upon hearing the cries of a dog, instructed the villain to stop the assault. "Stop, for in the pup's yelps I can hear the voice of a friend," Pythagoras supposedly said. This is taken to be an explanation of metempsychosis. However, others interpret it as Pythagoras' acceptance of the dog as an equal friend, whose cries he hears.

Literary evidence for the vegetarianism of Pythagoras and his followers is provided in the fifteenth book of the epic poem *Metamorphoses* by Ovid, the Roman poet born in 43 B.P. Although there is no evidence that Ovid actually practiced vegetarianism, it is apparent that he was sympathetic to the views of Pythagoras. "He [Pythagoras] was the first to ban the serving of animal foods at our tables, first to express himself in such words as these—wise words, indeed, but powerless to convince his hearers:

> O my fellow-men, do not defile your bodies with sinful foods. We have corn, we have apples, bending down the branches with their weight, and grapes swelling on the vines. There are sweet-flavored herbs, and vegetables which can be cooked and softened over the fire, nor are you denied milk, or thyme-scented honey. The earth affords a lavish supply of riches, of innocent foods, and offers you banquets that involve no bloodshed or slaughter; only beasts satisfy their hunger with flesh, and not even all of those for horses, cattle, and sheep live on grass. . . .
> . . . It may be that originally the reeking swords were stained with blood from killing wild animals, and I admit that creatures trying to kill us may be killed, without involving us in guilt. But that should have been enough. It was wrong to eat them as it was right to slay. . . . [Translated by Mary M. Innes]

The meals of Pythagoreans are described by Diogenes as bread and honey for dinner and raw and cooked vegetables for supper. Iamblichus, the Neoplatonist biographer of Pythagoras, depicts him as a man who paid fishermen to return their catchings to the sea, who stroked wild bears, lived on maize and corn, and abhorred animal sacrifices and wine.

Perhaps the most famous food taboo of the Pythagoreans was their

---

* Plato later expressed his approval of male and female equality. Vegetarian groups in nineteenth-century America, such as the Oneida Community and the contemporary Vegetarian Feminists, have also advanced sexual equality.

denunciation of beans. Pythagoras supposedly inspired such reverence for this anti-bean principle that ten of his disciples who might have escaped from an attack by crossing a beanfield died rather than tread down the beans, which were supposed to have a mystic affinity with the root of sensual and impure desires.

Other taboos concerned touching a white cock, and gluttony. Eating was necessary for life, but not its main focus. Vegetarianism contributed to peace as well as the suppression of animal passions; bathing and ample exercise in the open air were also encouraged.

"Wretches, utter wretches, keep your hands from beans!" wrote Empedocles, who flourished around 440 B.P. The noted philosopher, who advocated that there were four roots to all things—fire, air, earth, and water—and who discovered air as a separate substance, practiced vegetarianism and followed the principles of Orphism and Pythagoreanism. Born in the Greek city of Akragas, in Sicily, he founded the Sicilian school of medicine. Empedocles also advised avoiding marriage and procreation, regarding celibacy as a fundamental part of the philosophic life. Like many other Greek philosophers, his life is surrounded in legend: it is said that he controlled the wind and met his death by jumping into the crater of Etna to prove he was a god.

Socrates is known only through the writings of his pupils Xenophon and Plato, and a caricaturization by Aristophanes in *The Clouds*. Although Socrates and Plato are usually considered vegetarians, there is little supporting evidence for this view. Rather, they endorsed the simple life and a "natural" diet as the logical components of the ideal state. Temperance, not vegetarianism, is a consistent theme in *The Republic*. Socrates condemns drinking; he advocates simple food, and an equal education for women, since if dogs do not differentiate between the sexes, why should men?

Antistenes, a disciple of Socrates, lived within an aristocratic circle for most of his life. However, right after the death of Socrates he gave up his excessive ways and became one of the working people; he also adopted a simple vegetarian diet. Perhaps the tragic death of his philosophical mentor prompted the change? Or the defeat of Athens? Or "male menopause"? Whatever the reason, he advocated a return to nature where neither marriage, established religion, slavery, or government were necessary.

His pupil, Diogenes, was even more of an ascetic than Antistenes. The name "cynic" is ascribed to the school that Diogenes founded because the leader decided to live like a dog; *cynic* means *canine*. To Diogenes animals, as well as men, were his brothers. To attain his goal of self-sufficiency it was necessary to relinquish all worldly possessions. As a dramatic expression of his simple life he made his bathtub his home, even tossing aside a cup for the more natural way of drinking—clasped hands.

Roman Sympathy

Although the Romans were not universally vegetarian, they concentrated on vegetables, fruits, and nuts. The diet of the Italian peasant was as much a meatless one in ancient times as it is today because of the scarcity of flesh food. Although cattle slaughter was never a common practice, mutton, pork, and goat's flesh were available. As time went on, culinary tastes became more sophisticated and the craving for flesh accordingly increased. The taste for game was even more rapid: hare, wild goat, boar, and ass were highly esteemed. Eventually vegetables became the food fit for animals, rather than men, although by necessity the staple products were still bread, wine, and oil. Beans and onions, though extensively raised, were considered too heavy a food except for blacksmiths, gladiators, and farm hands.

Of course, each strata of society had a varied diet, for the table of the opulent or the soldier's rations differed considerably from the simple uncooked foods of the poor. A well-endowed table was the sign of wealth then, as now, and the soldier who was a model of discipline lived on grain and corn and vinegar diluted with water, which kept longer than wine.

There were a few "Roman" writers, as distinct from the Christian theologians, who were active vegetarians, providing references to the fact in their writings. In spite of Ovid's recording of the ways of Pythagoras, contemporary classicists do not consider Ovid to have been one of his followers. Quintus Horatius Flaccius, known as Horace, though not a vegetarian, did extol the simple life. Born in 65 B.P. at Venusia, a little town in southern Italy, he left Rome at the age of nineteen for Athens, where he could pursue his intellectual leanings. Horace learned the values of an ideal pastoral existence through the gift of a friend, Maecenas, of a Sabine farm in honor of the publication of Horace's first book of *Satires* in 35 B.P. In the *Odes*, translated by Burton Raffel, Horace writes:

> *Happiness sits in a battered*
> *Salt dish, on a thin-spread table,*
> *Lies in sleep too quiet for greed,*
> *Too soft for fear.*   [II,16]

Another Roman who toyed with a vegetarian diet was Seneca, a first-century Stoic who became tutor to the ten-year-old Nero. In Seneca's letter to Lucilius, translated by Richard M. Gummere, Seneca embodies the Stoic principles of anti-materialism and physical hardship as a means of strengthening the soul. His life, however, was quite contradictory to his principles since Seneca supposedly managed to accumulate about twelve million dollars by lending money in Britain at excessive rates.

Seneca tells Lucilius how through Sotion, one of his early teachers, he became acquainted with Pythagoras's avoidance of animal flesh. He expounds the theory of transmigration of souls as the basis for the Greek philosopher's diet. Seneca continues:

> . . . I was imbued with this teaching, and began to abstain from animal food; at the end of a year the habit was as pleasant as it was easy. I was beginning to feel that my mind was more active; though I would not to-day positively state whether it really was or not. Do you ask how I came to abandon the practice? It was this way: The days of my youth coincided with the early part of the reign of Tiberius Caesar. Some foreign rites were at that time being inaugurated, and abstinence from certain kinds of animal food was set down as a proof of interest in the strange cult. So at the request of my father, who did not fear prosecution, but who detested philosophy, I returned to my previous habits; and it was not very hard to induce me to dine more comfortably. . . . (*Epistle CVIII*)

Temperance, however, remained a firm principle in Seneca's life. He continues to explain to Lucilius the recommendation of his much-admired teacher Attalus, who endorsed the use of a pillow that "did not give in to the body." Seneca points out to Lucilius that now even as an old man he still uses one "so hard that it leaves no trace after pressure." In a similar fashion, he followed Attalus's example of denouncing excesses in food and drink, avoiding oysters and mushrooms throughout his life since "they are not really food, but are relished to bully the sated stomach into further eating, as is the fancy of gourmands and those who stuff themselves beyond their powers of digestion: down with it quickly, and up with it quickly!"

The one-time vegetarian gradually fell into disfavor with his former pupil, the Emperor Nero, and Seneca ended his eloquent life by his own hand in C.E. 65, supposedly philosophizing about his virtuous behavior even as blood flowed from his opened veins.

A Return to Greece

The "Golden Age" was over; there remained only a historical era of cultural glory, consumed by colonial expansion, militarism, and irreconcilable power struggles. As the country lay dying, the cause of vegetarianism was hailed in the writings of Plutarch, one of the last of the classical Greek historians, and by Porphyry and Plotinus, two eminent Neoplatonists.

In the collection of over sixty miscellaneous writings known as *Moralia*, Plutarch dealt with issues that went beyond the meatless diet. "The Cleverness of Animals, both of the Sea and of the Land" debates whether animals have souls and which species are more intelligent. Even in that essay, however, Plutarch has to control himself from delving into the subject of vegetarianism. He points out, through Autobulus's words, that "there is a view which holds that men became insensitive and savage because of the taste for bloodshed they acquired in hunting. . . ." Autobulus continues by describing Pythagoras's actions, based on "the contrary principle" that "consistent regular behavior is extraordinarily powerful, gradually infiltrating into the emotions and making men better . . ." (Rex Warner's translation).

"Odysseys and Gryllus," a dialogue with a mythological setting, satirizes the greed and gluttony of man but once again Plutarch expresses his high regard for animals for, he explains, even the poets describe "your mightiest warriors as 'fierce as a wolf' and 'lion-hearted.' "

Plutarch, known mainly for his widely-read biographical *Lives*, contributed some of the first ethical writings. In fact, to many they may seem even too moralistic. Plutarch traveled in Egypt and journeyed to Rome, and probably died some years after C.E. 120. However, his views expressed in a lengthy essay "On the Eating of Flesh," translated by Harold Cherniss and William C. Helmbold, are timeless:

> . . . Can you really ask what reason Pythagoras had for abstaining from flesh? For my part I rather wonder both by what accident and in what state of soul or mind the first man did so, touched his mouth to gore and brought his lips to the flesh of a dead creature, he who set forth tables of dead, stale bodies and ventured to call food and nourishment the parts that had a little before bellowed and cried, moved and lived. How could his eyes endure the slaughter when throats were slit and hides flayed and limbs torn from limb? How could his nose endure the stench? How was it that the pollution did not turn away his taste, which made contact with the sores of others and sucked juices and serums from mortal wounds?
>
> . . . It is certainly not lions and wolves that we eat out of self-defence; on the contrary, we ignore these and slaughter harmless, tame creatures without stings or teeth to harm us, creatures that, I swear, Nature appears to have produced for the sake of their beauty and grace.

. . . But nothing abashed us, not the flower-like tinting of the flesh, not the persuasiveness of the harmonious voice, not the cleanliness of their habits or the unusual intelligence that may be found in the poor wretches. No, for the sake of a little flesh we deprive them of sun, of light, of the duration of life to which they are entitled by birth and being. . . .

Another Greek, born about 232 in Tyria, Phoenicia, attacked meat-eating with equal vengeance and with the same application of doctrine to dietary practice. Porphyry, who changed his name from Malchus to Porphyrius (meaning the purple used for royal garments), devoted an entire four-part treatise to vegetarianism: *De Abstentia*. At the age of thirty, Porphyry traveled to Rome where he met another notable Neoplatonist, Plotinus. He became Plotinus' disciple and translated *The Enneads* of his master.

The literary output of Porphyry, a scholar who is usually seen in a secondary light to his master, was enormous. Voltaire mentions Porphyry in his *Philosophical Dictionary* as one who regarded animals as brothers and wrote an extensive treatise but failed to make any converts. One factor might have been the repetitious nature of *De Abstentia* and the monotony of his endless arguments trying to convince his friend Firmus that he should return to the meatless diet he had foolishly abandoned. There are four sections to the treatise: they contain arguments against animal sacrifice, moral persuasions, and historical evidence about communities, such as the Essenes, who lived on a meatless diet.

"Who is to say birds are irrational because they cannot speak," Porphyry asks. "Birds communicate with a language we cannot understand, nor can we understand the tongue of a foreigner—but do we pluck out his hair?" He continues: "A man who eats a harmless diet will be less inclined to slaughter another man's flesh since the idea would be unthinkable." Unfortunately, all his arguments are too one-sided and emphatic to be considered objective.

Porphyry, like Plotinus, was a moral and ascetic man, though he entered into a Platonic marriage with Marcella, a fellow philosopher and widow of a friend, so that he might provide an education for her five children. Plotinus, on the other hand, remained a bachelor. He too was a vegetarian and exceptionally moral. Porphyry relates that a senator, Rogatianus, was so taken with Plotinus that he gave up all his property, dismissed his slaves, and renounced all his dignities. Though a victim of gout, who had to be carried around in a chair, it was said that Rogatianus' new meat abstinence restored his health.

Although Plotinus is believed to have come from Egypt, where he was born about 204, his cultural and educational background was completely Greek. At the age of twenty-seven, overwhelmed by an interest in philosophy, he studied for eleven years under Ammonius Saccas. He arrived in Rome at forty and became the founder of a school. To Plotinus there were clearly two worlds: the material and the spiritual. To free oneself from the materialistic prison, contemplation and meditation were necessary. Although afflicted with intestinal problems, Plotinus refused all medicants that contained parts of wild beasts or reptiles. His health rapidly declined after the age of sixty and he retired to the home of a friend in Campania, where he died in 270.

4

Judeo-Christian
Ethics

Jewish Seeds

What did vegetarian Rabbi Chaim Zundel Maccoby do during the ritualistic Passover Seder since a shank bone is part of the symbolic meal? He substituted an egg. Rabbi Maccoby, renowned as the Kamenitzer Maggid, was born in 1858 in the Russian town of Kamenitz-Litovsk. He traveled throughout his country speaking out for emigration to Palestine, was subsequently denounced as a revolutionary and escaped, reaching London in 1890. Remembered as a dynamic speaker, who inspired Zionist organizations throughout England, Rabbi Maccoby was also the seed for the later Jewish Vegetarian Society in England.

At about the same time, Aaron W. Frankel, who lived in an overcrowded and unsanitary tenement in New York City, published an essay: *Thou Shalt Not Kill or The Torah of Vegetarianism*. He tried, unsuccessfully, to begin an American Jewish vegetarian movement.

Almost seventy years later, eighteen-year-old Vivien Pick wrote a letter that was published in *The Jewish Chronicle* (London), requesting Jewish vegetarians to write to her. An overwhelming response, as well as her mother's admiration for the Kamenitzer Maggid, led to the creation of the first society, with her father Philip as the first, still current, leader. The movement is strongest in England, with representatives of the society in Canada, Mexico, Jamaica, South Africa, Italy, Australia, the United States, Portugal, Holland, Greece, and Israel. An article written in 1967 lists 80,000 vegetarians in Israel, but precise or up-to-date statistics on Jewish vegetarians throughout the world are unavailable. For example, the society in Johannesburg boasts one hundred members, but there may be numerous other Jewish vegetarians who avoid joining a group. "Our greatest problem," says Joe Green of South Africa, "is to convince Jews who are vegetarian that there is a Jewish Vegetarian outlook. They obtain their ideological impetus from either the east or from the health movement."

Leaders of Jewish vegetarianism prefer to use the Old Testament as the inspirational source, including the commandment "Thou Shalt Not Kill." For in Genesis it is written that on the sixth day,

> God said, Behold, I have given you every herb bearing seed, which is upon the face of all the earth, and every tree, in which is the fruit of a tree yielding seed; to you it shall be meat. And to every beast of the earth, and to every fowl of the air, and to every thing that creepeth upon the earth, wherein there is life, I have given every green herb for meat. . . .

The first law in the Bible is a dietary one—do not eat the forbidden fruit. It is a *hukim*, or an unexplained edict, with the purpose of inspiring man's obedience and building his character. There is no reason to avoid that infamous fruit except that it is the "will of God." Significantly, it is only *after* Eve defies God and eats the apple that killing animals for food is recorded in the Old Testament. Then, until the time of Noah, he who killed an animal was as guilty as he who killed a man: Abel killed an animal; Cain slew Abel; and the chain of retribution for both crimes is, allegorically, responsible for all the evils that follow.

Right before the Deluge, the fable continues, man's character fell to its lowest level. As a consequence, the Flood is followed by a shortening of man's life span and an intensification of the life-and-death process. But man emerges from God's wrath as king:

> And God blessed Noah and his sons, and said unto them, Be fruitful and multiply and replenish the earth. And the fear of you and the dread of you shall be upon every beast of the earth, and upon every fowl of the air, upon all that moveth upon the earth, and upon all the fishes of the sea; into your hand are they delivered. Everything that liveth shall be meat for you; even as the green herb have I given you all things. . . .

However, animal food is seen in Jewish tradition, as in Hinduism, as a passionate food capable of exciting the "animal" side of man's nature.

Thus, to limit this effect, the rule of *noahide* was introduced—the prohibition against eating a limb torn from a live animal or bird. "But do not eat meat in which its life blood still runs," since blood was believed to contain the soul, instinct, and emotions of the animal. To avoid transferring that life force to man, meat was to be salted and boiled until all blood was removed.

The Old Testament indicates a preferential order of foods: garden pluckings are the most desirable, since Adam and Eve were intended to be vegetarians; next is the flesh of herbivorous animals; but the meat of carnivorous creatures is forbidden, since their predatory habits might become part of man's already too aggressive nature. Thus the orthodox Jewish dietary laws served two functions: to further unite a people whose only means of survival as a distinct religion was their cohesiveness; and to avoid arousing animal passions by digesting carnivorous creatures.

The Jewish dietary laws are quite extensive and can be explained on three levels: ethical, mystical, and symbolical. Within an ethical interpretation, the goal of self-mastery is the main emphasis behind the rulings.

"Why do we eat ham, Dad?"

"Because you should be kosher in your heart, not in your stomach," my father would say.

Orthodox Jewish interpretations, however, imply that God desired control of the *complete* being—not just the spiritual or philosophical aspects. No, God should be part of habits as basic as diet. Furthermore, moral discipline enables a man to be freed from his own instincts, impulses, and desires. Specific laws do not inhibit someone but free him from his own inclinations so he may hear a "higher" voice.

The implications of the prohibited animals, explicitly listed in Deuteronomy, may also be interpreted mystically: that flesh could affect a man's personality since the forbidden animals, or *tamei*, are unclean in both a moral and a metaphysical sense. They supposedly thrive by killing and aggression.

Symbolism is the underlying principle of dietary laws, but abstract ideas are often the least effective means of education. Specific injunctions, on the other hand, provide concrete guidelines to help Jews achieve a universal identity as well as a moral autonomy. Therefore, "In all thy ways acknowledge Him" includes what you eat as well as your soul, mind, and body.

The Old Testament has numerous rulings or tales that indicate a kindness to animals:

- When Isaac selected a wife, someone who showed kindness to a camel indicated similar compassion for man. (Genesis)

- A newborn animal is not to be removed from its mother for at least seven days. (Leviticus)
- An animal and its young may not be killed on the same day to prevent the possibility of a mother seeing the slaughter of its own child. (Leviticus)
- An ox and an ass may not plow together since they are unequal in strength; the weaker would suffer while trying to keep up with the stronger. (Deuteronomy)
- A man may not commence eating before his animals are fed. (Deuteronomy)
- While treading out the corn the ox, or any other animal, must not be muzzled. (Deuteronomy)

Meat-eating Jews feel that the *Shehitah,* or kosher slaughter, is the least painful method of obtaining animal food. Jewish vegetarians, however, fail to see the kindness in any form of slaughter. *Shehitah* is a very specific method of slaughter that is sanctioned for the permitted four-footed warm-blooded mammals and birds. Rather than the butcher being a lowly member of society or doing a debased job, the *Shohetim* must be a man of good character and he is highly regarded in the community. A dramatic account of the moral conflicts of a *Shohetim* is the theme of the compelling short story "The Slaughterer" by Isaac Bashevis Singer, who is a vegetarian. Yoineh Meir is appointed the town's ritual slaughterer but he is reluctant to accept the position. A rabbi, trying to convince Yoineh, writes to him: "When you slaughter an animal with a pure knife and with piety, you liberate the soul that resides in it." Yoineh Meir ambivalently accepts the position, but his desperate moral conflicts over the animal murders he performs drive him to suicide.

Tradition governs the act of *Shehitah,* which consists of a horizontal cut across the windpipe and gullet of the animal, using a faultless movable cutting instrument in a way that is designed for quick death and the fullest draining of blood. There are five rules:

- without interruption
- cutting by only one half of a movement to and fro and without pressure
- a knife with a perfect edge that is visible throughout the act and not covered by the hide of the cattle, wool of sheep, or feathers of birds
- within the specified space for cutting
- without tearing loose the windpipe and gullet before or during the cutting

Some say that the law of *Basar BeHabab*—or not consuming milk and meat together—stems from the fact that they are an indigestible combination. However, the reasoning goes deeper to the respect for parenthood. Three times in the Torah the ruling occurs, "Thou shalt not seethe a kid in its mother's milk." Similarly, the rule against eating an egg containing a blood spot is not because the egg is inedible or unclean but because blood indicates a new bird has already started to form.

There are other orthodox limitations on the diet of a Jew: he is required to examine fruits and vegetables for the presence of any insects or worms (*Sheratzim*). Such foods may not be eaten since the insects and worms themselves are prohibited. Fat and blood are distinct taboos because of respect for the spirit of the animal and the danger that the animal's instincts would be transferred to the body and personality of man.

Rabbis explain that meat-eating is a *punishment* to a Jew, not a reward. All the rules of kosher are attempts to make the punishment more palatable to the animals as well as man. It is as a consequence of the original sin that man eats meat; it is not supposed to be a pleasure, and throughout history Jews have rarely been hunters.

However, early vegetarian leanings were stifled by the writings of Rabbi Moses ben Maimon, known as Maimonides, who was born in 1135 to a distinguished rabbinical family in Spain. He became a leading interpreter of Jewish laws, as well as a physician. His guides to the sacred Jewish texts were written from a hygienic, rather than an ethical, vantage point. Maimonides argued that asceticism, including the rules against eating meat, drinking wine, and avoiding marriage, were evil roads. "Concerning these and similar excesses," he wrote, "King Solomon admonished: 'Do not be overly righteous nor overly wise lest you come to grief.'" To Maimonides, the middle road avoiding extremes was the best.

The Essenes

There were a group of ancient Jews, however, who embraced extremes. The Essenes were one of the three sects* that developed around 146 B.P. in opposition to the increasing rigidity of the Jewish religion. They also withdrew from the cities and organized temples because of such discouraging social and economic conditions as unemployment, excessive taxes, and famine.

Josephus and Pliny the Elder wrote about these communities, but

---

* The Pharisees and the Sadducees were the others.

most persons believed their ancient accounts were exaggerated since the Essenes were a peculiar male communal group that supposedly numbered about 4,000 in Palestine. King Herod regarded them as mystics for they even investigated the magical powers of plants and stones. However, in the early 1950's, the ruins of Khirbat Qumran were discovered about seven miles south of Jericho. In every way, they fit the description of the monastery of the Essenes that appeared in ancient writings and records of travelers. The *Manual of Discipline*, which was also unearthed, contained eleven columns explaining their specific rules. The Essenes were obsessed with cleanliness since they believed outward appearances indicated inner purity. In addition to digging their own latrines and washing frequently, they attended meals in white garments. They also grew and prepared their own simple vegetarian food. An official or master controlled their quiet and orderly daily life of prayers and silence. They claimed a heritage with Abraham, Moses, and the prophets, but rebelled against the extensive animal sacrifices that were practiced by the temple priests at that time. They were extremists who regarded themselves as the only true believers, through whom God's will had been revealed and through whom it would be fulfilled. "Among the Essenes," wrote Josephus, "there are some who claim to predict the future, practicing themselves in the Holy Books and in various purifications and in the utterances of the prophets, and it is rare that they are mistaken in their predictions."

It was a distinct community with its own charter, laws, rules, and rites. All decisions were debated and voted upon in a democratic way. Cooperation and sharing differentiated this group of celibate men. Slavery was noticeably absent. The term "Essene" comes from the Hebrew word *Esan*, "to be strong," since the members had strength of mind, enduring material suffering as well as repressing sexual passions.

There were two classes of Essenes: the first devoted themselves to a life of contemplation by studying the mysteries of nature as well as the holy writings; the second engaged in handicrafts. Not everyone could become an Essene; there were several trial stages a novitiate had to pass for three years before he was admitted to the order. While being considered, those youths were forbidden to attend the secret meetings or the sacred meal, called the Banquet of the Many.

A typical day was divided into three parts: devotion and worship of God and the relief of the needy and distressed; time to pursue their usual avocations, such as cultivation; and normal needs, such as simple meals and sleep. The *Manual of Discipline* reveals a strict penal code, with punishments for each diversion from their ethical rulings. For example, any man who lied regarding money would be excluded from the Banquet of the Many and could receive only one-fourth of his food for the next year. A lie knowingly spoken commanded six months' punishment. Interrupting the speaking of another Essene necessitated ten days of retribution; three months' punishment for saying a foolish word. Laughing aloud and stupidly brought thirty days' punishment; slandering a fellow Essene required one year of deprivation.

What do the remains of the monastery reveal? The ruin of an almost square building of about 100 feet with plastered inside walls. A pottery shop, kitchen, refrectory, and storeroom with the remains of foods in a thousand neatly stacked jars; an assembly hall over 70 feet long; and a scriptorium with inkwells. The nearby cemetery has more than a thousand graves and when they were unearthed there were bones of but a few women and children; the rest were men.

Essene monastery workshop in Qumran.

It is believed that Khirbat Qumran was built in the second century B.P. and that it lasted, without interruption, until 31 B.P. when an earthquake partly shattered the building. About thirty years later it was re-established and continued until the destruction of Jerusalem by the Romans in 70 C.E. when the Essenes mysteriously vanished forever.

Christianity

It is said that John the Baptist was a member of the Essene community. Some even believe that Jesus Christ spent his early years there. These are beliefs that are still historically unproven about the Essene cult. Others believe that the Teacher of Righteousness, an Essene who appears as a Messianic or ideal figure, was the prototype for Christ. All these questions go unanswered. Though the similarities between the Essene documents and the New Testament are significant, to date no one can conclusively explain what it all means. Both doctrines, however, rejoice in love of both the poor and one's neighbor, in humility, self-denial, and poverty. A more obvious similarity is the zealous way that the Essenes recruited new members, an indication of the later campaigns of the new Christians to increase their numbers. The Essene bodily purifications, possibly derived from the water cults prevalent along the Euphrates River, may have been the source for the Christian ritual of baptism. Further, more than any other Jewish group at that time, the Essenes believed that the Messiah would soon appear.

However, Jesus was not an ascetic like John the Baptist, who lived in the wilderness clothed with camel's hair and neither ate bread nor drank wine, but subsisted only on locusts and wild honey. Jesus seems to have eaten and drunk everything. Many persons who contemplate vegetarianism are hampered by the belief that Christ was a meat eater. There are too many references to Christ eating meat or fish in the New Testament for it to be oversight. Some try to explain these references to meat by the pointing out that Greek words for "meat" may simply mean food or nourishment. However, it is far more difficult to explain away the Last Supper or the Passover meal, for that would imply that Christ participated in the eating of the Passover Lamb, unless of course it is clearly proven that this could not have been the Passover meal since it occurred at an earlier date.

It is commendable that Jesus substituted bread and wine as symbols of the divine sacrifice rather than the actual animals that were then being used. But it is also a great historical irony that this advance for animals and men was only temporary—once Christianity was firmly established, fanatics would sacrifice disbelievers in "the name of" their God.

Although anti-meat injunctions are prevalent in the Old Testament, Jewish vegetarianism was not an early practice. However, several early Christian writers turned their attention to the moral and ascetic issue of flesh-eating. Tertullian, who lived from 160–240 C.E., composed numerous controversial pieces about the new religion he embraced. He wrote a treatise on dietetics to answer the common defense for meat-eating that no injunction against it appears in the Gospel. Tertullian explains that if man could not even follow a simple taboo against one fruit, how could he be expected to restrain himself from more demanding restrictions? Instead, after the Flood, man was given the regulation against blood; further details were left to his own strength of will.

Flavius Clemens, who lived about the same time as Tertullian, founded the famous Alexandrian school of Christian theology. His three major works are *A Horatory Discourse Addressed to the Greeks, The Instructor,* and the *Miscellanies.* One work that has been lost, *On Abstinence or Fasting,* might have contained valuable information on the early Christian view of fasting, an aspect of asceticism which eventually became more important than vegetarianism. However, at this point there were quite a number of early Christian fathers who protested against meat-eating because of the newly instilled Christian dogma of compassion to all living things. In *The Ethics of Diet* are passages from *The Instructor* where Clemens expresses his views on meat-eating:

> . . . the Instructor enjoins us to eat that we may live. For neither is food our business, nor pleasure our aim. Therefore discrimination is to be used in reference to food; it must be plain, truly simple, suiting precisely simple and artless children—as ministering to life not to luxury. . . . We must guard against those sorts of food which persuade us to eat when we are not hungry, bewitching the appetite. For is there not, within a temperate simplicity, a wholesome variety of eatables—vegetables, roots, olives, herbs, milk, cheese, fruits, and all kinds of dry food? . . . Accordingly the Apostle Matthew lived upon seeds and nuts and vegetables without the use of flesh. . . .

Other early Christian fathers who did not eat meat were Origen, who castrated himself and was a pupil of Clemens; and John Chrysostom, made patriarch of Constantinople in 398 and admired for his ascetic life. Fasting and abstinence from meat were encouraged as a means to increase willpower over mortal flesh and desires. However, meat was the consistent taboo, not fish. That association is exemplified in the Rule of St. Benedict, an Italian monk who founded the Benedictine Order and died around 547:

"Moreover, let the use of meat be granted to the sick who are very weak for the restoration of their strength, but when they are convalescent, let all abstain from meat as usual."

The Rule of St. Benedict is the chief rule in Western monasticism, used by Benedictines and by Cistercians as well. To this day the Cistercians abstain from meat not because of an ethical objection, or a hygienic motive. "It is precisely because meat is so good," says a Cistercian reverend, "that we do abstain from it. A meatless diet has a certain monotony about it and to forego the use of meat makes one's meals somewhat less attractive and enjoyable." Thus worldly goods will have less of a hold upon the monk and "he will have greater spiritual freedom to attend to the things of the Spirit and of God." Abstinence from meat was considered more important in earlier days; it is not presently an essential part of Cistercian life. In countries where other staples are harder to obtain than meat, for example in Argentina and parts of Africa, monks regularly eat meat.

The Trappists, a division of the Cistercian Order, still follow vegetarianism on an individual basis but it is not obligatory since there is a tendency to de-emphasize asceticism in contemporary monastic life. However, the Trappist production of natural jams indicates an appreciation of unadulterated foods.

Numerous other leaders in the development of Christianity, such as St. David, the patron saint of Wales who died about 588, St. Francis of Assissi, who died in 1226, and St. Clare, who died in 1253, did not eat meat. However, fish was never forbidden. Self-discipline was the main motivation for their dietary restrictions. For example, Rhigyfarch's *Life of St. David*, the primary source since he was a contemporary religious associate of St. David's, describes a typical scene at the monastery:

> . . . At length they assemble at table. Every one restores and refreshes his weary limbs by partaking of supper, not, however, to excess, for too much, though it be of bread alone, engenders self-indulgence; but at that meal, all take supper according to the varying condition of their bodies or age. They do not serve courses of different savours, nor richer kinds of food: their food is, in fact, bread and herbs seasoned with salt, whilst they quench a burning thirst with a temperate kind of drink. . . . [Chapter 24. Translated by J. W. James]

Later, in chapter 50, fish is mentioned: "But the holy bishop Dewi, foreseeing it with prophetic spirit, said to the brethren: 'This day, my breathren, very holy men are visiting us. Welcome them joyfully, and for their meal procure fish in addition to the bread and water.'" Likewise, St. Francis was a vegetarian most of the time although he relied on the words of Christ in the Gospels for guidance in rules for his Order; and it is written in Luke: "Eat whatever is put before you." Therefore vegetarianism was omitted from his rule for the Franciscans; but his biographers, Thomas of Celano and St. Bonaventure, cite instances of St. Francis's meat-eating as exceptions to his normal meatless meals.

Two of the most influential religions in Western civilization, Judaism and Christianity, have failed to enact one of the basic principles of their Gods: "Thou shalt not kill." Instead, Judaism evolved an intricate system of "kosher" slaughter and Christianity advocated "omitting meat on Friday."

5

Da Vinci and
the Dietetic Renaissance

Middle Phases

*T*here were only a few murmurs from vegetarian groups during the period from the fall of the Roman Empire until the submission of Constantinople to the Turks in 1453. With heretics casting bright hues as they burned on the stakes, Christendom, not independent thought, ruled Western Europe. One minor group, the Kathari, did have a meatless diet as a fundamental principle in their defiance of the Church from the eleventh through the thirteenth centuries. In order to gain entry into that puritan sect, a neophyte would have to answer the question: "Did you eat meat?" But even the Kathari ate fish, although the only creatures they would kill were threatening animals or reptiles. As early as 1052, two Kathari refused to eat a pullet, or young hen, and were hanged in Goslar, Germany; by the next century such defiance was a means of identifying these puritans. Then, in 1229 in Perugia, Pietra and Andrea, two leading members, made public admission of their heresy before Pope Gregory IX: eating flesh two days later they made formal display of their reconciliation with the established religion.

Eventually, because of the combined growth of individualism, and sociological and scientific advances during the fourteenth and fifteenth centuries, a philosophy that questioned the relationship of men and

66

women to "lower" creatures once again began to flourish. As a result, what one ate became a serious and controversial topic of conversation. Italy emerged as the main area for the rebirth of dietetics, just as it blossomed into a center for a renewed appreciation of the classical world. Of course the earlier years were not completely Aristotelian in thought, nor was the so-called Renaissance absolutely Platonic; but those generalizations are acceptable guidelines.

Aristotle's twenty years at Plato's academy left a lifelong impression on his philosophical outlook, but ultimately he encountered a theoretical conflict of focus. Aristotle was concerned with the concrete; Plato with the ideal. Though Aristotle died in 332 B.P., his influence would affect numerous aspects of the intellectual and moral probings of the following centuries. Significantly, Aristotle rejected Pythagoras' transmigration of souls and regarded man as superior to animals, specifying his ability to speak as the distinguishing feature. By Aristotle's proposal that some persons were by nature slaves, he gave credence to man as supreme ruler of the first, second, and third kingdoms. When he commended spending money and outward displays of wealth, he also encouraged a view that the pleasure of the palate, rather than simplicity and denial, might be a basis for formulating an acceptable life style.

In the *Ethics*, for example, Aristotle writes: ". . . Reasonably enough, therefore, we do not speak of oxen, horses, or any other animals being happy. . . ." And in the *Politics*:

> . . . Domesticated animals are superior in nature to untamed animals; it is better for all the former to be ruled by man, since in this way they obtain security. Also, as regards male and female, the former is superior, the latter inferior; the male is ruler, the female is subject. . . . There is only a slight difference between the services rendered by slaves and by animals: both give assistance with their bodies for the attainment of the essentials of living. . . . (Translated by J. L. Creed and A. E. Wardman)

The Renaissance was rekindling study of the philosophies of Plato, the cults of Orpheus, Zoroaster, and Pythagoras—all advocates of a simple or meatless diet. However, along with an intellectual reawakening came a dramatic growth in farming techniques that had subsequent beneficial effects on the diet of Renaissance man. Books on husbandry began to appear, although it would be many years before the principles that they set forth were universally applied. Yet these definite steps helped to transform a farming system that was certainly primitive and lagging far behind other parts of the "civilized" world. It was quite typical for a European cow of that time to weigh about one-third of a cow today; the results from shearing a sheep were equally diminished.

One of the reasons for the desperate conditions of the farm land was the sheer ignorance about necessary crop variation when planting. However, by the sixteenth century, mixed farming was introduced, prompted by the discovery that particular plants, such as the bean, significantly enriched and enhanced the soil. Alternative farming benefitted *all* classes since fresh meat was a true luxury and the excessive cost of fruit made it a dietary rarity as well. The nobility enjoyed their infamous feasts but they were more noteworthy as gluttonous experiences than epicurean displays. Though all types of meat—venison, beef, various game birds—and fish were present on the plates of the festive rich, the diet was rather monotonous because of an absence of varied vegetables.

Bread was surely the mainstay of the early Renaissance diet and a poor harvest was a tragic event for everyone. Wheat was so vital to daily meals that desperate measures were taken to provide a substitute, such as everyday grass seed, tree bark, acorns, or earth combined with some ounces of wheat flour.

However, the benefits of "New World" explorations began to materialize with a fruitful exchange of domesticated plants to Europe; carrots, cabbages, and cauliflowers entered that mundane diet. Potatoes and maize products soon replaced wheat in importance. The incidence of a strange skin disease, mistakenly called leprosy, began to decline because it was actually due to a lack of green vegetables. The practicality of existing without flesh foods was thus in the process of becoming feasible so that if and when the philosophy of vegetarianism re-emerged, it would be nutritionally possible as an alternative to the traditional mixed diet.

At this time there also arose a glorification of nature and an interest in plants for their own sake, culminating in the development of botany as a separate discipline: by 1542 the first botanical gardens were established in Padua. Doctors were using herbs for medicinal purposes. Animals were subjects for study, and were recognized as distinct and beautiful creatures, as evidenced by the publication of a *History of Animals* by the Swiss Konrad von Gesner, the results of thirty-six years of effort.

In contrast to the peaceful advances in agriculture and animal study was the development of more efficient and destructive weapons of warfare. During the Battle of Crécy in 1346, the cannon, probably the first, was used; within fifty years grenades and hand guns became standard military equipment. The Renaissance was also distinguished by the emergence of the mercenary army—staffed by men who were paid to fight for a predetermined period of time at a fixed salary. These mercenary soldiers, however, were less amenable to discipline; war became bloodier than ever.

Leonardo da Vinci

Into this atmosphere an illegitimate boy was born: Leonardo da Vinci. The eminent Renaissance artist, biographer, and historian, Giorgio Vasari, has described the Florentine genius as a beautiful, graceful, and brilliant man. The innovations of Leonardo in chiaroscuro or shaded drawing, in painting, flying machines, military weapons, and engineering are well known. Less well known is the fact that that prolific and complex genius was also the first vegetarian of modern Western civilization.

Leonardo's love of animals probably had its early roots in his childhood in the countryside near Anchiano, where he was born in 1452. This upbringing on a Tuscan farm amidst intriguing and colorful animal and plant forms could only foster a prolonged appreciation of nature. Until the end of his life, da Vinci devoted himself to drawing those creatures he so admired and loved.

In *Lives of the Artists* Vasari describes a well-known tale of the young Leonardo, who in order to paint a dragon on the shield of one of his father's peasants, brought butterflies, grasshoppers, crickets, serpents, lizards of varying sizes, bats, and similar animals into his room to facilitate his creation of a completely new creature. As in many instances in Vasari's biographies, it is difficult to prove if that shield existed anywhere but in his journalistic mind; but it is known that da Vinci continued to draw and depict fantastic creatures. Later, in his *Notebooks*, da Vinci even offers advice for drawing such an animal fantasy:

> . . . If, therefore, you wish to make one of your imaginary animals appear natural—let us suppose it to be a dragon—take for its head that of a mastiff or setter, for its eyes those of a cat, for its ears those of a porcupine, for its nose that of a greyhound, with the eyebrows of a lion, the temples of an old cock and the neck of a water-tortoise. . . .

There is definite confirmation for da Vinci's vegetarianism both in his *Notebooks* and a letter written from the Indies in 1515 by Andrea Corsali, a Florentine traveler, to Guiliano de Medici, da Vinci's patron and close friend. This is also the earliest printed reference to da Vinci. "Certain infidels," writes Corsali, "called Guzzarati do not feed upon anything that contains blood, nor do they permit among them that any injury be done to any living thing, like our Leonardo da Vinci. . . ."

Da Vinci drawings of a horse and flower.

Obviously da Vinci's compassion for animals and vegetarian diet were noted traits to his contemporaries, who undoubtedly regarded him as an enigma.

Only a few details of da Vinci's actual diet may be gleaned from his ambidextrous miscellaneous writings in the lengthy *Notebooks*, which fill over 7,000 pages. In explaining why he eliminated even honey from his diet, he writes: "And many others will be robbed of their store of provisions and their food, and by an insensitive folk will be cruelly immersed and drowned. O justice of God! Why dost thou not awake to behold thy creatures thus abused?" At another point, he notes that water is a better drink than wine.

Humanitarianism appears to be the main conscious motive for da Vinci's meatless diet. For example, it was well known that he would often pay for a caged bird just to set it free. Rejoicing in its freedom, da Vinci invented a contraption that he hoped would enable men to duplicate that supreme grace and ethereal experience of flying.

All life was sacred to da Vinci. "He who does not value life does not deserve it," he states. Claiming that nature did not intend for one animal to live by the death of another, he reiterates his outrage at the injustice of eating sheep, cows, and goats: "From countless numbers will be stolen their little children, and the throats of these shall be cut, and they shall be quartered most barbarously." Even more forcefully, da Vinci points out the waste and senselessness when oxen are eaten: "The masters of the estates will eat their own laborers."

In a society as eager to find medicinal cures for any and all ills as today's, da Vinci radically refused to take any medicines or even to allow veterinarians to care for his horses. This diversified man recognized the unity of body and mind—neither could be isolated and all functions were interrelated. "Just as eating contrary to the inclination is injurious to the health, so study without desire spoils the memory, and it retains nothing that it takes in."

Unlike Gandhi, most evidence for da Vinci points to a life *completely* devoid of sexual intercourse with women; the artist was apparently too busy juggling artistic mediums. It was probably not a *conscious* denial of sexuality, as is advocated by some vegetarian groups such as the present-day Natural Hygienists or Jain ascetics, but stemmed rather from unconscious conflicts disguised by an excessive commitment to his work and his intellectual life. "Intellectual passion drives out sensuality," da Vinci wrote, a theory to be subscribed to by Vincent Van Gogh and later a basic premise behind the principle of sublimation developed by Sigmund Freud. Da Vinci remained a bachelor until his death at the age of sixty-seven; the *Notebooks* demonstrate his emotional restraint and lack of excitement over conventional subjects. Instead, da Vinci's passion is aroused by the way the ocean flows or his technical rendering of a human embryo. There has, of course, been speculation that da Vinci was a homosexual, the most common source for this theory being the dramatic death by a gunshot wound of his beautiful thirty-eight-year-old pupil and model, Salai, when da Vinci was sixty-four. Significantly, the tragedy occurred the same year da Vinci left Italy to live in the court of Francis I of France in Amboise.

Certainly da Vinci has always been a complex man to the historians, who have alternately viewed his numerous talents as genius or as symptomatic of his inability to complete a project. One of the most confusing aspects of his character is the conflict between his well-known kindness to animals and vegetarian diet and his numerous designs for advanced and dangerous military weapons. Far from being a passing pursuit, da Vinci, in Milan, studied Roberto Valturio's treatise on war and attended a College of Ducal Engineers, gaining additional prowess in military techniques. Later he also served Cesare Borgia in bloody military campaigns. Any sign of remorse or emotional upheaval from these violent experiences is lacking in his *Notebooks.*

In a draft of a letter written in 1482 to the duke of Milan, Lodovico Sforza, da Vinci describes in extensive detail his plans to aid the duke with military advancements. There is even a bragging tone to the lengthy list of innovations that da Vinci will provide to enhance the killing power of the duke's army. For example, he would design a bridge over which the troops could travel to defeat the enemy; or he would think of ways to destroy the bridge of the opponent; or plans for building a cannon that would hurl small stones in a specific way guaranteed to cause extreme terror. He also listed his plan for an armored car and, resourcefully in case of sea attack, a ship that would carry guns.

Da Vinci, who condemned war and often called man the most violent and worst of any wild beasts, was the same outraged humanitarian who would accompany criminals to their execution to allow a first-hand study of their features distorted by fear. Or he would eagerly search for bodies that he might use for dissection to further his physiology studies. He designed a meat-roasting jack that would operate by water blown through a small hole. "One pound of charcoal, eleven ounces of sulphur, five pounds of saltpetre" are the ingredients in da Vinci's recipe for powder for a bomb that should be mixed well, moistened with "good brandy," and dried in the sun or at the fire.

How do you explain such drastic contradictions in so sensitive and innovative a genius? Leonardo da Vinci was the subject of Freud's one major monograph in what was then an infant field—psychohistory; he considered it one of his favorite works. More recently, Kurt Eissler has written an exploration of da Vinci appropriately subtitled *Psychoanalytic Notes on the Enigma.* Eissler, a New York psychoanalyst, quotes extensively to substantiate his interpretation, in confirmation with Freud's, that da Vinci's vegetarianism was a guard against "strong sadistic impulses," and a behavior pattern indicative of someone "involved in a severe oral-sadistic conflict."

I view da Vinci's vegetarianism as a probable manifestation of a very basic disruption in the primary infantile relationship with his mother. Numerous entries in his *Notebooks* compare killing animals for food to maternal situations. For example, he says: ". . . Of humility one sees the supreme instance in the lamb, which submits itself to every animal. And when they are given as food to lions in captivity they submit themselves to them as to their own mothers, in such a way that it has often been seen that the lions are unwilling to kill them. . . ."

Da Vinci describes in anthropomorphic terms the deprivations felt when the milk of a cow is taken to make cheese: "The milk will be taken from the tiny children. . . ."

More important, however, than an explanation of why da Vinci was a vegetarian is his historical position as the forerunner of subsequent modern movements whose followers still echo da Vinci's same sentiments—though rarely as succinctly, forcefully, or allegorically.

Enthusiastic Cornaro

A fellow Italian, Luigi Cornaro, was also a vegetarian, but his motivations were purely hygenic in his desire for the betterment of his own constitution. This separation of sentiments and digestion continues to widen until we reach the all-out health faddist groups of the nineteenth and twentieth centuries, who often considered the moral questions not even noteworthy. Cornaro is known now only to a select few; but at one time he was far more prominent, even appearing in Jakob Burckhardt's controversial treatise on the Italian Renaissance as an example of superior autobiographical writings. To Burckhardt, Cornaro's essays were classic examples of a literary motif that developed from the family histories of the fourteenth and fifteenth centuries to culminate in the intensely personal exploits of the infamous artist Benevenuto Cellini.

Cornaro was descended from a leading Venetian family; however, because of the "improper conduct" of a relative, he was deprived of his noble status. Then, after another disgrace, Cornaro retreated to Padua. His belated literary debut came in 1558, at the age of eighty-three, with the publication of his first and best-known essay, *A Treatise on the Sober Life*. Three years later, another essay followed: *A Compendium of a Sober Life*. Then, at the age of ninety-three, his third account: *An Exhortation to a Sober and Regular Life*. Finally, at ninety-five, five years before his death, his last work appeared: *Letter to Barbaro, Patriarch of Aquileia*.

Though similar hygienic exaltation of the meatless diet would appear within a hundred years, Cornaro was its first "modern" advocate; even more fundamental, English translations of his work were republished in America and Britain, and later read by the very men who would found organizations in their respective countries.

Cornaro's writing is refreshing, for he has an enthusiasm and evangelical zeal for saving other "bodies" as his had been saved. There is also a noticeable lightness of touch that is absent from da Vinci's sober *Notebooks*. In *A Treatise on the Sober Life*, Cornaro explains in his first chapter, "Of a Temperate and Regular Life," how he lived his early years burdened by intemperance, the "offspring of gluttony" that Cornaro believes caused more deaths in Italy than "the most cruel plague, or by fire and sword, and in many battles. . . ." Due to his youthful excesses, Cornaro passed the nights between his thirty-fifth and fortieth years in sheer pain. His physicians abandoned hope for his recovery. It was a bitter existence for Cornaro, whose ailments included stomach pains, colic, gout, an almost continual slow fever, and a perpetual thirst. "From these natural and acquired disorders," he writes, "the best delivery I had to hope was death, to put an end to the pains and miseries of life."

Cornaro was very skeptical about the last alternative: to begin a regular and sober life. Reluctantly he tried an innovative régime of simple food, leaving the table before he was full, and giving up his excessive wine drinking. To his great surprise, the results after a few days were an invigorated state of health; within a year he was entirely cured.

After that success, Cornaro experimented to determine which foods best suited his particular body. He challenged the premise that palatability equaled wholesomeness and nourishment, since wines, melons and other fruits, salad, pork, tarts, and pastry were pleasing to his taste but disagreeable to his stomach. Cornaro also permanently eliminated meat from his diet and continued to avoid heat, cold, extraordinary fatigue, any interruption to his usual hours of rest, and bad air. Violent passions, such as melancholy and hatred, were more difficult to abolish, but he believed those emotions had a powerful effect on the body. Their effect, however, was minimized if the *primary* rules of meat and wine avoidance were followed. Pursuing the sober life also negated his need for medicines. Thus, according to Cornaro, a man who follows a sober and regular life suffers little from disorders of any kind or from external accidents. A man would become his own physician, and the best one he had ever had. Cornaro gained a knowledge of his own individual limits; although wine aged more than a year upset him, new wine was agreeable.

The most unusual aspect of Cornaro's treatises are his joyous exaltation of being physically fit when one is old. Although in his "twilight" years, Cornaro still mounts his horse with ease and climbs hills as capably as he goes up stairs. His life contradicts the generalizations about the health or temperament of an octogenarian. Rather than a grumpy old man, Cornaro is gay, pleasant, good-humored, and free from "troubling thoughts." In his spare time he reads, converses with men of "good quality." Cornaro tells his meat-eating readers how at eighty-three he composed a humorous poem, although pleasant jesting is usually the vein of youth while tragedy is the style of the aged. His senses are highly perfected since his palate now enjoys simple food even more than it formerly prized rich dishes.

Though not a humanitarian plea for a simple diet, Cornaro's contribution is still laudatory; is not a body in tune with nature as noteworthy a motivation for a meatless diet as sparing the lives of animals? In fact, Cornaro's point is that one should be in harmony with his own body and a better life will follow. "Sobriety renders the senses clear," he writes, "the body light, the understanding lively, the soul brisk, the memory tenacious, our movements free, and all our actions regular and easy. . . ."

Another Italian, Antonio Cocchi, combined nutritional and ethical reasoning in a treatise written about two hundred years later, *The Pythagorean Diet*, published in Florence in 1743. Cocchi was an eminent professor of medicine and surgery as well as a student of old and modern European languages. He held chairs in both Philosophy and Anatomy at the University of Florence; included in his voluminous writings were a *Treatise on the Use of Cold Baths by the Ancients* and *Greek Surgical Books*, which contained many previously unpublished extracts from Hellenic writers on medicine and operations.

Cocchi's primary motivation in writing a book about Pythagoras was to show that indeed his philosophical mentor was a noble and important man. ". . . I wished to show that the first founder of the vegetable regimen," he said, disregarding all Eastern predecessors, "was at once a very great physicist and a very great physician . . . his motive in commending and introducing the new mode of living was derived not from any extravagant superstition, but from the desire to improve the health and the morals of men." Cocchi continued by expressing his belief that no one else had made Pythagorean dietetics the subject of a complete book and therefore he would be serving all contemporary and future dietetic reformers in presenting such a case. Later, his work was read and quite influential in France; his goal was therefore attained.

France

The French essayists, beginning with Michel de Montaigne, have often expressed a compassion for animals and a concern for kindness toward lesser creatures. However, there are few practicing vegetarians of note. Montaigne, born near Bordeaux in 1533, expressed a deep humanism in his epic-making *Essais*, but did not carry his beliefs past the printed page. Shocked by the death of his close friend and confidant, Etienne de La Boétie, Montaigne probably began writing these essays as a replacement for their friendly and soul-searching conversations. In "Of Cruelty," Montaigne expresses distress at observing an innocent and defenseless animal being killed. Like Pythagoras and da Vinci, he set caged birds free. Montaigne concluded that kinship between animals and humans exists much like that which transpires between people and plants. And a glorification of nature builds as a consistent theme in his work—in "Of Cannibals" he writes: "All our efforts cannot even succeed in reproducing the next of the tiniest little bird, its contexture, its beauty and convenience; or even the web of the puny spider. All things, says Plato, are produced by nature, by fortune, or by art; the greatest and most beautiful by one or the other of the first two, the least and most imperfect by the last. . . ."

Jean Jacques Rousseau was no vegetarian. Yet his writings on the subject influenced future dietary movements, such as Fruitlands, the nineteenth-century vegetarian commune founded by the Alcott family. In *Le contrat social*, Rousseau explains that man adapts himself to nature. But—he points out—this reasoning is illogical since it is nature which is already perfectly adapted to the needs of man. Thus man should try to live within the natural order of things—climate and seasons should not be violated. Vegetables, for example, should only be cultivated, weather permitting; artificial methods, like hothouses, are unwise.

It is easy to verify that Rousseau considered the vegetarian diet to be an ideal one.* In *Emile* (1757–60), his textbook for the ideal education of a child, he advocates a simple vegetarian diet for children. *Emile* evolved from Rousseau's primary thesis that nature is good, but society corrupts it. In the greatest detail, Rousseau outlines the process of educating a child from birth, a subject then ignored by educators since at that time children were usually regarded as smaller versions of men and women, rather than unique and separate persons with distinct constitutional and psychological needs.

In order to present his theories, the education of Emile, an imaginary orphan, is placed completely under Rousseau's jurisdiction. Temperance is necessary to maintain an ordered system. However, nutritional education begins with the mother or wet nurse, since Rousseau believed that the diet of those nursing the infant would affect the unborn child. Milk from herbivorous cows was sweeter and more wholesome than that taken from carnivorous animals. Worm trouble would be avoided if a child was not weaned too soon and was fed on a vegetarian diet by a foster mother or nurse who was also a vegetarian. Rousseau attempts to

---

* Sir Thomas More, in *Utopia*, also envisions his ideal society living a vegetarian existence.

dispel the common fears of curdled milk by pointing out that whole societies subsist only on milk diets. In any event, he argues, milk *always* curdles in the stomach.

In continuing his defense of a vegetarian diet, Rousseau notes that it becomes unwholesome only through flavoring. The reformation of cooking procedures, therefore, is necessary so that neither butter nor oil are used for frying; vegetables should be cooked in water and only seasoned when brought to the table.

Fresh air is essential for a child; crowds are to be avoided. "Diseases and vice are the sure results of overcrowded cities," he writes.

That meat is unnatural is substantiated by the indifference of children toward flesh food; their inborn preferences are for vegetable foods, such as milk, pastry, and fruit. It is not just the healthy aspects of a meatless diet that augment its importance: flesh-eaters are usually fiercer and crueler than other men. Therefore, a vegetarian diet will result in a more compassionate person. Butchers, Rousseau points out, although they are allowed to give evidence in law courts, may not serve on juries in criminal cases. He then reprints a lengthy passage from Plutarch where the Greek historian discussed the brutality of someone being compelled to eat the creature that he had murdered.

What do you do if a child eats too much? Rousseau suggests distracting him with his favorite games—you could easily starve a child that way without his even knowing it.

Rousseau continued his endorsement of a meatless régime in another work, *Julie: Ou la Nouvelle Héloïse*, which appeared in 1761. Here his heroine was a vegetarian who also protested against shooting and rod fishing.

Yet Rousseau himself did not adhere to a vegetarian diet because he had an unpleasant recollection of the Pythagorean system that he had once tried at Chambéry and Montpellier. In his *Confessions*, he admits: "I do not know what better fare than a rustic meal. With milk, eggs, herbs, cheese, brown bread and passable wine one can always be sure to please me." But in reality he ate everything except asparagus, which was offensive to his bladder—Rousseau suffered for years from a bladder ailment and probably died of uremia.

A man of intense contradictions, who extolled virtues but practiced deceptions, Rousseau in his youth blamed a young maid for stealing a ribbon that he himself had taken. His religious background was complicated: born to an orthodox Calvinist family, he then converted to Catholicism, and later reconverted to Protestantism. Yearning for his own purity, he retained a disgust for the flesh and said, "All that which makes me aware of my bodily needs saddens and spoils my thoughts."

Though Rousseau read the dietary treatises of two Italian physicians, Cocchi and Bianchi, his application of those simplistic régimes was to write about them for important foundations in ideal societies or educational systems. His own taste for wine increased over the years and later in life he and his wife finished at least one bottle with each meal. Rousseau's imagination was more rigid than his actual diet; he ate meat, drank ale and wine all his life.

Rousseau did have one immediate dietary disciple, however—Alphonse de Lamartine, the poet, who was born two years after Rousseau's death. Lamartine stated that *Emile* and Pythagoras' ascribed theories were his main education. Up till the age of twelve, Lamartine's mother raised him on a lactarian diet of vegetables, fruits, milk products, and bread. Although he later conformed to a conventional mixed diet, he wrote an epic poem in 1838, "La Chute d'un Ange," in which he denounced animal slaughter.

In spite of distinct Italian and French writings advocating a vegetarian diet from hygienic and humanistic viewpoints, cohesive modern movements did not begin in those countries. Instead, they would first appear in England.

6

British Advocates

Forerunners

Before the birth of modern organized vegetarian groups in England, a meatless diet was just another habit of notables involved in reforming society, protesting such causes as organized religion or even religion itself, birth-control taboos, vivisection, and prison conditions. The tradition begins in the eighteenth century with two distinguished Pythagoreans: John Wesley, co-founder of Methodism with his brother Charles and George Whitefield; and John Howard, prison reformer.

Wesley, the fifteenth child in his distinguished family, was ordained a deacon in the Church of England in 1725 and a priest in 1728. The next year, while a professor of Greek Literature at Oxford, the first step toward Methodism began in the discussion groups of the Holy Club that included his younger brother Charles Wesley and George Whitefield. Members would gather on Sunday evenings for debates and to read the Greek Testaments; they also fasted on Wednesdays and Fridays. The more formal origins of the religion took place in April 1735 when a small society made up of thirty of the serious members of his congregation in the British colony of Georgia gathered to discuss Wesley's views. These placed an emphasis on inner religion and on the effect of the Holy Spirit on the consciousness of such followers. The Wesleys had accompanied

James Oglethorpe to Georgia and during their two-year stay came under the influence of Moravian missionaries.

A vegetarian of indefatigable energy, Wesley traveled about 5,000 miles a year, preaching more than 15 sermons a week or about 40,000 in his lifetime. The growth of Methodism was outstanding: although there were only about 60,000 members in 1789, that number tripled within twenty-five years.

John Howard, a vegetarian and teetotaller who ate small meals at fixed intervals, returned from a trip to France and Italy to live in the style of a young man of leisure. He adopted a meatless diet to counteract his newly acquired consumptive nature and adhered to a meatless régime till the end of his life.

Though health motives were significant in Howard's lifelong adherence to a meatless diet, the tragic personal circumstances of his life must have also exercised an influence on his self-disciplined régime. Both his marriages were prematurely terminated by his mate's death. About 1750, Howard moved into the home of a widow, Sarah Lardeau. She nursed him through a bad illness that lasted two years. Though Howard was only 27, Sarah was 53; they married in October 1753 and seemed to live happily, although she was constantly sick. Then, in 1755, his wife died.

Travel provided a means for forgetting his grief: Howard set out for Lisbon in January 1756 to try to aid the victims of an earthquake that several months previously had claimed more than 20,000 victims.

Upon his return, Howard met Henrietta, who was about his age. They were married in 1758. Then, in 1765, four days after she bore him a son named John, Henrietta died. For the rest of his life, on the anniversary of her death, Howard fasted and prayed and tried to spend the day in silent meditation as well.

After her death, Howard settled near Bedford and in 1773 became the high sheriff. That position led him to investigate the state of prisons, a quest inspiring journeys through France, Germany, Holland, Italy, Spain, Portugal, and Turkey. In 1777, he published *The State of the Prisons in England and Wales* and dedicated it to the House of Commons. Edmund Burke, in a speech to the freemen of Bristol, praised the originality, genius, and humanity of Howard's work.

In 1809, two major events for vegetarianism took place. The first was the establishment of a vegetarian coalition in Manchester, when members of the Bible Christian Church under the leadership of the Reverend William Cowherd pledged themselves to abstain from alcoholic drinks and flesh foods. The second was the publication of Dr. William Lambe's report on the *Effects of a Peculiar Regimen in Scirrhous Tumors and Cancerous Ulcers*. His "peculiar regimen" consisted of a meatless diet, with a liberal use of distilled water. "We may conclude," Lambe wrote in his influential paper, "that it is the property of this regimen, and, in particular, of the vegetable diet, to transfer diseased action from the *viscera* to the exterior parts of the body—from the central parts of the system to the periphery. . . ." Lambe listed the various ailments that may be eliminated by adopting a vegetarian diet—brain disease was just one of them.

John Frank Newton read Lambe's essay, adopted his program, and subsequently recovered his failing health. The publication in 1811 of Newton's *The Return to Nature* is credited by many as the beginning of the modern era of vegetarianism. Lambe and Newton became friends. In fact, Newton dedicated his book to Dr. Lambe:

> . . . Convinced as I now am, not only by my exemption from attacks of the complaint under which I laboured, but by the improvement of my spirits and comfortable sensations, that a vegetable regimen and the use of distilled water have conquered a chronic illness with which I had been from childhood afflicted, allow me to lay on your table this feeble attempt to render more generally known a medical discovery, which, I am confident, will place your name at some future, and perhaps no distant period, at the head of your profession. . . .

Newton recounts a brief history of vegetarianism from the Book of Genesis to the myth of Prometheus, pointing out that man is constitutionally adapted to a vegetable diet. In the two years that he and his wife, four children, and their nurse were eating meatless meals, all experienced health improvements.

Newton's most famous alleged convert was Percy Bysshe Shelley,* a frequent guest at the Newton table where no flesh was served, nor butter and eggs, except when the latter were used for cooking. Shelley ate infrequently and simply even during his earlier Oxford days, roaming around and reading a book while nibbling on bread, pudding, raisins, or dried prunes.

On March 14, 1812, Harriet Westbrook, with whom Shelley had eloped the previous year, wrote from Dublin to an Elizabeth Hitchiner: "You do not know that we have foresworn meat and adopted the Pythagorean system. About a fortnight has elapsed since the change, and we do not find ourselves any the worse for it."

Shelley is a dramatic and sensual literary figure whose romantic image

---

* More intense investigations by David L. Clark point out that Shelley actually adopted a vegetable diet several months before he made his acquaintance with the Newtons.

is still powerful, providing many moments of fantasy for modern high-school students who traditionally read his verses. Two years after Shelley and his friend Thomas Jefferson Hogg co-published their pamphlet, *The Necessity of Atheism* (1811), which resulted in Shelley's expulsion from the sacrosanct university, he published another booklet, *A Vindication of Natural Diet.* It is a detailed and forceful defense of the Pythagorean system that begins: "I hold that the depravity of the physical and moral nature of man originated in his unnatural habits of life." Shelley points to the eating of the forbidden fruit by Adam and Eve as allegorical proof of the "disease and crime that have flowed from unnatural diet."

Carefully, Shelley substantiates his dietary preferences by demonstrating that man's comparative anatomy is indeed close to that of frugivorous animals; alien to carnivorous ones. However, Shelley cautions his readers that a simple diet fails to provide Utopian solutions to all the ills of the world, although many critics of that essay overlook his subtle concessions to the complexities of a dietetic view of the world and instead regard Shelley as another vegetarian fanatic.

By far the most inventive aspect of Shelley's essay is his political application of vegetarianism. If a country could become self-sufficient by utilizing available land to cultivate grains, rather than using grazing animals who are eaten only by the wealthy, who then pay for the privilege by "subjection to supernumerary diseases," England could become independent of commerce and the "caprices of foreign rulers." Then his beloved homeland could not be bribed into following the political leanings of other nations. Thus, if a natural diet were adopted, there would be no need to get spices from India or wines from Portugal, Spain, France, or Madeira.

Shelley states that dietary reform "strikes at the root of the evil." One must be realistic about the physical gains, since no one is spared from hereditary diseases; nevertheless, new diseases may be avoided and there will also be a diminution in the predisposition to genetic illnesses. Shelley recommends that as soon as the decision to adopt a natural diet is reached, a change should follow immediately. Easier breathing and heightened energy are just two of the numerous benefits Shelley describes. He concludes his essay by repeating the premises of John Frank Newton, namely, that one should not take into the stomach anything that once had life and one should drink only distilled water.

Shelley suffered conditionally from the strain of the numerous tragic experiences in his life: the suicide of Harriet Westbrook, followed a few months later by the self-inflicted death of Fanny Godwin, half sister of Mary Godwin who later lived with him and eventually became his legal wife. Shelley himself, during a visit to his friend Leigh Hunt, fell from a chair which resulted in a continual pain in his side. He concealed his suffering, however, believing his condition would be blamed on his innovative dietary methods.

Shelley's poem *Queen Mab*, subtitled "A Philosophical Poem, with Notes," and dedicated to Harriet, expresses in stanza 8 his views on a natural diet:

> *Immortal upon earth: no longer now*
> *He slays the lamb that looks him in the face,*
> *And horribly devours his mangled flesh,*
> *Which, still avenging Nature's broken law,*
> *Kindled all putrid humours in his frame,*
> *All evil passions, and all vain belief,*
> *Hatred, despair, and loathing in his mind,*
> *The germs of misery, death, disease, and crime.*
> *No longer now the wingèd habitants,*
> *That in the woods their sweet lives sing away,*
> *Flee from the form of man; but gather round,*
> *And prune their sunny feathers on the hands*
> *Which little children stretch in friendly sport*
> *Towards these dreadless partners of their play.*

Another essay that defends his Newtonian diet, *Essay on the Vegetable Diet*, followed *Queen Mab*. In it Shelley pleads that just as slavery and "the madness of ambition" are overlooked as a cause for evil in society, so to there is a disregard for the implications of the close relationship between the body and the mind. A man who is concerned about his health certainly cannot be bothered with high considerations. Thus, intoxicants and "irritating food" both disturb the mental faculties. Besides these points, Shelley covers little new ground in this essay, mainly repeating and adding extra emphasis to his comprehensive earlier treatise on naturalness.

In a letter dated November 14, 1883, Sir Percy F. Shelley, son of the poet, replied to the inquiries of Mr. Kegan Paul about his father's vegetarian diet:

> . . . I *think* I remember my mother telling me that he [Shelley] gave it up to a great extent in his later years—not from want of faith, but from the inconvenience. I made two attempts when I was young myself—each time I was a strict Vegetarian for three months—but it made me very fat and I gave it up. That was my only reason, and it took me several days to overcome my disgust for animal food when I returned to it.

The Burning of Percy Bysshe Shelley's Body, from the painting by L. E. Fournier. Shelley was drowned on 8 July 1822 while sailing in the Bay of Spezia, near Lerici.

Some authorities believe that Shelley acquired his views on vegetarianism from Lord Byron, but there is little indication that they discussed this particular subject. Byron, noted poet and lover, practiced a meatless diet sporadically throughout his life, not because of deep ethical or political ideals but out of vanity—to enable him to keep his weight down and preserve his thin, appealing stature, which was almost as memorable as his strikingly handsome features.

In Canto II of *Don Juan*, Byron does discuss the subject:

> *For we all know that English people are*
> *Fed upon beef—I won't say much of beer*
> *Because 'tis liquor only, and being far*
> *From this my subject, has no business here;*
> *We know too, they are very fond of war,*
> *A pleasure—like all pleasures—rather dear;*
> *So were the Cretans—from which I infer,*
> *That beef and battle both were owing her . . .*
>
> (Section CLVI)

Modern Organizers Flourish

Soon vegetarianism became institutionalized, rather than the occasional subject of notable philosophers, reformers, and poets: in 1847, when the word "vegetarian" first appears, a vegetarian society was established under the leadership of Joseph Brotherton as a separate organization from the Church. On September 30th of that year, vegetarians from London, Manchester, and various parts of England gathered at a conference of the new British Vegetarian Society at Northwood Villa in Kent. Many persons traveled over 300 miles to participate in the proceedings of enthusiastic believers who had all abstained from flesh food for periods ranging from one to thirty-five years. "Closet" vegetarians from that day on had a sympathetic homogeneous group to identify with, and could now discuss their mutual ethical and nutritional dietary biases.

Anna Kingsford, a noted vegetarian and women's rights leader, recognized the awe for physicians that was already widespread during that phase of English history termed the Industrial Revolution. It was to emphasize her point about vegetarianism and, in addition, to show that it was possible to study medicine and receive the necessary training without resorting to animal experimentation, or vivisection, that Anna Kingsford decided to become a doctor.

A bright and attractive girl, daughter of a well-to-do London merchant and shipowner, Anna attended a finishing school in Brighton that she loathed. By twenty-one she was married and a mother. In those early years, her chief goal was to become a writer and some of her stories were published in magazines.

She enjoyed riding and fox-hunting until one vivid day when she returned from the kill envisioning herself as the fox. Never again did she hunt and her adoption of a vegetarian diet was based on the cruelty involved to the animals in slaughtering them. ". . . My mode of life is that of a fruit-eater," she later wrote. "In other words, I have a horror of flesh as food, and belong to the Vegetarian Society. . . ."

The rights of women concerned her as much as those of animals. She collected signatures for a petition to Parliament for the protection of the property of married women. Though in England entrance to medical school was then denied to women, Anna Kingsford was determined and therefore, at the age of twenty-six, began her course of study at the Faculté de Médecine in Paris. "Much, you know, is permitted to men which to women is forbidden," she wrote. "For which reason I usually write under an assumed name."

By early summer of 1880, Anna Kingsford had passed all the required examinations and needed only to present her thesis, *L'alimentation végétale de l'homme*, a scientific treatment of vegetarianism. Dr. Kingsford devotes explicit chapters to anatomy and physiology, as well as to a country-by-country discussion of how the poor have always managed to live on a diet of only vegetables and plants. She could not resist the temptation, however, to conclude her controversial study with moral arguments.

Not only was the thesis accepted by her medical school, but it created such a sensation in France that it went into a second edition. In England, it was published as *The Perfect Way: A Treatise Advocating a Return to the Natural and Ancient Food of Our Race.* It is still considered a classic basic handbook to the subject, though her own sentiments are recognizable throughout the serious attempts at objective reporting.

Dr. Kingsford became passionate about the vegetarian and anti-vivisection movements in Britain, which saw the creation of the Victoria Street Vegetation Society and the first movement of international scope. Her activities caused some conflict as they overlapped with the vegetarian principles of the Theosophical Society, then expanding under Madame Blavatsky's direction.

Another woman of importance to the development of vegetarian doctrine was Annie Besant, a radical for her times, born in 1847 and married at the age of twenty to a Reverend Frank Besant. After a few years of disharmony, Annie Besant separated from her husband; within a year she completely embraced atheism. The next event in her sensational life was the famous trial of 1877, in which she and Charles Bradlaugh were prosecuted for republishing Charles Knowlton's *Fruits of Philosophy.* Both the trial and the accompanying publicity are credited with initiating the modern birth-control movement in England, but Annie Besant paid dearly for her beliefs: her husband was able to obtain legal custody of their daughter.

She joined the Fabian Society and in the spring of 1889 her best-known phase began with membership in the Theosophical Society and the beginning of her extensive efforts for that international movement.

In addition to numerous pamphlets on political and social issues, such as *The English Land System* and *Socialism: For and Against,* Annie Besant contributed *Vegetarianism in the Light of Theosophy.* "Theosophy," she writes, "regards man as part of a great line of evolution; it regards man's place in the world as a link in a mighty chain." That chain began for Annie Besant with the mineral kingdom, and proceeded through each evolutionary link until it reached man, who was at the top. Theosophy, a mystical cult incorporating Eastern spirituality and still a philosophical force today, believes in universal brotherhood, forbidding slaughter of all living things. Besant cites another reason for the condemnation of flesh-eating: ". . . It is clear that neither you nor I can eat flesh unless we slay it for ourselves or get somebody else to do it for us; therefore, we are directly responsible for any amount of deterioration in the moral character of the men on whom we throw this work of

Annie Besant, president of
the Theosophical Society, London, 1911.

slaughtering because we are too delicate and refined to perform it for
ourselves. . . ."

Annie Besant never vacillated from either theosophy or vegetarianism
from 1889 until she died. Her conversion to theosophy agitated her
Fabian colleague since 1884, George Bernard Shaw. In reply to Shaw's
inference that she had lost her mind, Annie Besant hinted jokingly that
perhaps it was vegetarianism that caused her unbalanced state.

George Bernard Shaw

Certainly if anyone were asked to name a famous vegetarian, Shaw,
that witty, despised, adored, controversial literary figure, would be the
first to come to mind. For over eighty-four years of his life, Shaw
practiced a meatless diet.

Shaw's sincere attitudes on vegetarianism are complicated by the humorous and sarcastic answers he provided for even simple inquiries; some took him too seriously. For example, he once said about his meatless diet: ". . . It seems to me, looking at myself, that I am a remarkably superior person, when you compare me with other writers, journalists, and dramatists; and I am perfectly content to put this down to my abstinence from meat. That is the simple and modest ground on which we should base our non-meat diet. . . ."

What prompted Shaw's adoption of vegetarianism? At the end of his teen-age years, Shaw avidly read all of Shelley's poetry and prose. When F. J. Furnivall founded a Shelley Society at University College, Oxford, Shaw joined and at the first meeting proclaimed himself to be, like Shelley, a socialist, athiest, and vegetarian. Shaw formally implemented a meatless diet in January 1881 philosophically because of Shelley, but physiological factors also played a part. He was experiencing severe headaches about once a month and hoped a vegetable diet might provide some relief or even a cure.

The bad cooking available at home was another factor, since Shaw remained a bachelor until his middle forties when he married Charlotte Payne-Townshend. In the meantime, he remained a struggling writer, who journeyed to London in 1876 to spend nine years writing five unacclaimed novels, being supported by his mother's income from music teaching and a small allowance from his father. At the time of Shaw's conversion to vegetarianism, there was a sudden spread of inexpensive vegetarian restaurants in London. There Shaw could enjoy cheap, edible meals. Diary entries mention how he took meals at the Wheatsheaf Vegetarian Restaurant in Rathbone Place, rarely spending more than 9 or 10 pence. In 1889, Shaw wrote that because of a dearth of funds he had to dine on bread, butter, and apples. Yet his first letter that year to the renowned actress Mrs. Patrick Campbell applauds his health: "I was told that my diet was so poor that I could not repair the bones that were broken and operated on. So I have just had an Xradiograph taken; and lo! perfectly mended solid bone so beautifully white that I have left instructions that, if I die, a glove stretcher is to be made of me and sent to you as a souvenir." Years later, Mrs. Campbell cried out during an exasperating moment when rehearsing *Pygmalion*: "Shaw, some day you'll eat pork-chop and then God help all the women!"

Shaw's sexual habits are far less identifiable than those of Gandhi or da Vinci: both celibates might have been active behind the scenes, but the surface accounts seem to verify their abstinence. Of course it is known that Shaw did not lose his virginity until the age of twenty-nine— a fact Shaw himself writes and jokes about. But what followed is unclear, in spite of the somewhat dubious references to numerous other women in Frank Harris's biography of Shaw. It is also known that Shaw's marriage to Charlotte Shaw did not include sex; they even slept in separate bedrooms. The evidence seems to point to Shaw's celibate existence from 1898 until his death fifty-two years later.

The reasons Shaw generally gave for his vegetarianism were aesthetic and nutritional ones; he preferred to avoid the moral issues. But Emarel Freshel and other vegetarian advocates have ascribed a poem to Shaw, "Living Graves," that provides a penetrating and moral approach to the issue. The poem opens:

> *We are the living graves of murdered beasts,*
> *Slaughtered to satisfy our appetites . . .*

It continues in a similarly violent vein to condemn animal slaughter as well as war. However, there are no references to this work in any of Shaw's manuscripts, notebooks, correspondence, or diaries. That it was created by Shaw as an adventure in rhyming is possible but improbable.

More concrete expressions of Shaw's motives are provided by the postcards that his secretary was instructed to mail to correspondents who inquired about his vegetarian diet. It is a pointed example of Shaw's imaginative way of saving time and his sensitivity that even the most redundant fan letter should receive some sort of response. The postcards that follow are taken from a large collection of similar printed statements on such topics as capital punishment, temperance, and phonetic spelling.

Shaw was also unwavering in his disapproval of human violence, unlike Gandhi who tangentially supported the Boer and First World Wars by providing his services to the medical corps. War was a blatant example to Shaw of the irrationality of the human animal. His biting words against mankind were not indicative of hostility, but of a deep, gnawing idealism. In an 1898 issue of a magazine entitled *M.A.P.* (*Mainly About People*), Shaw contributed these comments.

> . . . A critic recently described me as having "a kindly dislike of my fellow creatures." Dread would have been nearer the mark than dislike; for man is the only animal of which I am thoroughly and cravenly afraid. I have never thought much of the courage of a lion tamer. Inside the cage he is at least safe from other men. There is less harm in a well-fed lion. It has no ideals, no sect, no party, no nation, no class: in short, no reason for destroying anything it does not want to eat. In the Mexican war, the Americans burnt the Spanish fleet, and finally had to drag wounded men out of hulls which had become furnaces. The effect of this on one of the American commanders was

Mr Bernard Shaw's vegetarian correspondents are reminded that vegetarianism does not mean living on vegetables. Vegetarians eat cheese, butter, honey, cod liver oil (on occasion), and eggs He does not ignore the fact that if we stop killing animals and insects they kill us. Squirrels, rabbits, tigers, cobras, locusts, white ants, rats, mosquitos, fleas, and deer must be continually slain even to extermination by vegetarians as ruthlessly as by meat eaters. So should incorrigible criminals, dangerous lunatics, and idiots. He therefore advocates the exercise and public organization of the powers of life and death necessary to civilization, but never as retaliatory punishment, expiatory sacrifice, or deterrent. The operation should never be avoidably cruel.

As Mr Shaw reached the age of 82 before he experimented with liver injections after 50 years without eating flesh, fish, and fowl, the inference that his diet was insufficient is silly. He had already lived longer than most meat eaters, and is still (1947) alive. He experiments freely with new bio-chemical foods whether they are animal, vegetable, or mineral.

His objection to carnivorous diet is partly aesthetic, partly hygienic, mainly as involving the unnecessary waste of the labor of masses of mankind in the nurture and slaughter of cattle, poultry, and fish for human food.

Ayot Saint Lawrence,
Welwyn, Herts.

VEGETARIAN DIET

Mr Shaw's correspondents are reminded that current vegetarianism does not mean living wholly on vegetables. Vegetarians eat cheese, butter, honey, eggs, and, on occasion, cod liver oil.

On this diet, without tasting fish, flesh, or fowl, Mr Shaw has reached the age of 92 (1948) in as good condition as his meat eating contemporaries. It is beyond question that persons who have never from their birth been fed otherwise than as vegetarians are at no disadvantage, mentally, physically, nor in duration of life, with their carnivorous fellow-citizens.

Nevertheless Mr Shaw is of opinion that his diet included an excess of protein. Until he was seventy he accumulated some poison that exploded every month or six weeks in a headache that blew it off and left him quite well after disabling him for a day. He tried every available treatment to get rid of the headaches: all quite unsuccessful. He now makes uncooked vegetables, chopped or grated, and their juices, with fruit, the staple of his diet, and finds it markedly better than the old high protein diet of beans, lentils and macaroni.

His objection to carnivorous diet is partly aesthetic, partly hygienic, mainly as involving an unnecessary waste of the labor of masses of mankind in the nurture and slaughter of cattle, poultry, and fish for human food.

He has no objection to the slaughter of animals as such. He knows that if we do not kill animals they will kill us. Squirrels, foxes, rabbits, tigers, cobras, locusts, white ants, rats, mosquitoes, fleas, and deer must be continually slain even to extermination by vegetarians as ruthlessly as by meat eaters. But he urges humane killing and does not enjoy it as a sport.

Ayot Saint Lawrence,
Welwyn, Herts.

From the collection of printed statements
that Shaw sent to correspondents.

to make him assemble his men and tell them that he wished to declare before them that he believed in God Almighty. No lion would have done that. On reading it, and observing that the newspapers, representing normal public opinion, seemed to consider it a very creditable, natural, and impressively pious incident, I came to the conclusion that I must be mad. At all events, if I am sane, the rest of the world ought not to be at large. We cannot both see things as they really are. . . .

Throughout his life, Shaw clashed with numerous friends, hosts, and hostesses over his vegetarian diet. For instance, he was a close friend of William Morris, poet, printer, and artist, and visited his home to meet his daughter May. Jane Morris, her mother, was immediately annoyed with Shaw. It was not his socialist views or eccentric clothes that alienated her but his meatless diet. Shaw later remarked that "to refuse Morris' wine or Mrs. Morris' viands was like walking on the great carpet with muddy boots." William Morris, on the other hand, was sympathetic to vegetarianism, maintaining that a chunk of bread and an onion was a suitable meal for any man, but he insisted on a bottle of wine to wash it down. Mrs. Morris, on the other hand, was indifferent if someone drank water or wine, but a meatless diet was to her a suicidal fad. Thus Shaw alienated both Morrises.

Shaw had associates in numerous organizations, such as the Fabian Society, through which he met his future wife, and knew many vegetarians noted in the movement, such as Henry Salt and his wife Kate (Salt later published a monograph on Shaw). Shaw also befriended Curtis and Emarel Freshel, two founding members of a vegetarian group in America known as the Millennium Guild. Their considerable correspondence has unfortunately been lost but the wealthy Freshels were frequent guests of Shaw when they traveled to England.

Charlotte Shaw sympathetically tried vegetarianism right after their marriage, but she soon gave up her efforts. Cicely, her younger sister, was married to a military man completely shocked by his brother-in-law's freethinking ideas of atheism, vegetarianism, and socialism; but Shaw's most annoying crusade in his eyes was the one against hunting or shooting. Eventually Shaw did meet the couple, and he was so impressed with the tactful and charming way Cicely maneuvered her husband that he made it the theme of *Captain Brassbound's Conversion*, in which the heroine is called Cicely.

Grace Hegger Lewis recalls a party she and her former husband, the novelist Sinclair Lewis, gave in London which was attended by Mr. and Mrs. Shaw. "Mr. Shaw came late," she says, "in a blaze of protest at not being recognized by the doorman of our flat. There was tea and lots of useful bottles, and Mrs. Shaw murmuring, 'Mr. Shaw does not drink, Mr. Shaw does not smoke, Mr. Shaw does not eat meat.' Mr. Shaw drank tea and presumably avoided the sandwiches which were non-vegetarian, and talked with enchantment."

Archibald Henderson, author of a three-volume biography of Shaw, recorded an appropriate conversation with him in 1924, when Shaw was already sixty-eight; it appears in *Table-Talks*, a collection illustrating the outspoken and witty side of the prolific playwright:

Henderson: So be a good fellow and tell me how you succeeded in remaining so youthful.

Shaw: I don't. I look my age; and I *am* my age. It is the other people who look older than they are. What can you expect from people who eat corpses and drink spirits? . . .

Henderson: Our time is running short. You will have to be off to speak on behalf of the Labor Party, or Vegetarianism, or Communism, or Fabianism, or what not. You are such an incorrigible publicist that I have not yet got round to literature, or to drama which is popularly supposed to be one of your chief interests. . . .

Shaw had no desire to blend with the masses, nor would he allow his dietary differences to cause him unnecessary inconvenience. Therefore he would often arrive at formal dinners where he was scheduled to speak *after* the meal since vegetarian foods were rarely provided. Or, if he did attend, he brought along his own supply of nuts and fruits. Charlotte Shaw prepared a menu and made certain it was distributed to the chefs of hotels and ships during their travels:

Mr. Bernard Shaw does not eat MEAT, GAME, FOWL or FISH, or take TEA or COFFEE. Instead he will want one of the undermentioned dishes at lunch and dinner. He will eat green vegetables, puddings, pastry, etc., cheese and dessert like other people. He likes oranges and salads and nuts—especially walnuts.

For breakfast.	Oatmeal porridge or other cereals and always grape-fruit. For drink "Instant Postum."
Other meals.	One of the following dishes at lunch and dinner.
(Haricot Beans dry, white)	May be plain, boiled, with a sauce; or curried or formed into cutlets.
(Butter Beans)	
Lentils	(as above)
Macaroni	*au gratin;* or with tomato, cheese or other sauce—or curried.

Spaghetti	(as above)
Welsh Rarebit	
Yorkshire Pudding	
Rice	Savoury; or Milanese (no ham): or curried with haricots or eggs or nuts, raisins, etc.
Pease pudding	
Eggs (not too often)	
	Curried; cutlets: mayonnaise: *Espagnoli: en cocotte à la crème:* omelette, etc.
Gnocchi	
Sweet corn	
Curried Chestnuts	
Minced Walnuts	
Soups	Any thick vegetable soup such as: Lentil Haricot Pea (*St. Germain*) Barley (*crème d'orge*) Rice (*crème de riz*) Artichoke (Palestine) Celery Onion Tomato

It is no coincidence that Shaw lived to ninety-four. He was careful about his health, watching his diet and constantly exercising—usually by taking long walks outside his estate, Ayot Saint Lawrence, in Hertfordshire. He also carefully calculated the calories in every meal and weighed himself each morning to verify that his weight remained consistent. Yet he enjoyed eating and spent nearly three hours over breakfast and again over lunch, and a little over an hour for dinner, his lightest meal. Since Shaw refused tea, he substituted a large glass of milk with chocolate biscuits or slices of fruit cake for the traditional English tea time.

After Charlotte Shaw died in 1943, Shaw needed a cook who could perpetuate the culinary delights that he was used to. Alice Laden, who nursed Mrs. Shaw during her final illness, was a good choice since she had studied vegetarian cooking at the Domestic Science Training Guild in Aberdeen before her marriage. Mrs. Laden's rich desserts pleased Shaw's sweet tooth. His puddings were usually made with honey, and he often ate plain sugar by the spoonful.

George Bernard Shaw, in his late forties, dining in Charlotte Shaw's ancestral home in Derry, Ireland. Shaw took the photograph himself by using a long exposure.

Certainly Shaw enjoyed good cooking and his vegetarian régime was far from a "return to nature" diet. Some of the foods served at Ayot Saint Lawrence from 1943 on were: cheese strudel, soups such as vegetable, lentil, leek, and tomato—all made without an animal-based stock—Russian salad, cucumber salad with yogurt, cream cheese and fruit salad; main dishes such as cabbage pie, zucchini au gratin, tomato and mushroom pie, stuffed eggplant, nut cutlets, lentil curry, poached eggs and rice; numerous sauces such as walnut, cranberry, apple, bread, tartar, and gooseberry; and desserts that included baked apples stuffed with almonds, vanilla, strawberry, and coffee ice cream, lemon mousse, baked bananas, and apricot mold.

As early as the middle 1940's, there were indications of a furor to follow. Alexander Woollcott, drama critic, visited H. G. Wells just before going to see Shaw. Wells told him that Shaw cheated on his meatless diet.

"Cheats!" exclaimed Woollcott.

But he could not imagine the author of *Candida* and *St. Joan* secretly succumbing to beefsteaks.

"Yes," said Wells, "he takes liver extract and calls it 'those chemicals.'"

This fact, when publicized, led to a furious battle between Shaw and the vegetarians for the rest of his life. Shaw's penetrating intellectual perspective further alienated fellow lactarians. The letter that follows was addressed to Geoffrey L. Rudd, former editor of *The Vegetarian*; it was printed in the Spring 1947 issue and incited intense controversy as well as a peculiarly vindictive cartoon taking its caption from Shaw's letter.

IN A LETTER FROM MR. SHAW...

" What is needed is a Vegetarian journal that will ruthlessly separate fleshless diet from Humanitarianism, anti-War, Abolition of Capital Punishment, and all the usual sentimentalities that are associated with it. ONE THING AT A TIME.

Edible animals, leather and fur-bearing animals, milk-making animals owe their lives to the use we make of them; and their deaths can be made painless, which is more than can be said for fishes. But their breeding costs much labor in which masses of men and women become the nurses, valets, and accoucheurs of animals, and even come to resemble them somewhat.

In any case, however, civilization is largely founded on killing. If we do not kill multitudes of living things, from lice and microbes to tigers, cobras and locusts, they will kill us. Squirrels, foxes and rabbits must be ' kept down,' as every farmer and fruit grower knows.

Men who insure women's lives and murder them, women who poison and throw vitriol must not be punished; but they must be liquidated. Christianity will revise the Inquisition and kill the useless, mad and mischievous.

On these iron lines a diet paper is needed and might succeed. I repeat, One Thing at a Time."

" . . . . AND EVEN COME TO RESEMBLE THEM SOMEWHAT."

The British Vegetarian. 1948 edition.

Symon Gould, founder of the American Vegetarian Party, began an unrelenting ten-year battle with Shaw about the "violations" of his vegetarian diet. This became such a well-known and violent argument that it provided the main gossip for Earl Wilson's August 16, 1948, column "It Happened Last Night" in the *New York Post*. It seems Gould was infuriated to receive one of Shaw's traditional postcards in reply to a lengthy letter. Instead of satisfying Gould's curiosity, the printed statement maddened him. No doubt the standardization of the reply angered Gould because he believed he warranted personal attention. Earl Wilson describes how Gould, fuming over the postcard, was at Gus & Andy's 47th Street Restaurant, where "he had gone to spy on members of his own family who were reportedly eating hamburger steak. . . ." In his column, Wilson and Gould discuss the implications of Shaw's admission that he once took liver extracts. Gould believed that Shaw's argument in favor of killing exposed him. Wilson inquired if Gould favored mosquitoes. Gould would not give in, saying: "You've heard of people who wouldn't hurt a mosquito? That's us. If it BIT us, we might injure it so it wouldn't bite anybody else. But we wouldn't kill it."

It was not a new controversy to Shaw, for he had already published a letter several years earlier in *The New York Times* as a public record of his need to take liver extract when, in 1938 at the age of eighty-two, he developed a hemoglobin deficiency and had "no more scruples about trying it than I have about eggs and butter," other animal products Shaw always included in his diet although he was not dependent on them. When the liver extract failed, Shaw explains, he ceased the injections and took diluted spoonfuls instead. Soon his blood regained its hemoglobin.

Seven years later, Gould revived the controversy and wrote two lengthy letters, amounting to 17 typed pages, in which he restated and repeated his belief that Shaw was a phony vegetarian.

With his typical candor, Shaw replied and Gould published his comments in the February 1953 *American Vegetarian*, in his article "G.B.S. and His Latter Day Vegetarian Abuses":

> Ayot St. Lawrence, Welwyn
> Herts, 31st Aug. 1948.

Dear Mr. Gould:

Please stop sending me long letters telling me what I have known for sixty years, long before you were born.

Please stop telling all the old vegetarian lies, with the new one that I am living on cod liver oil. I do not know the taste of it. Possibly I was dosed with it as a child 87 years ago; but I have never taken it since, nor am ever likely to. But vegetarians give it to their children without scruple, as they give them honey, cheese, eggs and milk.

Liver extract you would take if you developed pernicious anemia. If you were diabetic you would take insulin. If you had edema you would take thyroid. You may think you wouldn't; but you would if your diet failed to cure you. You would try any of the gland extracts, the mineral drugs, the so-called vaccines, if it were that or your death.

Please stop telling the blazing lie that vegetarians are free from disease. Ask Josiah Oldfield (if you have not heard of younger authorities) whether he can cure rheumatism, or arthritis, or cancer. I know of no disease from which vegetarians are exempt.

As to longevity and health, my late friend and colleague, Sidney Wenn . . . had his mother put a bit of raw meat into his mouth when he was born. He lived on animal products every day of his life and was more healthy and worked harder than I, and lived far into his eighties. My parents, both carnivorous, were longlived and never ill.

Human adaptability to different diets and circumstances puts all such lying advertisements of vegetarianism out of court. Thoreau, though a vegetarian, said he could live on tenpenny nails. Scott Haldane, father of J. B. S. Haldane and a really scientific doctor, worked out that this power of adaptation is psychological and not corporeal. Gauchos live on tea (mate) and horseflesh: nine pounds a day. . . . People can live on anything eatable, provided they eat enough and not too much. This was well known 100 years ago; and it is time you found it out.

Today people are brought up to believe that they cannot live without eating meat, and associate the lack of it with poverty. Henry Salt, a champion vegetarian, said that what was needed in London were vegetarian restaurants so expensive that only the very rich could afford to dine in them habitually, and people of moderate means only once a year as a very special treat.

What you have to rub in is that it is never cheap to live otherwise than as everybody else does; and that the so-called simple life is beyond the means of the poor.

Your main point should be not that vegetarians are healthy and longer lived than meat-eaters, or that vegetarianism means living on vegetables, but that it is possible without eating fish, flesh, or fowl to live just as long and as well and as capably as by swallowing all three at least twice a day, with bacon and eggs for breakfast, and tea at 11 and more tea and cakes at 16 [4 P.M.]. Not too much or too little of either. I know of women in the prime of life who have seven meals a day and can hardly walk. Italian peasants who cannot afford meat nor enough cereals and pastas, suffer from pellagra.

Finally for the moment I urge you to stop lying and bragging about vegetarianism and stick to the facts. There is plenty to be said for it on its merits without dishonest nonsense, and plenty of its enemies to fight without attacking every well known vegetarian who does not share your delusions about it.

(signed) G. Bernard Shaw

P.S. Your printed article is a tissue of crazy nonsense and reckless

mendacity, but it shows that you can write, which is a considerable gift.
Until you have learned your business as a controversialist, your safest rule will be to do exactly what I tell you and nothing that you are bursting with yourself.

G.B.S.

Today

Though few British vegetarians since Shaw have attained his literary immortality, there is a continued interest in the humanitarian advantages of a meatless diet. Malcolm Muggeridge, noted author and television interviewer, Brigid Brophy, novelist, Sir Stafford Cripps, politician, and Lady Cripps, pacifist, are only a few famous contemporary British vegetarians. Certainly Britain is one of the most vibrant countries in regard to the rights of animals: active societies championing veganism, vegetarianism, anti-vivisectionism, cosmetics manufactured without cruelty to animals, and the reformation of factory farming practices are just some of the contemporary efforts.

Since that first society in England, similar groups have been organized all over the world. Today there are vegetarian coalitions almost everywhere: Montreal, Toronto, Buenos Aires, Bolivia, British Guiana, Paris, Amsterdam, Milan, and so forth. Rarely are they politically active or powerful groups, for their interests are quite narrow—to provide friendship for those united by dietary convictions that differ from the mainstream and to seek additional converts through repetitious literature. Perhaps their comparative lack of success emphasizes that morality cannot be preached. Certainly in contemporary times, postulates about health are accepted with less skepticism if they are advanced by nutritionists and men of science who seemingly lack emotional attachment to animals or "causes."

7

Wagner, Hitler, and Germany

Early Converts

Until we come to Richard Wagner, the names of advocates of vegetarianism are known only within that small group in Germany devoted to the practice and philosophy of dietetics. Yet from the middle of the nineteenth century, Germany was marked by a growing national militarism and anti-Semitism on one hand, and tightly knit vegetarian and health organizations on the other. One early leader of the second faction was Gustav von Struve, who was appointed attaché to the Bunderstag Embassy in Oldenberg. He gave up his position, sought political refuge in England, and arrived in the United States in 1850. During the American Civil War, von Struve despite his beliefs fought eagerly on the side of the North.

Later he returned to Germany and wrote several works on vegetarianism, of which the major ones are *Vegetable Diet, the Foundation of a New World-View* and *The Soul Life, or the Natural History of Man.* Von Struve stressed that animal slaughter, as well as being brutal to the creatures, also sets an example of a demoralizing life that includes cruelty and murder: "Doubtless the majority of flesh-eaters do not reflect upon the manner in which this food comes to them, but this thoughtlessness, far from being a virtue, is the parent of many vices. . . . How very different are the thoughts and sentiments produced by the non-flesh diet!" Later he founded a vegetarian society in Stuttgart, where he continued preaching humanity toward animals without recording an explanation of his own killings of men, a double standard that often marks the German vegetarian movement.

Another influential figure in these early days of the movement was Dr. Heinrich Lahmann, a contemporary of von Struve. Lahmann traced many illnesses to an over-reliance on meat and unnatural medications. One of the first German physicians to use natural healing methods, Lahmann called animals his brothers and refused to use them for his experiments. Instead, he used himself as a guinea pig. His régime consisted of fruits and vegetables, and fresh air. Water was endorsed for its strengthening powers, and loose and porous clothing were recommended so that air might circulate freely. To provide goods that followed his progressive ideas, he designed shoes, boots, and clothing for all ages. He also recommended pillows filled with plants, rather than feathers.

Lahmann's major books on these subjects were *Natural Healing, The Natural Way to Care for Your Health*, and *The Dietetic Mixture of Blood*, in which he recommended a well-composed blood mixture that could be achieved by living in a calm, spiritual way, bathing in the open air, and taking sauna baths. His sanitorium generated much enthusiasm, and, at the turn of the century, he founded a vegetarian society in Dresden.

Eduard Balzer, however, is generally recognized as the father of German vegetarianism, since he founded the first society in 1866 and was a prolific and popular writer on the subject. Although he continued his position as preacher at St. Nikolas's in Nordhausen, he also edited the *Vegetarier-Verein* and devoted himself to monographs on Greek advocates of vegetarianism, such as Pythagoras, Empedocles, and Porphyry.

Right before Balzer's conversion to vegetarianism at the age of fifty-two, he was a cigar-smoking preacher living on a typical mixed diet that included meat. However, he invited a vegetarian friend to dinner. Balzer was nervous about the visit since he could not serve his friend meat. The situation necessitated his exploration of the subject; he read books by Theodore Hahn on the natural way of living. Through his studies, Balzer became involved in the ideas. Once converted, he did not waste a moment in spreading the word of vegetarianism throughout Germany.

Richard Wagner

Richard Wagner had a lifetime love of animals: he was never without a dog or a parrot. Wagner's views against vivisection experiments are expressed by his son-in-law, British-born Houston Stewart Chamberlain: "Nothing that Wagner has written throws such a light upon his inmost soul as the letter on vivisection. Here he only attacks the dogma of utilitarianism which dominates our entire civilization and he proposed, as the moral principle of life, 'sympathy with all that lives.' " Chamberlain, author of the racist *Foundations of the Nineteenth Century*, could have added "except the Jews," a "minor" prejudice of Wagner's.

The letter Chamberlain refers to is one that Wagner wrote for the October 1879 issue of *Bayreuther Blatter*. It was addressed to Ernst von Weber, author of *The Torture-Chambers of Science*, and a former African explorer and diamond miner. At that time, public opinion was sharply divided on the issue of animal experimentation. Claude Bernard, a doctor and medical professor in Paris, had become infamous for his use of creatures in both the lecture hall and laboratory. *In Pity and In Anger*, the history of vivisection, tells how even Bernard's children turned against him because of his surgical operations on animals in the name of science. "It is necessary, so to speak," wrote Bernard, "to take an organism to pieces in successive stages, in the same way that one dismantles a machine, in order to recognize and to study its working parts. . . . After dissecting the dead, one must therefore go on to dissect the living, and to uncover and see functioning those parts of an organism that are hidden or concealed. It is to operations of this character that one gives the name of vivisections. . . ."

Today, except for a few sentimental groups, most people find it difficult to debate the moral questions which were then raised, since animal experimentation is largely unquestioned for scientific studies in medicine and psychology. However, in the nineteenth century science was still developing into the god it would become for twentieth-century man. Von Weber had founded in Dresden one of the most influential anti-vivisection societies. Though it enjoyed Bismarck's favor, Wagner was the most prominent member.

In his letter, Wagner equates the activities on the dissecting table to those in the weapons factories. Both productions are part of the utilitarianism that is sanctioned by the State. Because Wagner believed the issue of vivisection to be so strongly concerned with all aspects of humanity and feeling, he agreed to give his name to the cause.

Wagner did not join existing societies for the protection of animals, he explains, because their method of convincing the public was to demonstrate the usefulness of being kind to lower creatures. Yet, "animals can advance no valid argument against the most inhuman cruelty to beasts, now practiced in our licensed vivisection chambers, as soon as it is defended on the plea of usefullness." Pure humanity and compassion can be the *only* motives for kindness toward animals, claims Wagner, citing Arthur Schopenhauer as the philosopher who had to prove that "pity deeply-seated in the human breast is the only true foundation of morality."

By the time men realized that animals were their equals, Wagner continues, meat-eating had corrupted the race; there could be no returning to a more sympathetic and compassionate world. The same man who had condemned the Jews in his earlier essay on music could write, ". . . yet the love and fidelity of the grossly maltreated animal to its tormentor are not thereby diminished. . . . That even in the sharpest pangs a dog can still caress its master, we have learnt from the studies of our vivisectors. . . ." Yet this pity toward animals should not camouflage a mistrust and contempt for certain men, for Wagner (falsely) blames Jewish doctors for the horrors of vivisection. His real view of mankind is more accurately expressed by his sarcastic conclusion that man is superior to animals only in his ability to deceive.

Some persons incorrectly view Wagner's animal liberationist sentiments as a natural outgrowth from similar sympathies of Friedrich Nietzsche. The real situation was quite the reverse. In fact, Nietzsche disapproved of vegetarianism. And he disapproved even more emphatically after his brother-in-law, Dr. Förster, adopted it in emulation of Wagner since Nietzsche, very attached to his sister, was bitter that Förster had deprived him of his constant servant and companion.

A passage from *The Gay Science* entitled "Danger for Vegetarians" is one of numerous places where Nietzsche expresses his true feelings on vegetarianism:

> A diet that consists predominantly of rice leads to the use of opium and narcotics, just as a diet that consists predominantly of potatoes leads to the use of liquor. But it also has subtler effects that include ways of thinking and feeling that have narcotic effects. This agrees with the fact that those who promote narcotic ways of thinking and feelings, like some Indian gurus, praise a diet that is entirely vegetarian and would like to impose that as a law upon the masses. In this way they want to create and increase the need that they are in a position to satisfy. [section 145. Translated by Walter Kaufmann]

Wagner continued to expound his theories on vegetarianism and diet

Richard Wagner.

in a series of essays written from 1880 until his death in 1883, although he had revealed an interest in nutrition and food as early as 1850. Hoping that a new religion would evolve in which a meatless diet would play a significant role, Wagner ordered his followers to be herbivorous. The opera singer Lilli Lehmann was one of the many who carried out his iron will.

But did the innovative composer and political revolutionary follow his own preachings? His prose writings confirm his approval and enthusiasm for a fleshless dinner plate, but Wagner never brought his commitments to the table. His closest living relation, Winifred Wagner, widow of his son Siegfried, explained during our interview in February, 1972 that Wagner would have liked to have been a vegetarian for ethical reasons, but his poor health prevented him from changing his diet: he suffered from a weak heart and eczema of the face, *gesichstrose*.

Was Wagner's wife Cosima, the object of Nietzsche's unrequited attentions, a vegetarian?

"She was too great a character—on the same level with Wagner—," says Frau Wagner, "to do anything just because he believed it."

Wagner, like Jean Jacques Rousseau before him and Albert Einstein after him, embraced vegetarianism as an ideal—on ethical and physiological grounds. But he failed to apply his convictions, although his consciousness of the suffering of animals was originally roused when he was staying in Venice and saw a poulterer's bloody shop. In addition, the publication in 1871 of Darwin's *Descent of Man* was proof that man and animals had common ancestral roots. Wagner became convinced that *all* creatures were sacred.

Wagner did incorporate his intensified beliefs about animal treatment into his last opera, *Parsifal*. He seems to have recalled that scene in Venice: Guermenanz, knight of the Holy Grail, asks, "Who shot the swan?" Parsifal answers, "Yes, I! In flight I hit all that flies." Guermenanz rebukes Parsifal for murdering such a peaceful bird that is also harmless and faithful. Then, in the next scene, the bread and wine of the feast are treated symbolically as the flesh and blood of Christ, although Wagner's belief that Christ suffered for animals as well as men is omitted from his libretto.

Religion and Art is one of Wagner's most controversial writings. Musicologists regard it as the rantings of an old man, biographers consider it irrational prose, and vegetarians extol it as an idealistic essay. Formulating ideas that range from probable to fictitious, Wagner praises the Brahmans and Buddhists for their condemnation of animal slaughter. In times of famine, only after the master died did the creature also perish. Wagner believed that prehistoric man originated in the temperate zones and became brutalized when he began eating meat. His proposal as to how to convert the flesh-eating world to a vegetarian one was to force migration to the South American and South African lands, where it would be easier for a person to be sustained on a fruitarian diet.

"Taste such alone, in memory of me," are the words Wagner suggests Christ intended when he offered his disciples wine and bread at the Last Supper. Although a great advance brought about by Christianity was the castigation of the practice of spilling blood in the execution of a heretic, nothing was said in opposition to the burning of one at the stake. Man's journey away from a meatless diet led to the failure of the early Christian religion. The sight of animal sacrifice became abominable, but the devouring of the carcasses of murdered household beasts dressed up beyond recognition was endorsed.

Wagner argued that floods and ice forced the flight of early man from the tropics to the freezing northern zones. There, necessity and self-preservation initiated the slaughter of animals. What followed, Wagner says in a cloud of emotion, was "that thirst [for flesh and blood] which history teaches us can never be slaked, and fills its victims with a raging madness, not with courage. . . ."

He also provided examples of the success of a vegetarian diet in various parts of the globe. The long life of the vegetable-eating Russian peasant was the basis of his argument that meatless diets are even possible in a cold climate. The Japanese, who Wagner contended—incorrectly—eat nothing but vegetables, are acclaimed for their warrior valor and intellectual prowess.

Wagner concluded that vegetarianism could save mankind. The "long-lost Paradise" could be regained if man were to return to his natural diet. Then results might be expected, like those shown by the experiments in American prisons where the cruelest criminals were transformed into the mildest and most conscientious men by a meatless régime.

It is only possible to conjecture the effect that Wagner's animal liberationist views would have had on all his operas if he had explored the subject thirty years earlier than his first letter against vivisection. However, these ideas and writings do indicate Wagner's all-consuming passion for a new idea—that a natural diet would be the cure-all for society just as the Jew had been the lone villain.

Adolf Hitler

The Führer was late, as usual. His official colleagues waited hungrily until three o'clock for a luncheon prepared by a special cook who was superb at meatless dishes, as well as rich, fattening pastries. It was past noon, but Hitler was just rising. Insomnia had kept him awake until four o'clock in the morning. For breakfast he zealously ate a slice of zweiback as he gulped a glass of whole milk. This was just the daily routine at the headquarters of the vegetarian dictator.

Yet Hitler's name would scarcely come to mind in listing famous vegetarians, and the mere mention of his avoidance of meat initiates heated arguments among those who deny flesh foods. Numerous people have even advised me to omit his name from this book because it might hurt the cause of vegetarianism. This was not always the case. In 1933, when Hitler became chancellor, he was hailed by German vegetarians as the first to bring victory, fame, and serious journalistic exposure to their esoteric movement.

Hitler practiced vegetarianism, with increased faithfulness, from 1911 until his death in 1945. What motivated him, and how he applied his dietary theories, are far more significant than the indisputable fact that he was a vegetarian. Today many of his nutritional concepts are again echoed by health faddists.

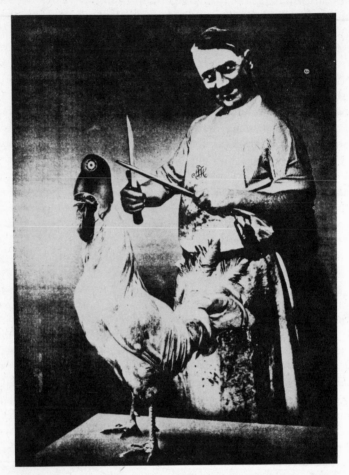

"Nur Keine Angst—Er Ist Vegetarier" is a photomontage by John Heartfield that says, "Have No Fear—He Is a Vegetarian."

The earliest roots of Hitler's later renunciation of meat lie in his relationships with his mother and father. Adolf was born a year after his three older brothers and sisters all died in a diphtheria epidemic. Klara Hitler seemed to overindulge her son to compensate for her loss. The intense relationship between mother and son has been substantiated by both August Kubizek, a childhood friend, and Dr. Eduard Bloch, the

Jewish doctor who treated Klara Hitler for cancer of the breast in 1907.

This over-reliance on his mother, which continued until Klara's death during Hitler's adolescence, indicated his probable fixation at the earliest phase of development, the oral stage. Throughout his life, Hitler showed this arrestment; he even sucked his little finger when aggravated. He was overly loquacious, sometimes giving 1,500 speeches in a year and exhausting his guests with repetitious, lengthy monologues. He was excessively nationalistic: the German nation became his mother figure.

At the oral stage, according to Melanie Klein, the infant perceives that a mother's breast is consumed along with the milk. If Hitler unconsciously made that association, he would have feared that he would consume his own mother if he ate meat. Interviews with neighbors of the Hitler family have verified Hitler's ambivalent love-hate feelings toward his mother. Later, on many occasions, he described meat eaters as corpse eaters, or carrion eaters. Both terms describe a savage preying upon his own kind and link his vegetarianism to cannibalism: man-eating is frequently motivated by magical thinking. The child has such thought patterns but soon passes to higher stages of development. The Führer did not.

Hitler's meatless diet was also a defense against unconscious passivity, his conflict an expression of the poor relationship with his father. He wrote in *Mein Kampf,* "Then barely eleven years old, I was forced into opposition for the first time in my life. . . . Neither persuasion nor 'serious' arguments made any impression on my resistance . . . I yawned and grew sick to my stomach at the thought of sitting in an office."

Hitler consistently struggled against a positive identification with his father. Alois Hitler enjoyed drinking, married three times, respected authority, conformed to society's demands for a dependable life, and indulged in pleasures of the flesh. His son, on the other hand, never drank, avoided marriage until the eve of his suicide, detested authority in any form, shunned formal work, and was an ascetic.

There is little proof that Alois Hitler was the hostile, aggressive father his son describes in *Mein Kampf.* Yet ample evidence from psychoanalytic sources indicates that Hitler identified his father with the Jews. He expanded the Jewish dietary law which prohibits the consumption of the milk of the cow with the flesh of its offspring to include *never* consuming the calf. Yet though Hitler followed Jewish dietary laws in some respects, he killed those very people to whom his avoidances were most closely linked.

Richard Wagner replaced Alois as Hitler's father figure, and the ardent worship of the composer was the strongest underlying cause of Hitler's later dietary conversion. This passion for Wagner was all-consuming: he adored Wagner's music, agreed with his philosophical beliefs, and accepted his political interpretations. Hitler developed the concepts that Wagner highlighted in his prose writings to the level of strict, lifetime principles. Wagner's essays on vegetarianism and anti-Semitism stimulated Hitler to extreme conclusions. Hitler spared animals because of Wagner's love for them, and annihilated men because he was provoked by the master's attitudes on anti-Semitism; his perverted philosophy enabled him to see Jews as lower than animals.

In the beginning of *Mein Kampf*, Hitler describes his introduction to Wagner's opera:

> The provincial capital of Upper Austria had at that time a theater which was, relatively speaking, not bad. Pretty much of everything was produced. At the age of twelve I saw *Wilhelm Tell* for the first time, and a few months later my first opera, *Lohengrin*. I was captivated at once. My youthful enthusiasm for the master of Bayreuth knew no bounds. Again and again I was drawn to his work. . . .

August Kubizek provides the next account of the continuous Wagnerian strain that was through Hitler's life, and furnishes one of the few descriptions of the formative years in Linz and Vienna. Kubizek and Hitler met in Linz in 1904 when competing for standing room at the opera house. Their friendship developed as they continued meeting at every opera performance. Kubizek paints a colorful portrait of the unfriendly, moody, fifteen-year-old transformed by a performance of Wagner's *Rienzi* into a boy with convictions. It was as if Adolf had incorporated Rienzi's character into his own. At first this narrative seems embroidered, since Kubizek's writing is flamboyant and embellished. Yet for the rest of his life, that same spiritual uplifting from Wagner's music was reported by those closest to Hitler.

At seventeen, Hitler left Linz and went to Vienna, sending postcards to Kubizek. In these brief notes he described his rapture and delight at seeing Wagner's operas at the Hof Opera House. That he thought the operas important enough to write about is significant since Hitler rarely wrote any personal communications. Later, he settled in Vienna and Kubizek became his roommate. They went to the opera without overcoats, in spite of cold weather, to avoid the cloakroom fee. *Lohengrin* and *Tristan* appeared to make the youths indifferent to freezing temperatures. Hitler once boxed the ears of the leader of a claque, who was paid by a singer to clap, because he was so outraged by the interruptions during *Tannhaüser*.

These operas enabled Hitler to enter a fantasy world and become entranced. Even his constant tenseness was gone. He remembered this effect when years later he played these nationalistic preludes over loudspeakers to hypnotize the crowds. Kubizek vividly describes the transformation Wagner's music produced on him, saying, "When he listened to Wagner's music he was a changed man: his violence left him, he became quiet, yielding, and tractable. His gaze lost its restlessness; his own destiny, however heavily it may have weighed upon him, became unimportant. He no longer felt lonely and outlawed, and misjudged by society. He was intoxicated and bewitched. . . ." The depiction could fit the effect of a religious revival meeting on a fervent follower of Billy Sunday or Billy Graham.

The two impressionable adolescents were ill-matched roommates. Friction resulted between Kubizek's normal working schedule and Hitler's erratic pattern of sleeping all morning and functioning in the afternoon while Kubizek practiced music. Hitler wrote plays, stories, and advertisements for storekeepers. In the early morning hours, he began to write the music for *Wieland, the Smith,* a drama that was found among Wagner's posthumous writings. In spite of a lack of musical training, he set out to imitate his hero. Kubizek joined him in this venture: the two worked together for several days. Hitler also made charcoal sketches for the scenery. Then Kubizek realized that the half-finished opera, which had echoed Wagner's works, had been put aside. A musical facility, however, did persist. In later years, Hitler would astound guests by his ability to hum or whistle entire operatic scores, such as *Die Meistersinger,* an opera he had seen dozens of times.

Although Dr. Karl Leuger, mayor of Vienna, leader of the Christian Social Party, and an anti-Semite, was his strongest political influence, Wagner was the only emotive predecessor that Hitler recognized. In 1933 he summarized Wagner's philosophical views for Hermann Rausching, an early figure in the Nazi Party who understood Hitler's master scheme and tried to warn the world. Hitler said:

> . . . Did you know that Wagner had attributed much of the decay of our civilization to meat-eating? I don't touch meat largely because of what Wagner says on the subject, and says, I think, absolute rightly. So much of the decay of our civilization had its origin in the abdomen—chronic constipation, poisoning of the juices, and the results of drinking to excess. He [Wagner] did not touch meat or alcohol, or indulge in the dirty habit of smoking; but his reason had nothing to do with considerations of health, but was a matter of absolute conviction. But the world was not ripe for this advance. . . .

The link between Wagner and Hitler was strengthened when Hitler met Frau Wagner and was accepted by her family. Frau Wagner, an orphan from England, was adopted by Karl Klindworth, a pianist and friend of Wagner's who wrote the score for the *Ring*. Klindworth lived in a vegetarian colony outside Berlin and, until she was eighteen, Frau Wagner was forced to follow a meatless diet. Wagner's operatic home, Bayreuth, was frequented by Hitler before the war; he often spent the entire opera season as her house guest. In the more English style, Frau Wagner turned over the entire guest house to Hitler, his servants, and compatriots. The Wagners resided in the adjoining Haus Wahnfried. In the living room of the guest house, right in front of the fireplace, Hitler asked Frau Wagner if she were a member of the Nazi Party. "I couldn't say no," she has said. She read one of the first copies of *Mein Kampf* and even provided the future dictator with the paper and pencils on which he wrote the work. After an opera, he went to the theater restaurant where he sat at Frau Wagner's table. While he ate vegetables and several fruits and drank milk, Frau Wagner was granted permission to smoke, in spite of Hitler's well-known contempt for the habit. Hitler knew her four children, who were among the few persons allowed to address him informally.

When Nazi putschists murdered Chancellor Dollfuss of Austria on July 25, 1934, Hitler was attending the Bayreuth Festival. In 1940 he heard his last opera, *Götterdämmerung*, at Bayreuth. Its theme, the death of the gods, was a fateful symbol. His association with the Wagner family continued throughout the war, however, despite the fact that one daughter, Friedilend, fled first to England, then to South America, finally settling in the United States where she wrote a book criticizing the Führer. Frau Wagner helped Hitler furnish his summer home. Of greater significance was her decision to remain in Germany and approve of the Führer's actions. Even today she will not accept that Hitler carried out such aggression against the Jews. "It was Martin Bormann," she says.

The powerful grip that Wagner had on Hitler's development was that of hero worship by an adolescent for his ego-ideal. Alois Hitler died a year after Hitler first heard a Wagner opera. The master fulfilled the need for a father figure that still persisted in the fifty-six-year-old ruler. Alois, a customs official, was an illegitimate child, and grew up using his mother's last name, Schicklgrüber, until he was thirty-nine. It is probable that Wagner was also illegitimate. His father, Karl Friedrich Wagner, a police clerk, died a few months after Wagner's birth. His mother soon married Ludwig Geyer, actor-playwright-painter, who was reputedly of Jewish blood. Six months later they had a daughter. Wagner believed that he was Geyer's son since his mother had been Geyer's lover before her husband's death. Until his fourteenth year, Wagner was known as Richard Geyer. He changed his name to Wagner to curtail rumors about his parentage.

In *Mein Kampf* Hitler describes his anguish and despair at having a father who could not appreciate his artistic temperament or genius. Alois wanted his son to follow his own secure profession as a civil servant. Wagner's pursuit of music and culture appealed to Hitler and he adopted the composer as his fantasy father. A bust of Wagner, by Arno Breker, was always on display in Hitler's private workroom; there was no picture of Alois.

There are many other similarities between the two Germans. Both regarded music as the highest art form. Each saw France as Germany's mortal enemy. When Hitler professed that idea in *Mein Kampf*, he was repeating Wagner's view, expressed in his pamphlet *German Art and Politics* published in 1868.

Both men embraced anti-Semitism. Wagner's essay on Jews and music and his writings against them in the *Bayreuther Blatter* were the forerunners of Alfred Rosenberg's *Der Volkische Beobachter* (*Racial Observer*) and Julius Stricher's pornographic *Sturmer*.

Hitler and Wagner also saw themselves as revolutionizers of German tradition. In *Mein Kampf*, Hitler ranked Wagner, along with Frederick the Great and Martin Luther, as one of the "great reformers." Later, in a speech made at Leipzig in 1934 when laying the foundation stone of a new national monument to Wagner, he said, "Among those embodying the best there is in the German people, and rising from national to transcendent greatness was Richard Wagner, the greatest native of Leipzig and the mightiest master of German music."

Hitler was content to live on his mother's pension as a widow while he was in Linz. He considered having a job unnecessary, since he believed himself a creative artist. Wagner also lived on his mother's pension during his adolescence. Later he told his first wife, Minna, that it was far better to have others support one than to have to work and deny one's art. He told Liszt that he was better at squandering money than at earning it. Hitler shared Wagner's view of work as a middle-class value that was not applicable to him. Even the title of Hitler's autobiography, *Mein Kampf* (*My Battle*) reminds us of the title of Wagner's autobiography, *Mein Leben* (*My Life*). The exaggeration implicit in both works has been noted by numerous scholars.

Wagner's wives and mistresses were compelled to be totally self-sacrificing for their master. Many of his mistresses were married when they became involved with him. Yet he disregarded all feelings but his own. When Cosima bore Wagner two children, her husband, Hans von

Bulow, who was also Wagner's student, said that he would have killed any other man. Hitler treated Eva Braun, his mistress for over a decade, with similar neglect of her public image or personal sympathies. Both Wagner and Hitler preferred women from the artistic world; Eva Braun was an assistant to Heinrich Hoffmann, Hitler's photographer, when they met. Neither man encountered any difficulty in attracting or keeping women at their disposal since their personal magnetism was overwhelming. Eva Braun's diary, discovered after the Allied invasion of Berlin in 1945, describes the cruelty and sadism in Hitler's relationship with her. Sometimes he would not talk to her for months, and then he would slip her an envelope with some money in it, though she would have been happier if he had said just one kind word. Yet these words were written in 1935 and she remained the secret "Mother of Germany" until the end of the war.

Wagner's music was Hitler's tranquilizer. When he was fatigued at night, Ernst Putzi Hanfstaengl, an early Nazi and Harvard graduate, would be summoned to play selections from Wagner on the piano. When the sessions of the Reichstag convened in the Kroll Opera House in Berlin, whole performances of Wagner's opera ended the government meetings.

Linked to Wagner's music and theories on vegetarianism are Hitler's belief in an élite group of Teutonic knights. Just as Mussolini sought a regression to Roman times, Hitler sought a regression to feudal times. Hitler was very much a snob. He shunned his lower-middle-class heritage and sought to become part of the aristocracy. Of the very people that adored him, he said, "The great masses . . . only want bread and circuses; they have no understanding for ideals of any sort whatever. . . ." When Hitler first came to Vienna, there were many small groups of eccentrics, each preaching a way of thinking and living. One group leader with whom Hitler had a great deal of contact was a vegetarian named Grill. Joseph Greiner, who came from Graz and knew Hitler, has said that Hitler discussed vegetarianism with Grill, a Jew. Hitler was also influenced by Lanz von Liebenfels, a founder of the Order of New Temple, a monastery near Vienna. Not only were there dietary rules at this monastery but the brothers baked their own special health bread.

Lanz von Liebenfels wrote for magazines that Hitler read from 1905 to 1909. Separate cheeses and liquors were prepared at the monastery. Through a vegetarian diet, Hitler sought to separate himself from the masses. Discipline and self-control would help him to attain the superiority that he sought so ravenously.

Hitler's health, which was never robust, was another of the reasons he shunned meat. At fifteen he was forced to drop out of school because of a lung ailment. In *Mein Kampf* he refers to the seven years he later spent in Vienna as the most miserable time of his life. His diet then was very inadequate, since he preferred to spend any extra money on the opera. Even when he did have a few extra cents, he cooked a large platter of rice and milk and covered it generously with sugar and grated chocolate.

The earliest document by Hitler in which he states his conversion to a vegetarian diet was a letter written to an unfamiliar addressee in 1911. "I am pleased to be able to inform you," he wrote, "that I already feel altogether well and have resumed my wanderings through the lovely countryside. It was nothing but a small stomach upset and I am trying to cure myself through a diet of fruits and vegetables. Since the doctors are indeed all idiots, I find it ridiculous to speak of a nervous ailment in my case. . . ."

The stomach pains that Hitler suffered had a long history of treatment by a meatless diet. Yet his diet was very unwholesome, as Reinhold Hanisch, a German Bohemian who stayed with Hitler in the Viennese men's hostel, has verified. He depicts his acquaintance as a lazy, moody youth. On unproductive days, Hitler would stay around the night shelter living on bread and soup. If he earned a little money, he would stop drawing, loaf for days, and go to a café, eat cream cakes, and read a newspaper.

Hitler sometimes frequented a canteen that attracted many Jewish students. The specialty, his favorite dish, was a kind of nutcake. This posed a dilemma for a lad who already had anti-Semitic beliefs, but the nutcake always won.

From 1911 on, Hitler's diet consisted of little protein and large quantities of sweets, fruits, and vegetables. His craving for sweets was intense. Indeed, his tastes in food generally reflect an intense ambivalence and contradictory character. Later, he would be filled with medicines and strange injections to "supplement" his diet.

In 1914 Hitler was called up by the Austrian Army, but rejected because he was "too weak." When the war began, he joined the Bavarian Army, but his sweet tooth persisted. If he discovered some artificial honey, not even enemy shells could prevent him from getting to it. Following a fierce British attack, he was seen soothing his nerves with large helpings of marmalade and sweetened tea. Richard Hauser, who knew Hitler during the First World War, concluded that sweets were the only food he cared about.

Hitler was temporarily blinded by mustard gas during the war. This experience, together with his unbalanced diet and nervousness, left his stomach in an extremely sensitive state. Since many doctors prescribe a dairy diet for gout and stomach disorders, Hitler continued to believe it to be a safer diet. Because of his nervous stomach, he could not digest meat or the fat in meat.*

Hitler believed a variety of medical notions; he also had many physiological problems on which he based his adherence to a meatless diet. He thought that vegetarians did not sweat as offensively as meat eaters. Meat-eating, in addition, contributed to objectionable flatulence and fostered bacteria in the colon, and underwear stains, he believed, were increased by the consumption of flesh foods. Furthermore, he was afraid of death and believed that being a vegetarian would help him to live longer, for as he told his secretaries, did not the elephant far outlive the lion?

Though some of Hitler's ideological or medical reasons for changing his diet were unsound, they were attitudes that he felt were rational. His stomach condition gradually became a preoccupation, to the extreme of forbidding X rays because of a fear that he might develop stomach cancer, a fear that had begun with his mother's death, in 1907, from breast cancer. Dr. Eduard Bloch, a Jewish physician, treated her for cancer. Finally a breast had to be removed. But Hitler believed that she died from the treatment as much as from the cancer itself.

His niece's death in 1931 brought out the associations of meat and corpses even further. Hitler told his secretaries and Göring that on September 18, 1931, the morning she died, he looked at the ham that was served for breakfast and declared, "It is like eating a corpse!" After that, no power on earth could make him eat meat again. Though he had made such remarks previously, this time it seemed to have had traumatic significance. The deeper meaning lay in the relationship between Hitler and his niece, Geli, his half-sister Angela's child. He fell in love with Geli soon after they met in the summer of 1928. Various party leaders who were familiar with Hitler at this time have verified his emotions for this blond, twenty-year-old girl. Geli's feelings for her uncle are difficult to ascertain, but it is certain that a rift between them began. Geli wanted to study voice, and Hitler, jealous and possessive, forbade her to go to Vienna. There are many connections between this situation and the one caused by his mother's death in 1907. Both are concerned with incestuous relationships, a fantasy in the case of his mother, but actuality with his niece. She wanted to go to Vienna, just as Hitler had done, and

---

* Medical necessity also forced Benito Mussolini to become a vegetarian in 1925, following a gastric hemorrhage, although he would occasionally eat chicken, rabbit, and fish. Mussolini's reasons for adopting a meatless diet were based solely on his stomach condition, however, and lacked any philosophical motivation.

where he had known suffering and grief. Another factor was Geli's reaction to the publicized involvement of her uncle with Winifred Wagner, although Frau Wagner still claims this was all "rubbish."

Neighbors witnessed a scene between Hitler and Geli on September 17, 1931, and the next morning she was found shot dead. After an investigation, suicide was ruled the cause, although suspicion has fallen on Hitler and his circle. Hitler's nephew, also Adolf, told his mother, Brigid Hitler, that Hitler and Geli reportedly had a violent fight during which Hitler physically abused his niece. The next day she was dying of her wounds. His nephew spoke to the priest who buried Geli and asked him whether he thought the cause of death had been suicide or murder. The priest answered him indirectly, saying that he would never permit a person who had committed suicide to be buried in the church courtyard.

Hitler was inconsolable for months. Whether Geli's death had been self-inflicted or another Nazi murder, he was responsible for killing the one person, since his mother, for whom he had complete devotion. It has been reported that he left Geli's room in his large apartment as it had been during her life, and that he always put flowers on her grave when he passed by the cemetery. William Shirer sees Hitler's devotion to Geli's image as continual, and a strange contradiction in his otherwise emotionless character. Shirer also asserts that "From this personal blow stemmed, I believe, an act of renunciation, his decision to abstain from meat; at least, some of his closest henchmen seemed to think so."

Yet Otto Strasser, a journalist who met Hitler for the first time in 1920, has written an account of that meeting in which Hitler said that he did not eat meat. When he saw the trouble that Gregor Strasser's wife had gone to in preparing a lunch of sliced beef, he put aside his principles. Perhaps the entwinement of Wagner and Hitler though Geli's jealousy of Winifred Wagner reinforced the composer's belief that man's downfall stemmed from his deviation from a herbivorous diet. Thus Geli's death probably strengthened Hitler's belief in vegetarianism. Beginning in 1931, the attitudes that he had stated and usually adhered to since 1911 became rigid, definite convictions. From this point on, he would rarely deviate from his disapproval of meat-eating, or compromise, as he had done in Strasser's household. Although Geli's death was not the direct basis for Hitler's revulsion at meat, it did cement his determination to be a vegetarian. Thus, his vegetarian diet freed him of any guilt for her death, and this sacrifice further reinforced his strong defense of asceticism.

The Puritan Führer

In addition to eating meat, Hitler opposed smoking, drinking, vivisection, and hunting. On the subjects of nicotine and alcohol, he was outspoken. The first and last time Hitler got drunk was after he had to leave grammar school. He vowed that that would be his last time, and he kept to his promise. Later he recalled that he had been found at dawn, spread out on a country road. A milkmaid assisted him back to town. The combination of losing control and being assisted by a woman were associations that probably remained in his mind.

When Hitler lived in Linz and Vienna, he was radically opposed to alcohol. Kubizek redecorated some rooms in the office building of a firm that manufactured a coffee substitute, and Hitler visited him there. The firm provided a delicious drink at a very low price. He enjoyed the beverage, speaking about it often, saying that inns would be unnecessary if every household had this inexpensive and nutritious drink. In a country where youngsters accompany their parents to beer halls to consume a quart of beer mixed with juice, this was a radical proposal.

Yet his attitude did win him support from a small group. In 1933, the Good Templars Order, a group prominent in the temperance movement, sent Hitler a telegram: "To the first abstinent Chancellor of the Reich: We assemble in the cause of abstinence and pledge our faith and loyal support in the struggle for the health and youthful strength of the nation."

Hitler was embittered at the countries that had created tobacco monopolies. The State, he believed, was ruining the health of its own subjects. He proposed to close all tobacco factories and forbid the importation of tobacco, cigars, and cigarettes. Yet in the early years when he was still unknown in Germany, he would campaign for popularity by stopping cars on the highways and handing out packs of cigarettes or small sums of money. These practices were soon replaced by a violent opposition to smoking and the realization that the future of the German nation depended on an élite generation of healthy young people.

The motive in avoiding both pleasures was his growing concern about his health. Heinrich Hoffmann, Hitler's photographer, always related a story that showed his leader's antipathy toward nicotine. At the time of the Nazi-Soviet pact of 1939, Hoffman showed Hitler a group of photographs in all of which Stalin was smoking. The Führer, therefore, rejected them. Hoffmann objected because Stalin's cigarette smoking befitted his personality. "The signing of a Pact is a solemn act," Hitler said, "which one does not approach with a cigarette dangling from one's lips. Such a photograph seems frivolous. See if you can paint out the cigarettes before you release the pictures to the Press."

Pictures like this were typical of ones placed inside cigarettes during the 1930s.

The year 1938 was hailed by the Nazis as one of vast gains because the Hitler Youth were beginning to emulate their Führer in their personal lives. The campaign against smoking and drinking culminated in a conference in Frankfurt on March 4, 1939, held by the National Health Department of the Nazi Party, to substantiate their slogan that "THE WHOLESOME LIFE IS A NATIONAL DUTY." Twelve aims were cited:

1. Alcohol and tobacco would be prohibited for German youths.
2. Pregnant women, nursing mothers, and ill persons would not be allowed either alcohol or tobacco.
3. Those driving after drinking would be severely punished.
4. Government controls for both habits would be introduced.
5. Any advertisements which implied that either tobacco or alcohol was beneficial were prohibited.
6. One-third of alcohol taxes would be utilized for the establishment of "settlements for hereditarily sound families composed of numerous children."
7. Public restaurants would be founded that would serve only non-alcoholic beverages.
8. There would be an increase in the manufacturing of non-alcoholic drinks at low prices.
9. Scientific experiments on non-alcoholic beverages would be promoted.
10. A publicity campaign would be initiated, exposing the nature of alcohol, misuses of tobacco, and the dangers of both to the German people and race.
11. Youth must be educated to understand that wholesome conduct is a national duty.
12. Emphasis was to be placed on physical exercise for the entire nation.

The campaign was against more than just stimulants; playing and dancing to swing music, particularly the "animalistic hopping" of the Lambeth Walk, were also forbidden in some sections of Germany. Increased work capacity was one of the goals of these measures. Hitler and his henchmen believed the glory of a strong Germany to be the greatest personal pleasure. On the other hand, they built the Autobahn and manufactured the Volkswagen as methods of distracting the public from political activities.

Opposition to the use of animals in experimentation was another philosophy professed by Hitler. Before the war, he often discussed the protection of animals. Germany's laws regarding the treatment of animals are among the most humane in the world.

Women applauded Hitler's views on vivisection, for he often spoke at ladies' luncheons. He ascribed the ability to think to animals, and permitted their scientific use only if it served a military purpose. Yet his reasons for caring about creatures were not humanitarian, for he regarded that attitude as an expression of stupidity and cowardice. Wagner, once again, was at the root of Hitler's disapproval of vivisection.

Göring, Himmler, and Goebbels also expressed a concern for animals. Although Göring was a hunter and had a personal hunting preserve, Rominten Heath, it was said that he loved animals and felt that they should be protected. He kept lion cubs as pets, calling them all, regardless of their sex, Caesar. To ensure national concern for animals, he wrote hunting and forestry laws for the Reich. In a radio speech to his fellow Germans, he explained the anti-vivisection law that he had put into effect: his preference for animals over people is seen in his statement, "I have forbidden vivisection in Prussia with immediate effect and have put it under punishment, for the time being until the law itself puts it under severe penalties, of being thrown into a concentration camp."

Hitler criticized Göring's fondness of hunting. One opera season at Bayreuth, he invited Göring to hear *Parsifal*. Then he discussed the scene about shooting the swan, in an attempt to dissuade Göring from hunting. This incident greatly impressed Frau Wagner, who was present and said, "Imagine someone caring that much to try to convince someone else to stop killing. That is the one good side of Hitler that I know."

Himmler, also an animal lover, chastised Göring for his hunting passion. In a speech at Nuremberg, described as one of the most vicious statements ever heard, Himmler declared: "We Germans, who are the only people in the world who have a decent attitude toward animals, will also assume a decent attitude toward these human animals [Czech and Russian women], but it is a crime against our own blood to worry about them and to give them ideals. . . ." His colleague Goebbels, who poisoned himself, his wife, and his children, was also known for his affectionate treatment of his dogs.

Mealtime for Hitler

From his first days as chancellor until his suicide as dictator of the Third Reich in 1945, Hitler dined in four main places: the Chancellery in Berlin; the Berghof, his country lodge in Obersalzberg; the teahouse near the Berghof; and the bunker in Berlin built deep beneath the surface where the beaten, angry man ended his life. Each situation had a particular mood, tradition, and group of visitors. The shifts in the power structure of Nazi Germany are shown by the changes in the list of dinner guests. His gradual desocialization and the decline of Germany as a world power are revealed by those meals . . .

Hitler called the dining room at the Chancellery the "Merry Chancellor's Restaurant." The large, 40-foot-square room was designed by the architect Ludwig Troost, and the interior decoration was carried out by United Munich Workshops. Simple wooden chairs with red leather seats surrounded a massive round table, capable, when fully extended, of seating sixty persons. The Führer's chair was identical to his guests' seats. A floral centerpiece embellished the table. In the corners of the room were four smaller tables, each with chairs that matched those of the host's table. Adjutants and persons of lesser importance sat at these tables. Three glass doors opened onto the Chancellery gardens. Completing the furnishings were a big wooden buffet, and above it on the back wall an unfinished painting 20 feet across entitled "The Entry of the Sun Goddess" by F. August Kaulback, and two nude statues by Josef Wackerle.

The light, plain china and unadorned glassware blended in with the pale, cream-colored table napkin. The napkin was monogrammed with a drop-winged eagle above a swastika. The swastika, typifying Party and State, was a curious symbol, because Hitler inverted this Eastern iconograph, thus changing the meaning from endless life to floor and flame of life leading to a violent destruction. The initials *A H* surrounded this dramatic symbol. All the silverware, which Troost designed, was embossed with a small replica of the table-napkin pattern.

In the early years, political topics were discussed at meals by Hitler and the founders of the Nazi Party: Greggor Strasser, Rudolf Hess, Captain Ernst Röhm, and others. But by 1932, politics were banned

Hitler's
table napkin
and soupspoon.

from the mealtime discussions, along with military leaders. Lunches and dinners were reserved for casual conversations that were monopolized by the repetitious Führer. Certainly he spoke about food and diet more often than the average person. He would dwell on the differences in foodstuffs and their preparation in various parts of Germany, and on the vitamin and caloric content of assorted dishes. He would bring the doctors in on the discussion, and argue with them in favor of a vegetarian diet, claiming, as Wagner had in 1870, that it had been the primeval diet of the human race, and was desirable for the future because it was both wholesome and economical. He stressed that he was a vegetarian mainly because it increased his working and intellectual capacities.

Hitler exaggerated when he said, "I eat everything that nature voluntarily gives: fruits, vegetables, and the products of plants. But I ask you to spare me what animals are forced to surrender: meat, milk, and cheese. Thus from animals, eat only eggs!" Yet without statements from his cooks it is inappropriate to judge how strict a vegetarian Hitler was. Did he eat fish? When Frau Goebbels, who often cooked special meals for him, asked the Führer if he ate fish, since it was not meat, he replied, "I suppose then, that fish, in your opinion, dear lady, is a plant!" He did eat caviar for a few weeks until he learned how expensive it was. Numerous accounts by his contemporaries affirm that he was a lacto-ovo-vegetarian—that is, his diet consisted of dairy products, eggs, vegetables, fruits, grains, and sweets, but neither meat, fish, nor fowl.

What type of etiquette did he observe at these lunches? The atmosphere was informal, and he greeted his visitors with a handshake and *Guten tag* (Good day) rather than the official *Heil Hitler!* Once everyone was assembled in the dining room, he would choose who would sit next to him. He always sat on the window side of the room. When the food arrived, his left hand remained on his thigh as he lowered his worn-looking face to the plate. Then his right hand stuffed vegetables into the thin-lipped mouth. Between bites he guzzled mineral water or his favorite drink, chocolate prepared in the strong Viennese manner. Rather than reserve conversation for the end of the meal, he spoke constantly while eating. Perhaps that was a cause of his constant indigestion, for Hitler could rarely speak without getting into an emotional rage. His persistent chattering posed a problem for his interpreter, Dr. Paul Schmidt. When Schmidt first began interpreting, he rarely had a chance to eat. Finally he worked out a system with his leader whereby Hitler would eat while Schmidt translated, and vice versa.

There were two simple menus for each meal. The meat one included a soup, meat with vegetables, and potatoes, a dessert, and a choice of mineral water, bottled beer, or a cheap wine. The vegetarian bill of fare consisted of a soup, starchy dish, vegetables, cheese or fruit, and Fachinger mineral water. A salad was part of all meals.

Martin Bormann, Hitler's secretary, never missed a meal and was the only guest to imitate his leader's vegetarian habits. Yet the other secretaries often found him eating meat in the kitchen. Göring, whom Hitler in 1939 designated as his successor, rarely came to meals at the Chancellery because he disliked the food and the dullards from Munich. Heinrich Himmler, a chicken farmer who became leader of the S.S. and Gestapo, was seldom a guest. Yet Himmler developed his own health food ideas. Hess came once every two weeks until Hitler learned that he was having special vegetarian meals served to him. The Führer said that he had a first-class diet cook who could prepare anything that Hess's doctor prescribed. After that episode, Hess rarely came. His only outside interest was faith healing; in fact he founded a hospital in Dresden and one in Stuttgart based upon faith cures. Dr. Joseph Goebbels, Minister of Enlightenment and Propaganda, was a prominent guest at lunch.

Sometimes Hitler tried to convert his associates to his own diet. In 1937 Hans Bauer, his personal pilot until Hitler's death, was told that he should become a vegetarian because it would soothe his nerves and make him healthy. Bauer answered, "I'm already very healthy and my nerves are all right too. . . . I'm not one of those hypocrites who come here and eat a vegetarian meal and then go afterward to Kannenberg the steward and have a proper meal. I'd sooner have one good meal of roast pork with potato dumplings than all the nut cutlets in the world. . . ."

The steward, Arthur Kannenberg, was the former chef of the Braune Haus in Munich, the early official headquarters of the party. There Kannenberg and his wife prepared meals to fit every palate, from Hitler's plants to Göring's gluttonous feasts. Like Himmler, Röhm, and Göring, the cook was plump. He was the son of the proprietor of a once famous wine restaurant in Berlin. Kannenberg opened a little *Lokal* (pub) in Berlin which Hitler and Dietrich Eckhart, a poet and early Nazi, frequented in the early 1920's. Hitler chose this comic man, who had a pumpkin-shaped face, a double chin, and mustache, to run the mess. Then in 1933, he and his wife began residing across the hall from the Führer in the Chancellery.

What were dinners with Hitler in the Chancellery like? Lunch lasted for two hours, until four o'clock. Then selected persons would be invited to dinner, which would start in two hours' time. The guests were his adjutants, his doctor, his photographer, one or two Munich acquaintances, Hans Bauer, and Bormann. Kannenberg sometimes served better food for these more intimate meals, but dinner usually consisted of simple dishes. The after-supper routine has been dramatized in many Hollywood movies. Hitler stretched out his legs and relaxed while movies were shown, such as one of his favorites, *King Kong*. Sandwiches, beer, and wine were passed around until the evening ended at 2 A.M. Women were invited to these parties, but that practice stopped suddenly in 1935. Perhaps Hitler felt that his image, that of the ascetic, clean-living man, was being damaged. Even during his Bohemian years in Munich he knew that the masses would be drawn only to someone who seemed to spring from common roots, and who lived in a similarly humble way.

Hitler had admired Berchtesgaden since 1923, when he accompanied Dietrich Eckhart to a small town there so that Eckhart could hide from the authorities. In 1925, after his release from Landsburg Prison, the new martyr returned to the mountains in Obersalzberg, which were conveniently situated near the Austrian border. He was still an Austrian citizen, so he was secure in knowing that he had a quick escape route if flight became necessary. In 1928, Hitler rented a villa, Haus Wachenfeld, and invited his widowed half-sister, Angela Raubel, to come from Vienna to keep house and cook. Her mother was Alois Hitler's first wife, Anna. She brought her two daughters, Geli and Friedl. Cooking had been Angela's trade. After she left home to marry Raubel, she earned a living as a cook in the Jewish Student's Charity Hall in Vienna. She remained the cook at Haus Wachenfeld until she moved to Dresden to marry an architect.

After Hitler assumed power, he bought Haus Wachenfeld and remodeled it to accommodate the numerous visitors from political and theatrical circles. In 1934, the house, renamed the Berghof, was completed. In spite of its lavish size, it looked modest against the three surrounding Alpine peaks. When Hitler took a stroll, villagers flocked to catch a glimpse of the man they worshipped.

In 1936, Bormann bought land around his leader's home and transformed the area into an artificial park, with gravel paths. High fences kept the villagers away. Soon the town of Obersalzburg was demolished, to be replaced with barracks for an entire S.S. guard battalion.

The Führer rarely ate breakfast before nine, and Bormann was instructed not to begin blasting until noon. Often Hitler ate alone in a small breakfast room that had a northeastern view of the slope. Sometimes he would join guests in the dining room. Oatmeal porridge and prunes, or whole-meal rye and honey were typical dishes. As usual, his guests did not have to observe his vegetarian diet. After breakfast, if the weather was favorable, Hitler liked to walk on his mountain.

Having breakfast in the Berghof, Berchtesgaden,
Hitler looks out at the snow-capped Bavarian
mountains.

When the leader returned to the Berghof, he listened to his adviser's summaries of the significant events of the previous day. A staff member attended to the routine mail; Hitler replied only to those letters that exalted his image, such as a widow's request for her pension. Then he watched the news come out of the Siemens tape machine that he had installed. In the hour before lunch, callers were received, such as Göring and cabinet members.

The dining room of the Berghof was the heart of the house. The walls and ceilings were paneled in light wood. Bright red morocco leather chairs surrounded the 20-foot table by the window. A globe was placed next to the table. A long verandah with sliding glass doors led out onto the sheltered terrace. In addition to a massive clock was a large record collection.

The presence of Eva Braun, two or three women secretaries, and wives of Nazi officials made the Berghof atmosphere different from the Berlin Chancellery. Meals here were simple, but sample menus show that Hitler did indeed provide two choices for his guests.

MENUS OF DAILY MEALS AT BERCHTESGADEN*

July 13, 1937
Consomme with marrow dumplings
Stuffed peppers
Home-fried potatoes
Green salad
Vegetarian:
Soup
Noodles with cream of wheat
Green Salad
Cheese—Fruit

July 14, 1937 (Lunch)	*July 14, 1937 (Dinner)*
Potato soup	Asparagus soup
Baked fish	Potato puffer
Stuffed breast of veal	Cranberries
Potatoes	Mixed cold cuts
Mixed salad	Cheese—Fruit
Vegetarian:	*Vegetarian:*
Consomme with noodles	Consomme with noodles
Baked squash	Home-fried dumplings made
Potato salad	of rolls
Filling made of rolls	Green salad
Salad	or
Fruit tarts	Potato puffer
	Applesauce

Hitler's favorite dishes were asparagus tips and artichoke hearts with cream sauce, and eggs and cauliflower prepared in many ways. When Hitler saw artichokes served for the first time in 1922, he exclaimed, "But madam you must tell me how to eat this thing. I never saw one before." Scrambled eggs was his choice from among gourmet treats when he met Mussolini for lunch in Venice in 1934. Spinach, spaghetti, and green

---

* Albert Speer gave me these menu cards. He acquired them from a former adjutant of the Reich Minister for Clerical Affairs, Kerrl. Speer says he had similar ones in his own hand on many occasions; about 700 such menus were issued each year. (Translation by Frederick Stein)

vegetables formed a staple part of his diet. Gooseberry pie, well-made puddings, and chocolates were delights. G. Ward Price, a British journalist who shared a meal with Hitler, writes that he liked *Nuddel-suppe*, a soup with little dumplings in it; apple, baked or raw; and *Russische Eier*, cold hard-boiled eggs with mayonnaise.

Dinner was served at the Berghof at eight o'clock. The ladies wore evening dresses, but were advised against using bright red rouge or nail polish. In 1939 all the men, except Hitler, wore uniforms. He preferred a dark suit. The meal was served by white-jacketed S.S. men, as had been the procedure at the Chancellery. After dinner, coffee was offered in the central hall. During the winter months, the guests sipped their beverages in front of a blazing fire. Until the war, three hours of movies followed dinner.

A tea pavilion was built in 1937, and near it a group of farm buildings intended to serve as a model farm were erected. Hitler cared only for the hothouses, 300 feet high, which were his year-round source of fresh vegetables. Since he liked his table to be colorful, rows of tables lit by ultraviolet lights provided bright red tomatoes. In 1939, a new teahouse was built on Mt. Kelstein (6,000 ft.), nicknamed the Eagle's Nest. On a clear day, Salzburg was visible. The main room of the stone structure was round, 25 feet in diameter. Along the interior wall was a fireplace, and easy chairs surrounded a circular table. Those guests who could not find seats in this room went into a small adjoining one. Tea, coffee, or chocolate, and various cakes and cookies, followed by liqueurs, were served. The host drifted into familiar monologues. Two hours later this relaxed atmosphere ended and the guests and host were driven back to the Berghof. Hitler usually withdrew to the upper rooms and Bormann to the room of one of the younger stenographers.

A meal served at the Berghof in 1940 was even simpler than those offered three years previously. Dishes of tomato ketchup, mushroom, curds, and yoghurt were prepared. Hitler's close associates tried to avoid the dreary days of conferences and meals at Obersalzburg. During the war, even the after-dinner movies ceased as his expression of sacrifice for the war effort. The lull was filled by hours of Wagnerian operas and other operettas, and the same records were played over and over again. Whoever tried to stay away and was caught, however, incurred the master's strong disfavor.

From 1937 Fraulein Manzialy, from Vienna, was the vegetarian cook. Hitler often praised her cooking and pastries. She had been trained at the clinic of Dr. Werner Zabel, who delivered vegetarian meals to the Führer at the Berghof. Fraulein Manzialy came from a school for dieticians in Munich. She was about twenty years old when she began her employment for Adolf Hitler. Hitler liked her, and she liked him because he always took time to speak with her. More than a cook, she would often join Hitler for meals if Eva Braun was unavailable, and she was one of the eighteen people with him during the final days in his bunker.*

All of the members of the inner circle, except Hitler, had been or would be patients at Dr. Zabel's clinic. Albert Speer was put on a vegetarian diet after he became ill. He did not like the diet, but it was part of Dr. Zabel's treatment at that time. Bormann, Eva Braun, Hess, and the others also stayed at the clinic and ate vegetarian meals. The clinic still stands in Berchtesgaden today, although it was closed in 1971.

The Berghof exists only in photographs; just a few low foundations of the basement remain. Hitler ordered the S.S. troops to destroy it in 1945, and it was gutted. Then an American plane bombed it, and the occupying army completely demolished what was left, clearing the site in an unsuccessful attempt to keep away tourists and Nazi worshippers. They still flock to his Bavarian retreat to climb on the ground where the structure once stood.

Once the war began, Hitler proclaimed that Sunday meals would be *Eintopfgericht*—having only one dish. His own table followed that ruling; however, few guests came. The two or three visitors who did appear would be asked to sign a list to pledge a donation to the war effort. Toward the end of the war, Germany's production rate of military parts was at a lower level than expected. One reason was the reluctance of non-military factories to cease production of luxury goods. The Führer was the only member of his circle who made such a sacrifice at the dinner table. Although some writers believe the one-dish meals were a propagandistic brainstorm of Goebbels's, this asceticism was in fact genuine.

Fraulein Christa Schröder, one of Hitler's personal secretaries for eight years, has related in *Twenty-two Cells at Nuremberg* the changes that the war made in Hitler's mealtime guests:

> . . . Even during the war he continued with his habitual afternoon and evening teas. At the beginning of the war, he took his meals in the headquarters dining room in the company of the general staff officers. He discontinued this suddenly in the year of 1941, because several generals had disagreed with him during the meal time. He was of the opinion that the generals forgot the limits of respect because of the common meals, and from then on he ate by himself. When this became too boring for him, he sometimes invited a guest who

---

* The others were Hitler, Eva Braun, Goebbels, Frau Goebbels, their six children, Goebbels's adjutant, Schwaegermann, Dr. Stumpfegger, Heinz Linge, Otto Guensche, and Hitler's two secretaries, Frau Christian and Frau Junge.

Hitler and Goebbels at a one-pot meal.

happened to be at headquarters. After a while, however, he was sorry, because these guests would always carry on official conversations while eating; so he discontinued those invitations. The way I heard it from the guests was that it was Hitler himself who always started talking about official things. . . .

Most of the recorded statements Hitler made on his diet come from the war years, because in 1941 Bormann convinced him to have all his conversations recorded by a team of reliable stenographers. The Führer was to use this material for the books he planned to write after he had conquered the world. Admiral Fricke, chief of the Navy War Staff Operations Division, was his special guest on January 22, 1942. Early in the conversation, Hitler discussed Germany's production of fish. Hitler told his guests:

> Germany consumes, yearly, an average of twelve kilogrammes of fish per head. In Japan the average is from fifty to sixty kilos. We still have . . . to make up! . . . Above all, don't go believing that I'll issue a decree forbidding the navy to eat meat! Supposing the prohibition of meat had been an article of faith for National Socialism, it's certain our movement wouldn't have succeeded. We would at once have been asked the question: "Then why was the leg of the calf created?" . . .

Hitler continued by giving an economic argument for vegetarianism: more crops would feed all the population. "At present," he said, "the base of our diet is the potato—yet only one per cent of the soil in Germany is devoted to growing the potato. If it was three per cent, we'd have more to eat than is needed. Pasturages cover 37 per cent of the surface of our country. So it's not man who eats grass, it's his cattle."

Hitler mentioned the increased work capacity of herbivores. He cited examples: the vegetable-eating Turkish porter, who can move a piano alone; the elephant that can outrun the lion; the plant-eating Japanese wrestlers who are amongst the strongest men in the world. Other defenses for a vegetarian diet, he said, was that a child will never choose meat if it can select from meat, an apple, or a piece of cake; that meat-eating is imitative, like drinking and smoking; and that the consumption of meat decreases as soon as a greater choice of vegetables is presented.

Finally, he summarized his theory as to why man was led away from a vegetarian diet. "I suppose man became carnivorous because, during the Ice Age, circumstances compelled him. They also prompted him to have his food cooked, a habit which, as one knows today, has harmful consequences."

A further conversation between Goebbels and the Führer is recorded in Goebbels's diary and *Hitler's Secret Conversations*. Goebbels wrote: "He believes more than ever that meat-eating is harmful to humanity. Of course he knows that during the war we cannot completely upset our food system. After the war, however, he intends to tackle this problem also."

Hitler delivered an extensive monologue in reply to Goebbels's asking whether a pound of potatoes had the same nutritive value as a point of meat. He explained that the food of the soldiers of ancient Rome consisted mainly of fruit and cereals and they had a horror of meat. Yet their teeth were good, and the "intervening centuries do not appear to have caused any changes. Travelers in Italy have noticed that the masses still feed on the same things, and that they still have excellent teeth. . . ." Hitler then claimed that the vegetarian's endurance is a further argument for that régime since the dog, a carnivore, cannot compare in performance with the horse, a vegetarian. He also extolled the virtues of raw foods, saying: "It is in their raw state that vegetables have their greatest nutritive value. The fly feeds on fresh leaves, the frog swallows the fly as it is, and the stork eats the living frog. Nature thus teaches us that a rational diet should be based on eating things in their raw state."

In 1943, Hitler once more used his table to air political gossip. He invited Speer and Goebbels to lunch and dinner, and used the situation to make derogatory comments about all his associates who were absent. From autumn on, dining with the Führer was an aggravating experience. In the midst of his negative opinions on such relatively unimportant matters as the weather bureau came consistent praise of his cook and her vegetarian cuisine. Although he was endlessly worried about his weight, since he gained weight easily, he ate pastries eagerly.

By this time, the diet that he had begun in 1911 to counteract an imaginary stomach condition was beginning to take its toll, largely because of the huge quantities of drugs he was taking. Three doctors were in attendance: Dr. Karl Brandt, Dr. von Hasselbach, and Dr. Theodore Morell. Morell was a fake who had been expelled by the German Medical Association. All the experimental drugs that he invented were tried on the Führer. There were some twenty-eight combinations of drugs, including Ultraseptyl, which had been condemned by druggists.

Drugs took over his body and his mind. Injections became a daily ritual. Hitler was in fact slowly poisoned. It is ironic that the fate he had always feared he finally imposed on himself: contamination by a foreign substance.

By 1944 Hitler began to bar certain persons from his table, a sign of his distrust of the leaders of the German people. He blamed the loss of the war on the incompetence and lack of self-sacrifice of his countrymen. After his quarrels with his commanders, Keitel, Jodl, and Halder, military associates were not present at his table. Soon Hitler retreated to the bunker that he had built below the Berlin Chancellery. He lived with his personal cabinet, secretaries, and cook. Eva Braun joined him on April 15, 1945. There were twelve rooms in the first part of the bunker, including bedrooms, servants' quarters, and the *Diaetkeuche* or vegetarian kitchen. At the end of the central passage, which served as the general dining area, was Hitler's room.

In these final days his lifelong erratic habits persisted. Meals took place at irregular hours as night and day finally became one. Refusing to visit the front or any of Germany's bombed cities, he ate pastry by the platterful and continued to talk about the benefits of his diet. He remained a sick enigma until the end, having Eva Braun's brother shot for being an accomplice in Himmler's betrayal. Then, in his last hours, he married his mistress, a romantic act performed only to please her. (Or was it planned with the same eye to posterity that had carefully analyzed every other phase of his career, except, of course, the military defeats?) That same afternoon, he had his favorite dog, Blondi, poisoned. The officer who looked after the other two dogs of the household shot them.

Hitler asked his personal staff to leave the bunker and flee to safety. Yet they chose to stay with their leader as a last act of dedication. Fraulein Manzialy was not allowed at the Führer's wedding ceremony, which took place between one and three in the morning on April 29. But she did partake in the party that followed. She and three secretaries joined Hitler for his last lunch, at two o'clock, after Eva Braun declined, remaining in her room to polish her nails. Hitler reportedly avoided discussing his immediate intentions.

Soon after lunch, Hitler and Eva Braun died from poisoning. Before his death Hitler had planned every detail for the burning and destruction of their bodies to prevent them from falling into Russian hands.

What happened to the German vegetarian movement during the Nazi years? Followers of Eduard Baltzer helped Hitler to gain power and became part of the early Nazi movement. But after he became chancellor, he turned his back on the vegetarians, just as he ignored the dozens of other groups to whom he had made promises. Like a real politician, he forgot those who gave him his power.

Vegetarian societies were declared illegal and were forced to become part of the German Society for Living Reforms. The magazine *The Vegetarian Warte* ceased publication in Frankfurt in 1933. The Mazdaznan movement, a modern vegetarian cult based on the teachings of the Persian prophet Zoroaster, was outlawed because Dr. Rauth, the leader, was Jewish. The last official meeting of the societies was held in 1935 in Nordhausen-am-Harz, later to become the sight of a concentration camp. The magazine *Vegetarian Press* was allowed to continue publication, but the notification of the time and place of meetings and the use of the term "vegetarian movement" were prohibited.

Members of vegetarian societies were subject to raids in their homes. Even those books that contained only vegetarian recipes were confiscated by the Gestapo. Soon pressure forced the German vegetarian societies to leave the International Vegetarian Union. The vegetarians were viewed suspiciously by the Reich's Health Department because they might claim Hitler as a member of their own organization. The very use of the word "peace" was cause for suspicion.

The German Vegetarian Society in Munich, founded in 1898, decided to terminate its link with the German Society of Living Reform at a lecture at the Mathilda Hospital on May 13, 1936. On November 12, 1937, Dr. Werner Zabel publicly declared that the policy of the German vegetarians was to keep their health attitudes to themselves. Just because a meatless diet was adopted by those persons who tried to reach the highest accomplishment, this did not mean that vegetarians would suggest it for the entire nation. Some members of the Munich group began to meet secretly. Once all the participants at a lecture in the private home of a painter were arrested, but they were immediately released because the host was a Dutch citizen.

Shortly after the beginning of the war, Werner Altpeter, a vegetarian, was summoned by telephone to the Ministry of Propaganda, because he had mentioned in an article in his newspaper that Hitler was a vegetarian. They were angry because Altpeter had implied that Hitler was part of his dietetic circle. His experience was similar to that of many innocent persons who were interrogated; Altpeter tried to figure out what he had done wrong as he sat through long hours of hearings and discussions. Finally he was forced to pay 100 marks, in perspective a small sentence indeed.

Although vegetarians could not organize themselves or publish magazines during the years of Nazism, they were allowed to live according to their beliefs. For instance, at the beginning of the war in 1938, vegetarians could exchange their credit notes for meat for dairy products. About 83,000 vegetarians participated in this program.

Many vegetarians were members of the Wandervogel group, which existed as a youth organization before Hitler's ascent to power, although he attempted to transform it into a union of adolescent Teutonic knights. Eden, the vegetarian colony founded in 1893, which then comprised about 1,000 members and was located near Berlin, continued along familiar lines until May 8, 1933. On that day, the directors and executive council decided to work together with the Nazi Party to realize within the vegetarian community the same goals as those proposed for the entire nation. Some members withdrew to practice vegetarianism in private; many remained.

Throughout the Nazi period, there was no organized movement among vegetarians to oppose the inhumane actions of Adolf Hitler. It does seem strange that persons who were so outraged at the suffering of animals were not more outspoken on issues of injustices of such gross proportions.* After the war, in 1946, the German vegetarians reorganized at Hanover and founded the Vegetarier-Union Deutschland.

Albert Schweitzer

Although of German heritage, Schweitzer more than any other great contemporary figure belongs to all nations. Albert Schweitzer, whose name is synonymous with the phrase "reverence for life," was a

---

* The same phenomenon was true of the later India-Pakistan war.

Albert Schweitzer's childhood prayer: "Dear God, protect and bless all living things. Keep them from evil and let them sleep in peace."

theologian and philosopher, an accomplished organist, the author of numerous books, including the classic study *J. S. Bach*, missionary doctor in Africa, and the winner of the 1952 Nobel Peace Prize. "I never go to a menagerie," he wrote, "because I cannot endure the sight of the misery of the captive animals. The exhibiting of trained animals I abhor. What an amount of suffering and cruel punishment the poor creatures have to endure in order to give a few moments' pleasure to men devoid of all thought and feeling for them."

In *Memoirs of Childhood and Youth*, Schweitzer recalls a dramatic event in his childhood that laid the foundation for his later embracement of love for all creatures. A young friend, Henry Brasch, asked

Schweitzer to accompany him on an escapade to shoot birds. At the moment of attack, however, Schweitzer heard a distant bell that seemed to indicate a divine warning against his premeditated assaults. "Ever since," he writes, "when the Passiontide bells ring out to the leafless trees and the sunshine, I reflect with a rush of grateful emotion how on that day their music drove deep into my heart the commandment: 'Thou shalt not kill.'"

Schweitzer dined mostly on fruits and nuts, but he occasionally ate meat and it was always on his table. Anita Daniel, who shared many lunches and suppers with Schweitzer in his home in the village of Günsbach, Alsace, describes his belief that "life has to be respected at the utmost—except in cases where killing an animal is being done for a very important reason"; he cites as examples of such exceptions a dangerous snake or a wild beast attacking someone, or persons doing important brainwork who are thus in need of meat to keep up their strength. However, Schweitzer was convinced of vegetarianism as an ideal of reverence for life and regretted he could not fulfill that goal as completely as he would have liked. In his later years, he became a more consistent vegetarian.

The setting is Schweitzer's little garden in Günsbach. The lawn is being mowed. Daisies are growing near the cut grass and Anita is starting to pick them.

"How could you pick them?" Schweitzer asks excitedly. "Never, never pick field flowers!"

Ms. Daniel was startled and argued unsuccessfully for her point of view, finally saying, "Two minutes later they would have been mowed in any case!"

"This is completely different," Schweitzer replied. "This *had* to be done."

8

Back—and Forth—to Nature

Benjamin Franklin Experiments

*T*hroughout American history, there has been an epicurean clash between ethical convictions, nutritional fads, and positive advances, on the one hand, and the growing industrialization of food production, removing consumers even further from the land, on the other. To many persons, vegetarianism showed a way to rebel against the desensitization of nature and feelings as the god of Mammon overtook numerous aspects of life in the new land of promise and capitalization.

The first notable American vegetarian was the printer, statesman, inventor, and writer Benjamin Franklin. His dietetic experiment, although of rather brief duration, began from his own readings and contemplations—unattached to an organized movement. In his memoirs, published posthumously, Franklin says that at sixteen he read Thomas Tryon's *The Way to Health, Long Life and Happiness, Or A Discourse of Temperance*. That British publication inspired him to try a meatless diet. He was pleased by the two immediate results of his experiment: he saved money and since he began eating separately from his meat-eating brother James, he found extra time to devote to his favorite pastime, reading.

Franklin temporarily became a propagandist for Tryon's views: when he entered Samuel Keimer's employment as a journeyman printer, he made a pact with his gluttonous boss. Franklin writes:

> He agreed to try the practice if I would keep him company.
> I did so, and we held it for three months. We had our victuals dress'd, and brought to us regularly by a woman in the neighborhood, who had from me a list of forty dishes, to be prepared for us at different times, in all which there was neither fish, flesh, nor fowl, and the whim suited me the better at this time from the cheapness of it, not costing us above eighteen pence sterling each per week. I have since kept several Lents most strictly, leaving the common diet for that, and that for the common, abruptly, without the least inconvenience, so that I think there is little in the advice of making those changes by easy gradations. I went on pleasantly, but poor Keimer suffered grievously, tired of the project, long'd for the flesh-pots of Egypt, and order'd roast pig. He invited me and two women friends to dine with him; but, it being brought too soon upon the table, he could not resist the temptation, and ate the whole before we came. . . .

Until his first voyage from Boston, Franklin continued to be a vegetarian. Then, since the boat was stranded off Block Island, the travelers caught cod fish. Franklin still agreed with his dietetic mentor Tryon that each fish eaten was the result of an unprovoked murder since no sea creature could do anything to a man that would justify its slaughter. However, Franklin had always loved the taste of fish and the aroma of freshly-caught cod was irresistible. He rationalized that since within the stomach of a large fish one would find a smaller fish, for the larger to eat the smaller was really the natural order of life. Thus he dined "very heartily" on the cod and began to eat with other people, "returning only now and then occasionally to a vegetable diet." Franklin, an open-minded, all-seeing thinker, realized he could endorse either action, depending on his momentary point of view.

Temperance in eating and drinking, however, continued to be prime virtues to the inventor of the open stove and author of *Poor Richard's Almanac*. Franklin made a comprehensive list of thirteen virtues, ranking dietary reserves as the first ones. Some of the proverbs from the almanac advocating abstinence are:

He that lives carnally, won't live eternally.

Against Disease here, the strongest Fence,
Is the defensive Virtue, Abstinence.

To lengthen thy life, lessen thy meals.

A full belly is the mother of all Evil.

Hunger is the best Pickle.

Dine with little, sup with less: Do better still: sleep supperless.

Cheese and salt meat should be sparingly eat.

Franklin had boundless energy and was thoroughly organized; he provides a sample of his work schedule in his autobiography. A series of boxes represent the hours in the day and each section is allocated with an activity—a few squares are reserved for sleeping or procrastination. In addition to hard work, simple meals, and alcoholic temperance, Franklin preached the values of both drinking water and bathing in it. He opposed bathing in cold water, however, believing that too violent for his constitution. Franklin's suggestion instead was to bathe in cold air.

Unfortunately, Franklin eventually became less austere about food and drink until his physique finally rivaled that of his former boss whose corpulence he had found so offensive. In 1757, Franklin described himself to a friend as "a fat old fellow."

Almost one hundred years passed from Franklin's conversion to the development of a vegetarian movement in America. Reverend William Metcalfe, a Manchester clergyman and homeopathic doctor, was inspired by Reverend Cowherd and the Bible Christian Church movement in England. Metcalfe, who interpreted the Bible in terms of vegetarianism, vehemently denounced meat-eating and alcohol. He immigrated to America in 1809 and settled in Philadelphia, where he used the schoolroom and articles in newspapers as means to disseminate his liberal ideas. An essay, *Abstinence from the Flesh of Animals*, was published in 1821 although his major achievement was the conversion in 1830 of Sylvester Graham and Dr. William Alcott. Metcalfe continued to serve without pay at the Bible Christian Church.

Sylvester Graham, who had been a sickly child, became a Presbyterian minister in 1826 and traveled around the eastern states, developing into a fanatical prohibitionist while an agent for the Pennsylvania Society for the Suppression of the Use of Ardent Spirits. As the result of his meetings with Metcalfe, Graham added other platforms to his temperance lectures: sexual restraint, fresh air, baths, and vegetarianism. Followers, called Grahamites, began to apply his principles and hundreds started a regiment of Saturday night bathing, exercises before open windows, and sleeping on hard beds. According to Graham, excessive verbiage was also the result of a diet that was too concentrated; but it might be eradicated by putting the bran, usually removed, back into wheat flour. The *Graham Journal of Health and Longevity* appeared, reiterating the diverse health principles of a man who was by now rich as well as famous. Graham compared man physiologically to the orangutan, concluding that vegetable food was natural for both primates. Tea and condiments were to be avoided since the latter, like sexual indulgences, might cause insanity. Sylvester Graham, known of course for Graham crackers, is now considered the founder of the modern health movement in America—a faction that is often steeped in fanaticism and far-fetched claims, but whose members frequently have solid principles as the foundation for their extremist views.

When the British Vegetarian Society was founded in 1847, Metcalfe corresponded with Graham, Alcott, and others to begin a similar organization in America. The result was the first American Vegetarian Convention in New York on May 15, 1850. The following November, *The American Vegetarian and Health Journal* began under the editorship of Metcalfe, a position he held until his death in 1862.

Horace Greeley, founder of the *New York Herald Tribune,* was an early convert to vegetarianism but his interest eventually waned, although he continued to advocate such social reforms as temperance and women's rights. Mrs. Greeley, however, remained committed to the Pythagorean system of eating and other Grahamite views all her life.

In an article, "Temperance in All Things," Greeley describes his decision to give up liquor in 1824. Then, after attending a Graham lecture in New York in the winter of 1832, he gave up coffee. For years, coffee had been Greeley's chief luxury: "coffee without breakfast being far preferable to my taste, to breakfast without coffee . . ." Yet he felt better from that day forward. Greeley recognizes that the vegetarian diet he adopted during his poor and lean years was far better for him, but he still gave it up. Humorously, he notes that his wife could easily and quickly inspire guests to leave their household since they tired of her cooking—beans and potatoes, boiled rice, puddings, bread and butter, no condiments but salt, and never even a pickle.

A vegetarian diet had mixed effects on Greeley since his natural energies were so relaxed that he could not jump as high or run as fast as he could when he ate flesh foods. On the other hand, he did not feel as full or have headaches, and flesh wounds healed more easily when he was a vegetarian. "Other things being equal," he says, "I judge that a strict vegetarian will live ten years longer than a habitual flesh-eater, while suffering, on the average, less than half so much from the sickness as the carnivorous must."

Meatless Communes

The Alcott family were thoroughly enmeshed in vegetarian dogma. However, they were of course known for far more than that: Bronson Alcott was a noted advocate of radical teaching methods and friend of the Transcendentalists Emerson and Thoreau; his cousin, Dr. William Alcott, was a prolific writer about health; and Louisa May Alcott, Bronson's daughter, wrote the classic *Little Women*, which was not only the most popular novel of the time but helped support her struggling family.

William and Bronson, although cousins, were raised on farms in close proximity and shared a close childhood, exchanging books and ideas. William continued his higher education in Boston, where he came under the influence of Graham. His major work in the field of vegetarianism was *The Vegetable Diet As Sanctioned by Medical Men and By Experience in All Ages*. Many hail it as a scientific exploration of the subject, but it is far from that, being a compilation of letters in response to a query published by Dr. Milo L. North in an 1835 edition of *Boston Medical and Surgical Journal*, and later republished in *American Journal of Medical Science of Philadelphia*. In that letter, Dr. North asked his colleagues to reply to seven questions regarding a vegetarian diet, such as: Did it improve or diminish physical strength? Was the mind clearer? What was the length of the time of trial? Were constitutional problems aggravated or removed?

William Alcott answered with a lengthy letter. However, before North could compile his results, he became ill and eventually Alcott undertook to coordinate the project. *The Vegetable Diet* gives the unedited statements of one hundred physicians about their experiences on a vegetable regimen, with Alcott's comments after each entry. There is not one completely negative reply, which somewhat decreases the credibility of the study. At the conclusion of the letters, Alcott gives seven reasons for his own preference for vegetarianism: anatomical, physiological, medical, political, economical, experimental, and moral.

According to Alcott's thorough essay, vegetarians have superior appetites, which meant to him that they could eat at all times and under all circumstances. "The more perfect the appetite," he writes, "the greater should be our moral power of commanding it, and of controlling the quality and quantity of our food and drink, as well as the times and seasons of receiving it." He includes a brief historical survey of ancient vegetarian groups, such as the Pythagoreans and Essenes, and points out the moral arguments are his favorite. But he acknowledges that few persons would be convinced on those grounds alone.

In another book, *Ways of Living on Small Means*, William Alcott discusses the basic rules for avoiding cider, tea, or coffee. He developed that theme further in *Tea and Coffee*, a tiny book that is little more than a hard-covered essay. For example, he reports that Dr. Burdell of New York tried out an experiment using a yellow bird. It received one drop of tea extract upon its tongue; within fifteen minutes, it was dead. Although tea is known to relieve fatigue, Alcott points out, it achieves that delusionary benefit through nervous stimulation.

His cousin Bronson began following his dictums in 1835, when he completely eliminated meat from his diet. With William and several other persons, they founded Fruitlands, the vegetarian commune in Massachusetts that lasted only seven months. It was developed on land purchased by Charles Lane, a prominent figure in the nineteenth-century Utopian community movement. In May of 1843, against Alcott's advice, Lane purchased the Wyman Farm for close to $2,000.

Fruitlands consisted of a house and 11 acres of land, cultivated with beans, rye, oats, potatoes, barley, and maize. In addition to vegetarianism, the members were forbidden to use sheep for the production of wool; therefore, only cotton was worn. Oxen and horses were similarly not employed to till the soil since that was considered slave labor. Only food that grew above the ground could be eaten, and baths were in cold water. "In apparel," wrote Bronson, "we cannot as yet dispense well with cotton and leather, the first a product of slaves and the last invasion of the rights of animals."

In addition to Bronson Alcott and his family, other original members were Charles Lane and his son William, Isaac Hecker, Christopher Green, Abraham Everett, Anna Page, Joseph Palmer, Abram Wood, Samuel Larned, H. C. Wright, and Samuel Bower. Numerous other people visited for short intervals, but failed to stay. The major issues at Fruitlands, which eventually led to Bronson's abandonment of it, were marriage and the family. Lane, who was familiar with the nearby Harvard village of Shakers, thought the single family unit had to be absorbed into a large group family. The Alcott family was in firm opposition to this concession and Lane felt that Abigail May, Bronson's wife, was responsible for the failure of the communal experiment. Bronson suffered deeply from the conflicts at Fruitlands; he began staying in bed, refusing to eat, and losing interest in life. This proved a turning point in his life; later, he lacked the drive and enthusiasm which had marked his earlier experiments in teaching.

Of the 500 American communes founded during the nineteenth century, others were far more successful than Fruitlands. One of the most intriguing was the Oneida Community, founded by John Humphrey Noyes, a graduate of Dartmouth College who left Yale Theological School as a convert to Perfectionism—a branch of Wesleyan Methodism that preached complete sinlessness. Noyes, however, declared that he was free of any sins on February 20, 1834, regarded by the Oneida Community as the day of High Tide of Spirit. This blatant declaration of the supremacy of man over God led to Noyes's segregation from the Church and his many peers.

With Noyes's immediate family as the nucleus, the Oneida Community began in upstate New York. Gradually it developed satellite communities, such as one in Brooklyn. The basic principle was *coitus reservatus*, self-control, as a means of birth control. The general concept, known as Male Continence, was joined by another basic Oneida innovation: the Complex Marriage—each member was married to everyone else. However, they did not believe in "free love," although newspapers constantly applied that label to their way of life. Rather than "free" love, their sexual activities were strictly regulated and the sexes were even separated into distinct sleeping quarters.

This controversial experiment, which continued actively until 1881, operated on vegetarian lines for health rather than ethical reasons. Discussions of vegetarianism were known as "The Meat Question," and debates occupied many of the daily evening meetings.

"Do you become like a cabbage or a cow if you eat of it?" a member would ask.

No, someone would reply, you did not become like a cabbage or a cow. But, if you did, it would be far better to be like a cow than a cabbage.

Members of the Oneida Community also avoided tea, coffee, tobacco, and medicine. Although their diet was rather high in carbohydrates, the children seemed to thrive. After the community decided to become self-sufficient in its food production, there were several years of butter and cheese shortages. Yet there were little ill effects, and the shortages served to inspire experimentation with new dishes, as well as an increased appreciation of fruits.

The most astounding fact about this vegetarian community is the way they primarily obtained their income—by trapping animals for furs. By 1864, the trapping business had steadily grown over the past decade so that annual sales from furs amounted to about $100,000, with the manufacture of close to 300,000 furs. Noyes and members of the community took great pride in the superior efficiency of their traps.

These fur-trapping vegetarians were also innovative in the rights of women—up to a point. Equality was the word of the day. To the horror of unsympathetic neighbors, Oneida women cut their hair short so that they could do the same labor as men and shortened their dresses to knee length, adding loose-fitting pantaloons. The goal, though never realized, was to build a university where women and men would study the same subjects. By unanimous agreement the role of woman was redefined to state that she was *not* a child bearer; thus she should be free of the sexual and biological differences usually ascribed to women and men. A kibbutz-type educational system was established to provide women with free time to pursue their vocations. Then, after preventing the increase of population at the Oneida Community for twenty years, the stirpi-culture policy was instituted—a system of eugenic procreation developed "scientifically" to bring together the best examples for parenthood.

Basically, it was Noyes who provided the scientific part of the process; he decided who should procreate and when. The women even signed a statement about their beliefs: "That we do not belong to ourselves in any respect, but that we belong first to God, and second to Mr. Noyes as God's representative."

Gradually the community died out, probably because the children of the original founder grew up and drifted away from the communal pattern of their parents. Although their childhoods seemed happy and outwardly unaffected by the drastic changes in living arrangements and education, their displeasure surfaced since they took any opportunity to strike out on their own.

John A. Collins, an abolitionist from Boston, founded a commune in 1843 at Skaneateles, New York, where vegetarianism was also practiced. The Utopian community operated on a 300-acre farm and advocated the conventional monogamous family unit, growing out of "love and virtue." Another motto was "Reform in All Things." Organized religion was forbidden, since Collins was an atheist. Each family lived in a separate apartment, though meals were shared at a common table. Divorce was encouraged so that happiness within marriage was always obtainable and really practiced, rather than a Utopian goal. Eventually Skaneateles also disbanded because of the jealousies and petty arguments that developed among the colony.

Another commune advocating vegetarianism was established in Benton County, Arkansas, where a group of anarchists, consisting of ten men and seven women, settled in 1860 on a 500-acre plot of land. They called themselves the Harmonial Vegetarian Society. Neighbors labeled them "grass eaters." However, it was their advocacy and practice of free love that caused a sensation in conservative Arkansas, rather than their meatless diet. What might have happened to the commune is conjecture since the imminent Civil War between the states led to its disbandon-ment. Confederate soldiers took possession of the various buildings and seized their official publication, *The Theocrat*.

One would think the author of *Walden* would have embraced a simple, meatless diet. Yet Henry David Thoreau, who chose solitude rather than communal living as a means of experimentation, advocated vegetarianism but practiced it for only a few years. "I have found repeatedly," he wrote, "of late years, that I cannot fish without falling a little in self-respect." Thoreau objected to meat-eating on practical grounds—it was unclean, extensive time was necessary to prepare it, and it was inconvenient. A little bread or a few potatoes were equally as satisfying and involved less filth and trouble. "Like many of my contemporaries," he continues, "I had rarely for many years used animal food, or tea, or coffee; not so much because of any ill effects which I had traced to them, as because they were not agreeable to my imagination." Thoreau recognized that one's repugnance to animal flesh is mental rather than a genuine repulsion.

Simplicity was the main stress in his ideal life, with water the only drink for a wise man since a man's body is his temple and one that he builds daily by his actions. One meal was far better than three; eventually, Thoreau continues, a meatless diet will be part "of the destiny of the human race." But Thoreau did eat fish and once went as far as to slaughter a woodchuck for dinner. He recognizes that most sensitive men have, at one time or another, thought of abstaining from animal food. "It is hard to provide and cook so simple and clean a diet as will not offend the imagination," he continues,

> "but this, I think, is to be fed when we feed the body; they should both sit down at the same table. . . . The fruits eaten temperately need not make us ashamed of our appetites. . . . But put an extra condiment into your dish, and it will poison you. It is not worth the while to live by rich cookery. . . . Is it not a reproach that man is a carnivorous animal? True, he can and does live, in a great measure by preying on other animals, but this is a miserable way—as anyone who will get to snaring rabbits, or slaughtering lambs, may learn—and he will be regarded as a benefactor of his race who shall teach man to confine himself to a more innocent and wholesome diet.

Thoreau proceeds to explain that he is not a squeamish man for, when he had to, he enthusiastically ate a fried rat. He could also drink like anyone else, if he had to. But it is the control over one's palate that is gratifying: "He who distinguished the true savor of his food can never be a glutton. . . ."

Needless to say, Thoreau's exaltation of civil disobedience and the abandonment of the complexities of society have been far more influential than his contradictory views on vegetarianism. Another nineteenth-century innovator, Ellen B. White, had a greater influence on the national spread of the meatless diet.

The Seventh Day

Ellen B. White, who was then Ellen Harmon, was in the original group of New Englanders who began the Adventist movement, an outgrowth of the Millerite movement. The others were James White, her future husband, Joseph Bates, Hiram Edson, Frederick Wheeler, and S. W. Rhodes. The importance of this Christian sect in a history of vegetarianism may be explained by their present number of followers: there are about 2 million Seventh Day Adventists around the world and approximately 500,000 in the United States. Fifty per cent of all Adventists are lacto-ovo-vegetarians.

"The Second Advent of Christ is near at hand," William Miller told his followers.

"When?"

"About the year 1843," Miller said. He based his prediction largely on an interpretation of Daniel about the cleaning of the sanctuary as the end of the world.

Followers of Miller, known as Millerites, included Baptists, Christians, and Methodist ministers and their congregations. In fear they waited for the dreaded day, specified by Miller as October 22, 1844, for the scheduled end of the world. When it failed to happen, his followers were disappointed and called Miller a phony: his movement of about 100,000 believers dispersed.

However, the group that included Ellen Harmon reinterpreted the Scriptures and decided where Miller's error in calculation lay; final work of investigative judgment in the sanctuary was necessary before the Second Advent. The Seventh Day Adventist movement began quite slowly. The term "Seventh" came from the fact that they believed the Sabbath or seventh day was sacred and holy, a strict observance that inflicted social and financial hardships on many members who were bound not to work on that day.

By 1855, headquarters was established in Battle Creek, Michigan, with an important publishing company devoted only to the Seventh Day Adventists. The success of this sect is due largely to a tight web of educational programs that involves separate schooling—from elementary school through college—a continual magazine, book publications, and international missionary work. Contributions are authorized by a strict interpretation of the Bible.

Vegetarianism in the Seventh Day Adventist movement is the direct result of Ellen White, who believed the body to be God's temple and that therefore any abuse of one's body is also a violation of Him. With that principle in mind, she denounced tobacco, alcohol, and meat. The incorporation of vegetarianism was further promoted when Goodloe H. Bell, the first official Church school teacher, attended Oberlin College and became acquainted with health reform and meatless diets. Later, when he went to Battle Creek and was converted to Adventism, he agreed with their meatless philosophy and began teaching it to his students.

Basic beliefs of Seventh Day Adventists are that Jesus Christ ascended to Heaven, where he lives as "High Priest" as the lives of men are called into judgment; when Christ returns to earth the Millennium will begin and he will take the righteous living and resurrected ones back to Heaven with him for a "thousand-year" period. At the end of that time, Satan will be destroyed by the fire from God and all earth will be cleansed of sin and sinners. With the righteous inhabiting the "new earth," the original creation will be restored. To promote righteous living, attendance at movie theaters, dancing, and similar activities are discouraged.

Although not a nutritionist, Ellen B. White, a plump woman, applied common sense to various health problems that afflicted America during the nineteenth century, and of course many of the excesses she pointed to still apply today. A few of her remarkably modern beliefs follow:

- Puddings, custards, sweet cake, and vegetables, if served at the same time, will cause a stomach disturbance.
- It is unwise to eat fruit and vegetable at the same time.
- Avoid drugs.
- Eat plain food, prepared in the simplest manner.
- Increase physical exercise.
- Discard rich pastry. Fruit is a better dessert.
- Food should correspond to climate.
- Eat slowly.
- Overeating weakens the digestive organs, aggravates previous diseases, and leads to headaches, indigestion, and colic.
- Eat something warm, at least each morning.
- Warm food until it equals the temperature of the stomach.

A Seventh Day Adventist whose name is as well known as the cornflakes that he invented was the vegetarian Dr. John Harvey Kellogg. His involvement with the Adventists really began in 1864, when James White visited the Kellogg home. Soon twelve-year-old John, an excellent student, was an apprentice at the Review and Herald Press, the Seventh Day Adventist publishing company still in existence today. His duties began with sweeping the floors and cleaning, but eventually he was setting type, reading proof, and performing more advanced editorial tasks.

Kellogg received his medical degree from Bellevue Hospital in 1875. However, he did not immediately return to Battle Creek. Instead, he took private lessons with Dr. George M. Beard, an advocate of the use of electricity as medical therapy. In fact, Kellogg's medical studies continued throughout his life in terms of extensive reading and trips to Europe to explore radical techniques in water cures and exercise therapy. But in 1876 he returned to Michigan; it would remain his base of operations for the rest of his controversial life.

John Harvey Kellogg, M.D., lecturing on health in the old parlor of the Battle Creek Sanitarium.

Kellogg took over the Adventist sanitorium, which soon became a non-profit and non-sectarian health institute that reflected the personal stamp of Dr. Kellogg, inventor of the breakfast cereals that bear his name due to the business expertise of his younger brother.

For over sixty years, Kellogg edited *Good Health Magazine*, which promoted vegetarianism in almost every issue. His nutritional ideas were always undergoing modification. For instance, at first he was skeptical of all root vegetables since he believed they failed to receive the advantages of direct sunlight on their edible parts. At that point, legumes were the only vegetables he advocated. Later, he became a firm believer in such vegetables as potatoes. His dedication to fruits, nuts, and grains as the natural and best diet for man remained consistent throughout his life.

Kellogg wrote prolifically about his radical ways to treat sick people. In one book, *The Miracle of Life*, published in 1904, he describes his dietetic views in great detail. Chapters include "The Mystery of Life," "A General View of the Body," "The Miracle of Digestion," "Dietetic Sins: Shall We Slay to Eat?" "The Natural Way in Diet," "Drugs Which Enslave and Kill," and so forth. What is the oldest dietetic principle? ". . . the book of Genesis," writes Kellogg, "in which we are told that 'the Lord formed man of the dust of the ground . . .'"

Kellogg believed cow's milk was unnecessary because a milk made from the paste of filberts, almonds, and other nuts was completely equal to traditional milk. Of all the animal foods, eggs were the least objectionable to Kellogg. Meat was unquestionably the villain. He also advocated the free use of water as a beverage, not during meals. Kellogg believed fruits were essentials, rather than luxuries, and that nuts— pound for pound—were the most nutritious food. While traveling, he rarely ate more than bread and apples.

By 1901, there were seven hundred guests at the famous and influential Battle Creek Sanitarium. Five years later, there were 7,000 patients, who were cared for by almost as many staff, including 30 physicians. Kellogg introduced such health programs as morning calisthenics and open-air sleeping arrangements.

Fresh fruits and vegetables were always important foods in Kellogg's sanitarium. Women prepare them in the old main building in 1922.

A significant aspect of the endorsement of a meatless diet by the Seventh Day Adventists has been the development of meatless protein dishes, such as soyburgers, soy milk, and various canned plant protein foods flavored to resemble meats and poultry. Since their objection is based on biblical injunctions against meat-eating as well as nutritional disadvantages, many members want to comply with their Church dogma while still clinging to the taste of meat. Thus these high-protein canned foods offer substitutes that are both nourishing and convenient. The dietary explorations of the Worthington Foods Corporation, which is affiliated to the Seventh Day Adventist Church, has inspired researchers trying to find low-priced, high-protein solutions to the problem of providing nutritious and economical meals for schoolchildren in this country and around the world.

Loma Linda University, a Seventh Day Adventist institution of higher education, is conducting a study among the California population of White followers with the aid of a grant from the United States government because they are considered a low-risk group for cancer and other diseases that are related to smoking or drinking, although the reasons are still unknown. Approximately 100,000 California Adventists will participate in the study, which will explore these possible reasons for the better health of Adventists: non-smoking and non-drinking, careful dietary practices, socioeconomic factors, medical care, levels of stress or anxiety, hormonal factors, exposure to viruses, immunity level, and inheritance.

Upton Sinclair

In Upton Sinclair's obituary in *The New York Times* in 1968, twelve reforms that he advocated are listed: vegetarianism is one of them. In fact, Sinclair practiced a meatless diet for only about three years when he experimented with nutritional benefits in 1911; yet the label struck, even posthumously.

One obvious reason for this was his novel *The Jungle*, famous exposé of the fictitious "Packingtown." The brutal and unclean conditions of the stockyards of Chicago that Sinclair described in 1906 would seem logically to be the efforts of a man angered by animal slaughter. Yet Sinclair even stated that he was not opposed to flesh foods, just to the cruel and insanitary way they were produced. He cited abattoirs in England where cattle had leather covers placed over their heads and neither suffered nor were unclean.

Of course the meatpacking industry is simply the background Sinclair made use of in *The Jungle* to describe his central theme—the plight of the immigrant working class, and the contrast between rich and poor, dreams and reality. Yet the nation was ready for Sinclair's explosive and visual words about the meat industry, although they occupy only 12 pages of a 340-page novel. It was this material that gained instant national and international fame for the struggling novelist. As Sinclair often commented, he aimed for the hearts of Americans but reached them through their stomachs.

Sinclair uses the situation in the stockyard to philosophize about men. A particularly moving and powerful depiction of the death of hogs led him to ponder whether the demise of a hog is symbolic of "the hog-squeal of the universe." He pursues additional similarities: no two hogs are alike: and, unsuspecting of their fate, they live a trusting and harmless life. Wasn't there some place where the suffering hogs would be rewarded for their misery? Would no one appreciate their sacrifices and torments? Yet as the story of *The Jungle* develops, there apparently is no recognition of the traumas of Ona, the heroine, who eventually dies as painfully as the hogs. Ona and her husband Jurgis symbolize the plight of the American laborer.

In a tongue-in-cheek autobiography, *American Outposts*, Sinclair attributes his mother's influence as the fundamental one in developing his major character traits. His father, a drinker, caused the family endless pain, so his mother became Sinclair's model. If his mother abstained from drinking, learning arithmetic, drinking coffee or tea, or smoking— so did her son Upton.

The Baltimore-born boy read all of Shakespeare and Milton once in a period of two weeks; he entered college while still an adolescent. After graduation, Sinclair pursued graduate courses at City College. Originally he intended to be a lawyer, but he began to attend classes just for the sake of learning, while supporting himself by writing "potboilers."

Upton Sinclair in 1905, when *The Jungle* was written.

Saving money was not one of Sinclair's prime virtues. Thus he sank all of his earnings from *The Jungle* into a colony known as Helicon Hall, located in the back of the Palisades overlooking Englewood, New Jersey. For $36,000 he purchased about two acres of land and a house, but the Utopian dream only lasted from 1906 until 1907. The fourteen members of Helicon Hall included such influential persons as Edwin Bjorkman, critic and translator of August Strindberg; Edith Summers, who became a novelist; and an eager student, by the name of Sinclair Lewis, who took odd jobs. One day the entire house caught fire and burned to the ground; so ended the colony.

Throughout his life, Sinclair seemed to suffer physically when writing his ninety books. Psychosomatic but painful symptoms developed as he experienced the anguish of those characters he was fictionalizing. Sinclair's vegetarianism was a means of devoting even more time and effort to his writing—this way, cooking became inconsequential. Headaches, indigestion, and exhaustion were his common ailments. Immediately after the demise of Helicon Hall, Sinclair's first wife almost died from an attack of appendicitis. She recuperated at Battle Creek Sanitorium, which was successful, although Sinclair always remembered the exorbitant fees he had to pay: $90 a week.

That summer Sinclair decided to take his wife and young son, along with his friend Mike and his family, to the coral reefs of Bermuda. There his experiments with a meatless diet became an obsession and proved the inspiration for *Good Health and How We Won It*, published in 1919. Thirty years later, in *American Outposts*, Sinclair tells his readers that he is so ashamed of his dietetic treatise he will not reveal the title. In *Good Health*, Sinclair advanced numerous physiological reasons for giving up meat, basing many of his conclusions on the studies of Horace Fletcher at Yale University, and on the increased endurance of vegetarian, as opposed to meat-eating, groups. Sinclair described his régime: two meals a day, never eat before sleep, no drinking during meals, using only fresh foods, adequate ventilation, play as the best exercise, and careful chewing of food to allow enough nutrients, but in smaller quantities. He even provided daily menus and recipes.

Upton Sinclair remains an enigma. He wrote some of the most incriminating passages against slaughterhouse procedures, yet denied any ethical considerations for a meatless diet. In a chapter in *The Fasting Cure*, published in 1911, entitled "The Use of Meat," Sinclair expresses his views against vegetarianism quite harshly. He explains:

"And when ignorant people wish to live cheaply, the foods they eat are the sugar and starch foods. I remember in Thoreau's *Walden* he sets forth how he lived for many months upon five or six dollars' worth of food. He does not give the amount of the food by weight, so of course we cannot tell exactly; but he gives the prices he paid, and the leading articles in his diet were flour, rice, corn-meal, molasses, sugar and lard. One is, therefore, perfectly prepared to learn that Thoreau died of consumption. . . .

Fasting—a purely hygienic procedure to Sinclair—was a practice he pursued all his life as a cure for any illness provoked by overwork or other causes. He broke the fast with orange juice and advised against any solid foods until the third day. The social reformer certainly proved an advocate for vegetarianism indirectly through *The Jungle*, even though he avoided the label.

Vegetarians for President

When five hundred delegates to a convention of the American Naturopathic Association met at the Hotel Commodore in New York on July 28, 1947, it proved to be the birth of the American Vegetarian Party. At eighty-five, Dr. John Maxwell, a naturopathic doctor and vegetarian restaurant operator from Chicago, was nominated for candidacy in the presidential election of 1948. Symon Gould, public relations director and associate editor of *The American Vegetarian*, was nominated for Vice-President.

The admission of a vegetarian candidate to a Presidential election that already had ten candidates was more attention-seeking than effectual. Dr. Maxwell, who married a few months after his nomination, took the campaign quite seriously. Unfortunately, he was ineligible to appear on the ballot since he had been born in England, but that did not deter the group. Although a diet without the flesh of meat, fish, or fowl was the primary campaign motto of the party, there were other platforms, such as government ownership of all major natural resources and power facilities, worker ownership of factories, liquidation of the national debt, Congressional currency control, printing new money, and the financing of a network of eight-lane transcontinental highways to eliminate unemployment.

Symon Gould, familiar from his battle with George Bernard Shaw, was the force behind the American Vegetarian Party. Gould entered into another battle, this time with Jesse Mercer Gehman, president of the American Vegetarian Union. Dr. Gehman insisted that Gould belittled the vegetarian movement by connecting it with politics. Gould, on the contrary, felt he merely added "social dynamics" to an ethical movement.

The candidate for the 1952 presidential election was retired General Herbert C. Holdridge, a 1917 West Point graduate who was described in his yearbook as "an energetic fellow, generally getting what he strives for." This time he failed to achieve his goal, which had been to hire a vegetarian chef for the White House after his victory.

Another candidate was proposed in 1956; in 1960, Gould himself finally ran for President. He continued to keep vegetarianism and pacifism in the forefront of the public mind through his 1962 campaign for state senator from New York. His opponent, Jacob Javits, had been his classmate at Public School 40 in New York.

Gould's political career was a joke to some, annoying to others, and appreciated to only a few fellow believers, since he alienated so many other American vegetarians who believed that a meatless diet should take place at the dinner table, not in discussion after the meal. Gould died of cancer in 1963, at the age of seventy: the American Vegetarian Party died with him.

Modern Times

What is the situation in America today regarding organized vegetarianism? There are some notable advocates, such as Will Durant, author of the multi-volume *The Story of Civilization*; Dick Gregory, comedian and political activist; Scott and Helen Nearing, socialists and authors of *Living the Good Life*; and some actors and actresses, such as James Coburn and Susan St. James. Yet it is not a cause that is openly discussed and debated by the intellectual community. There are far more prominent vegetarians than it appears, but they share a personal belief that consistently instigates useless labeling rather than impassioned or philosophical debates. Thus many doctors, educators, and celebrities are silent about their meatless diet and ethics.

The groups that are in existence tend to be so emphatic about their beliefs that they alienate many potential followers. Vegetarian groups experience the same advantages and pitfalls as all organized coalitions— one leader trying to exercise strong control and create a unified value system that may erase the subtle differences which people cherish and prefer to retain.

One eclectic faction, located in New York City, is the Vegetarian Feminists, who are part of the Vegetarian Collective. A headline in the *Majority Report*, organ of the women's liberation movement, stated:

WOMEN, ARE YOU *STILL* HUMAN CHAUVINISTS?
THE ALL COMPASSIONATE FEMINIST IS A VEGETARIAN!

Their point is well taken and is of course a continuation of the crusade for female and animal rights advanced all the way from the Pythagorean religious communities to such notable women vegetarians as Anna Kingsford and Annie Besant. But once again the explosive and emotional nature of their literature fails to convince the non-believer and simply reaffirms the ideas of sister vegetarians who probably developed their outlooks independently.

More effective than their redundant brochures is a three-minute film the Vegetarian Feminists distribute, portraying the activities inside an actual slaughterhouse. Even thirty seconds of this gruelling film, showing the sheeps' throats being cut and their bodies hung upside down, is enough time to get the message.

Otoman Zar-Adusht Ha'nish, raised along strict lines in Tibet and Iran by monks, began the Mazdaznan movement in Chicago in 1890. This group, still active today, is a modern adaptation of Zoroastrianism. The four basic principles are: vegetarianism, distilled water, no tea or coffee, and sun worship.

Also located in Chicago are the headquarters of the Natural Hygienists, who bear the stamp of one man, Herbert Sheldon, although there are followers around the world as well. Their teachings state that man is constituted in perfect health, rather than being an unstable organism in constant struggle. Man's illnesses may be traced to a breach of naturalness: his symptoms are hidden by drugs and vaccines, and the best way to recover genuine health is by fasting.

The American Vegan Society, founded by Indian-born Jay Dinshah, follows similar views but enhances them with Jainist attitudes of *ahimsa* and the elimination of all animal products and clothing apparel. Freya, Dinshah's wife, helps to run the active organization that includes a retreat called Suncrest and a magazine, *Ahimsa*. Both groups are the extremist vegetarian sects in America today; no membership figures are available on any of these American organizations.

Since the national census does not record if someone is a vegetarian, it is impossible to know how meany people actually practice a meatless diet in the United States. Some estimates, however, go as high as 5 million persons. That vegetarianism is a growing movement in contemporary America is undeniable, as evidenced by the appearance across the country's college campuses of vegetarian alternatives for meals in dormitories and cafeterias. Why is it spreading? Is there a resurgence of ethical beliefs or is this just another passing fad? Vegetarianism offers idealistic youth a chance to show their parents that there *is* a way for each person to fight the unharnassed aggression and violence associated with earlier generations. It is also an expression of the growing affinity with Eastern philosophies. Furthermore, vegetarianism offers a way of returning to nature, an aspect of human existence that is quickly disappearing from the larger urban areas of contemporary America, once the frontier of the "New" World. In addition, the high cost of meat is forcing people to adopt a diet that consists of fewer animal products; starting under external impetuses, many persons choose to continue such a regimen when they discover that it is possible to eat both pleasantly and humanely.

Tolstoy and
the Doukhobors

From Hedonist to Celibate

lthough Russia of necessity was "vegetarian" for the impoverished peasants, who thrived on black bread and potatoes, vegetarianism did not become a cause until Count Leo Tolstoy adopted it in the later part of the nineteenth century.

When Princess Marya Nikolayevna Volkonsky married Count Nicholas Ilich Tolstoy, her dowry consisted of eight hundred serfs and Yasnaya Polyana, her estate. Count Tolstoy supplied only his name and aristocratic manner. Such were the "humble" origins of Leo Tolstoy.

In response to a request in 1903 by his friend P. I. Biryukov, Tolstoy described his life as distinctly divided into four periods:

That wonderful, especially in comparison to what followed, innocent, joyful, poetic period of childhood up to fourteen.

Then the second—a terrible twenty years or period of vulgar licentiousness, of ambition-serving, vainglory and, chiefly, lust.

Then the third, an eighteen-year period from my marriage to my spiritual birth, a period which from the world's point of view may be called moral . . . during these eighteen years I lived a proper, honest family life, not yielding to any of the vices castigated by public opinion, a period during which all my interests were limited to egotistic concern for my family, for augmenting my wealth, for achieving literary success, and to pleasures of all sorts.

And, finally, a fourth, twenty-year period in which I am now and in which I hope to die, from the viewpoint of which I see the whole significance of my past life and which I would not wish to alter in the slightest, except in those evil habits acquired by me in previous periods. . . .

Although, by his own declaration, Tolstoy was a hedonist for the greatest portion of his life, he also showed an early concern for self-discipline. When only eighteen, he began a diary of his thoughts and actions—a habit he would continue, although irregularly, throughout his life. In January 1847 he recorded some of his ideals: to rise by five o'clock and retire by nine or ten; to eat little and avoid sweets; and to kill desire by work. It would take Tolstoy about forty years to fulfill several of those goals.

Although his mother died in 1830, when Tolstoy was only two years old, he remained obsessed by her image the rest of his life—trying to imagine how she looked, holding her up as an ideal of womanhood; he had never heard an unkind word about her. Then his father, who drank a lot, coughed and spit up blood and died in the summer of 1837. The next year, his grandmother died; Tatyana Alexandrovna Ergolskaya, Aunt Toinette, raised the four Tolstoy children. Certainly it is not strange that Tolstoy became obsessed with death—a fear that would haunt him during various traumatic periods of his life.

Rousseau's philosophies had an early influence on Tolstoy, who was dissatisfied with the teachings of Descarte. Tolstoy empathized with Rousseau's moral struggles between instinct and doing the "right" act, as the Frenchman detailed in his *Confessions. Emile* also had an influence on the teaching methods Tolstoy applied to the school he began for the serfs of Yasnaya Polyana in 1848; he returned to this early interest in radical teaching methods repeatedly throughout his adult life.

Was there one specific event that changed the hedonistic Russian who passionately enjoyed hunting into a celibate, vegetarian pacifist? Turgenev wrote about Tolstoy's affinity with animals: "I could have listened forever. He had got inside the very soul of the poor beast and had taken me with him. I could not refrain from remarking, 'I say, Leo Nikolayevich, beyond any doubt, you must have been a horse once yourself!' " Yet as late as 1878, Tatiana recorded her father's hunting activities: "Papa went hunting, and got three hares and one fox. We counted up today how many Papa has got this autumn and it came to fifty-five hares and ten foxes. . . ."

The last volume of *War and Peace* was published in 1868—the result of eight soul-searching and emotionally absorbing years of research and dwelling within the tragic lives of his characters. Rather than experiencing elation over the fine critical reception of his masterpiece, Tolstoy suffered a deep depression for several years—unable to write or see a bright future. Then he devoted four years to the completion of *Anna Karenina*, published in 1877. But his penetrating novels failed to satisfy him. Tolstoy began to study the Bible, to the dismay of his wife Sofya, who enjoyed copying his novels in progress as a relief and distraction from her child-rearing and household duties.

Leo Tolstoy had money, literary fame, numerous children, and a devoted wife—but it was not enough. There was a gnawing sadness. He began to think that if he could believe in God, he might find inner fulfillment.

"At the thought of God, happy waves of life welled up inside of me," he wrote. "Everything came alive, took on meaning. The moment I thought I knew God, I lived. But the moment I forgot him, the moment I stopped believing, I also stopped living. . . . To know God and to live are the same thing. God is life."

Tolstoy, however, could not reconcile *his* God with conventional Christian dogma. In his treatise, *The Kingdom of God Is Within You*, Tolstoy tried to show that his version of Christianity was the true interpretation of the Gospels. This was the endorsement of non-violence that would become Gandhi's inspiration. Tolstoy stated some of the ideals expressed in the Sermon on the Mount which he considered absolute guidelines:

> . . . The ideal consists in having no ill-will against any one, in calling forth no ill-will, in loving all. . . .
> The ideal is complete chastity, even in thought. . . .
> The ideal is not to care for the future, to live only in the present. . . .
> The ideal is never, under any condition, to make use of violence. . . .
> The ideal is to love our enemies, who hate us. . . .

By the summer of 1882, Tolstoy had given up hunting with such vengeance and regret at his earlier pleasure that he felt completely alien to two sons, Sergey and Ilya, who would go hunting each day with the same disregard for morality that Tolstoy had experienced at their ages.

That fall, Tolstoy returned to Moscow to prepare a house that he felt would be more suited to the family's needs and budget than the one Sonya had chosen the year before. Tolstoy did not want to live in Moscow, but Yasnaya Polyana was too isolated for the growing children, who now needed to be near universities and advanced schools. The house Tolstoy purchased cost about $75,000, although Tolstoy considered it a bargain and an expression of his new decision to become less of a materialist. It was in an industrial area on the outskirts of the city—a concession to humbleness—although Tolstoy began supervising a massive and costly renovation of the twenty-room house.

Within a few weeks, the rest of the family arrived and began their routine. There was a chef for the parents and eight children; a woman cook for the twelve servants. At the large dining room table, only water was served in a homemade kvass. Tolstoy, who had resolved to go on a vegetarian diet, ate only oatmeal, and as much fruit jelly and preserves as possible. The meatless diet had three purposes: it aided his health, which was precarious from overwork and depression; it served his lack of teeth; and it alleviated his troubled conscience over his personal wealth in contrast to the conditions of the Russian peasants.

On the morning of June 18, 1884, Sofya gave birth to a daughter, Alexandra, called Sasha: it was her twelfth delivery. Tolstoy recorded in his diary the suffering his wife had experienced and also noted: ". . . I have stopped drinking wine. I drink tea and suck on a lump of sugar, I eat no meat, I am still smoking, but less. . . ."

Tolstoy's conversion to a vegetarian diet was gradual and he struggled with the decision for several years, vacillating back and forth. Three years later, a diary entry of Sonya's for March 9, 1887, discusses his diet: ". . . Last week he again took up his vegetarianism, and it is already having an effect on his frame of mind. Today he purposely started talking about the evils of wealth and money in front of me, and alluded to my desire to keep things for the children. . . ."

The following week, Countess Tolstoy continues, "He eats rich food one day and vegetarian food the next. . . ."

Tolstoy wrote on abstinence from alcohol and on meat-eating in essays that served as introductions to books by relatively unknown persons. Were it not for these writings, his unique viewpoint would be unknown except for isolated diary entries and journalistic accounts by some of the numerous visitors to Yasnaya Polyana. "Why Do Men Stupefy Themselves?" is a 20-page essay written on June 10, 1890, as an introduction to *Drunkenness* by Dr. P. S. Alexeyev, the brother-in-law of his friend and translator Aylmer Maude.

Of course people can offer typical reasons why they should stupefy themselves, Tolstoy explains, by using vodka, wine, beer, hashish, opium, tobacco and, less frequently, ether, morphia, and fly-agaric. "To while away time," "Cheer oneself up," and "Because everyone else does it" are common responses. But Tolstoy feels that such loathsome and destructive habits must have a deeper motivation:

> . . . When observing his own life, a man may often notice in himself two different things: the one is blind and physical, the other sees and is spiritual. The blind animal being eats, drinks, rests, sleeps, propagates, and moves, like a wound-up machine. The seeing, spiritual being that is bound up with the animal does nothing of itself, but only appraises the activity of the animal being; coinciding with it when approving its activity, and diverging from it when disapproving. . . .
> . . . The cause of the world-wide consumption of hashish, opium, wine, and tobacco, lies not in the taste, nor in any pleasure, recreation, or mirth they afford, but simply in man's need to hide from himself the demands of conscience. . . .

This major thesis, relating stimulants to a moral failing, continues throughout the essay. Tolstoy even points out how people inflict suffering on others by smoking in public, ignorant or unconcerned about the discomfort they cause non-smoking associates. ". . . No one would allow himself to wet a room in which people are sitting, or to make a noise, shout, let in the cold, hot, or ill-smelling air, or commit acts that harm others. But out of a thousand smokers not one will shrink from producing unwholesome smoke in a room where the air is breathed by non-smoking women and children. . . ." But he concludes the essay optimistically, asserting that not only will the emancipation from stupefication be "an epoch in the life of humanity," but his new world is soon at hand since the evil is now recognized.

One of the most thorough, soul-searching modern treatments of the moral reasons for vegetarianism is found in Tolstoy's preface, written in 1892, to a Russian translation of *The Ethics of Diet*, a historical survey of writers on humane eating by an Englishman, Howard Williams—a book that also impressed Gandhi.

". . . And not only does a man become morally better the more love he has for others and the less for himself," Tolstoy writes in the seventh chapter, "but the less he loves himself the easier it becomes for him to be better. . . . Instead of feeding others a man eats too much himself; by so doing he not only diminishes the possibility of giving away the surplus, but by overeating deprives himself of power to help others. . . ." Tolstoy concludes this section by praising self-control as the first quality necessary for a good life.

The sections most pertinent to vegetarianism begin with a praise of fasting, describing it as an art that one should understand fully, including "when to begin the fasting, how to fast, how often to eat, what not to eat." Tolstoy vividly describes a recent visit to a slaughterhouse in the city of Tula. He met with a butcher who was quite astonished at his asking whether he felt pity when he performed the killings.

" 'Why be sorry? This has to be done,' " the butcher replied. 'What is to be done? I have to make a living. At first I was afraid to kill. My father never killed a chicken in all his life.' "

Tolstoy outlines his visit in graphic detail:

> . . . We arrived. Even before entering we could smell the oppressive, detestable, rotten odor of joiner's glue or of glue paint. The farther we went, the stronger this odor. It is a very large, red brick building, with vaults and high chimneys. We entered through the gate. . . . By the wall of the little house, and to the right of it, sat six butchers in aprons, which were covered with blood, with bloodspattered sleeves rolled up over muscular arms. They had finished their work about half an hour ago, so that on that day we could see only empty chambers. In spite of the gates being opened on two sides, there was in each chamber an oppressive odor of warm blood; the floor was cinnamon-colored and shining, and in the depressions of the floor stood coagulated black gore.
>
> One of the butchers told us how they slaughtered, and showed us the place where this is done. I did not quite understand him, and formed a false, but very terrible conception of how they slaughtered, and I thought, as is often the case, that the reality would produce a lesser effect upon me than what I had imagined. But I was mistaken in this. . . .

The Doukhobors

Just how involved and sincere Tolstoy was about vegetarianism and pacifism became apparent in 1895 when the former soldier came to the aid of the Doukhobors, an ancient sect of Russian Christians. They called themselves "People of God" or just "Christians," implying they were the only true Christians. However, Archbishop Amvrosi Serebrennikov named them Doukhobors, or "spirit wrestlers," in 1785, to show they fought against God.

They shared many of Tolstoy's principals: vegetarianism; pacifism, or "non-resistance to evil," as Tolstoy called it; abstinence from alcohol and tobacco; and a belief that God is within each man and therefore the priesthood is unnecessary.

The origin of the Doukhobors is clouded in legend since they believe that the written word kills and so they pass on their traditions and doctrine orally through hymns and psalms. The most plausible story is that during the seventeenth century a deserter from the army established himself as a hermit in a cave on the shores of the Volga River. Peasants listened as he preached. By 1779, the first major governmental investigation of this heretical sect occurred, and soon began the exiles to Siberia. By 1890 there were 20,000 Doukhobors living in the Caucasus. In the spring of 1895, those Doukhobors in exile were instructed by their leader, Peter Verigin, who had read Tolstoy's works on resistance, to destroy their weapons and publicly refuse induction into the army. Cossacks rounded up the conscientious objectors and beat them with whips; their land was confiscated, houses pillaged, their leaders imprisoned, and 4,000 Doukhobors exiled to the mountains.

The route to vegetarianism was not a quick one for the Doukhobors. It was while Verigen was imprisoned that he turned vegetarian, deciding it was as wrong to kill creatures as men. At the same time, he reintroduced the old Doukhobor ban on drinking and added a smoking prohibition. When the announcement of the rulings reached the Caucasian settlements, there were ritualistic bonfires of tobacco and liquor was poured out. Giving up meat, however, caused a great deal of controversy and resulted in three hundred families breaking away to form a middle group, since the followers of Verigin became known as "The Fasters" and meat-eating dissidents were called "The Butchers." Verigin even added abstinence from sex as part of his platform.

Tolstoy felt personally responsible for the fate of the Doukhobor peasants since his writings had encouraged their defiant actions. Knowing a plea for the Doukhobors would not pass the Russian censors, he had an anonymous article published in *The Times* in London, under the title "The Persecution of Christians in Russia in 1895."

But the situation continued to deteriorate and by the next year, four hundred of the exiled Doukhobors had died of deprivation in the distant mountains. Tolstoy encouraged his disciples Chertkov, Biryukov, and Tregubov to write a manifesto, which they called *Give Help!*, to which Tolstoy added a postscript. The reaction to the publicly circulated booklet was immediate; even the Czar received a copy in the mail. Facing exile because of their participation, Chertkov left for England; Biryukov was sent to a little town in Kurland.

Tolstoy tried desperately to raise money for the Doukhobors, to the dismay of many of his own followers who felt he was now defying his own refutal of material wealth. The concerned writer even asked the recently established Nobel Prize Committee in Sweden, who were considering him for an award, to send money instead to the Doukhobors whom Tolstoy felt were genuine embodiments of peace. When that failed, he turned to making pleas in the foreign press and sent his son Sergey to England to be a liaison with a relief committee there.

Sergey was able to make contact with the Quakers and it became clear that the Doukhobors could emigrate to Canada, but there simply were not enough funds. Tolstoy, feeling a passionate need to help the living proof of his life's goals, violated his own recent principle of rejecting money earned by his writing and vowed to sell his next work to the highest bidder. Numerous followers felt cheated, although the money would be directly donated to the Doukhobors. With great speed Tolstoy completed *Father Sergey*, and also *Niva* was sold for about $3,000 for each 16-page sheet before he had even completed it.

Father Sergey, however, proved too close to Tolstoy and was not published until after his death. Thus he returned to his novel, *Resurrection*, as a means of aiding the Doukhobors. After months of agonizing writing, it finally appeared in 1899; the monies he received, which amounted to about $225,000, went to the fund for his followers.

The Doukhobors in Canada

Although some Doukhobors remained behind in Russia, most migrated to this new land where many began cultivating farms in the wheatlands of Saskatchewan and Alberta. These Doukhobors are mainly the Independents. The ones termed the Union of Spiritual Communities of Christ live in the interior of British Columbia, inhabiting the neglected orchard lands in the west Kootneys and the Kettle Valley around Grand Forks. Another sect, entitled the Sons of Freedom, is the most radical, known for parading in the nude, eating raw foods, and throwing incendiary bombs as a sign of its defiance of the organized government of Canada and of assimilating into the Canadian culture.

In Canada, however, the isolation of the Doukhobors is self-imposed, rather than State-instilled, as in the Soviet Union. Food has deep symbolical meaning to them: each religious meeting begins with a large loaf of bread, a jug of water, and a dish of fruit on the table. They eat their meals with hand-carved wooden spoons, often starting with a dish of cabbage and borscht, mixed with cream. Various fruits, blintzes, kasha, pirogi, and green beans are other favorite foods, as are fresh vegetables, large tomatoes, salads, and sweet corn, which they are particularly fond of. Other staples are the wholewheat and black bread that are so closely associated with old Russia. Though milk products are used freely, eggs are rare. Tea with lemon is the standard drink, but huckleberry and red-currant juices are common during the summer.

Maurice Hindus, a Russian-American journalist, visited the Doukhobors in the 1920's and was certain they would feel a debt to Tolstoy.

The first nude march in about 1907 of the Canadian Sons of Freedoms, a radical sect of the Doukhobors. Near Swan River, Manitoba, they were protesting against the increase of materialism among their members.

"Tolstoy?" asked the head of the household where Hindus ate a vegetarian meal. "Was he a general in the Czar's army?"

The Doukhobors do not fit into the Canadian way of life and long for a return to Russia. But they fantasize about a Russia that died after 1917. The "new" Russia would be as antagonistic to their eccentric and rebellious ways as the czarist régime they fled from.

Tolstoy's Later Years

By 1897, troubles with two of his daughters were added to Tolstoy's frustration over his disappointing marriage and his guilt feelings about his life. Masha followed her father in several ways: a vegetarian, she had relinquished her share of the inheritance in a Tolstoyan gesture; she was a stern and noble young woman. But that summer, she announced her plan to marry an impoverished distant relative, Prince Nicholas Leonidich Obolensky, who was handsome, irresponsible, and lazy. Masha then asked that her inheritance be reinstated. Her hasty marriage left Tolstoy bitter and hurt. A few months later, his eldest daughter Tanya expressed her desire to marry a middle-aged widower. Tolstoy recorded in his diary on November 20: ". . . Tanya has gone away—God knows why—with Sukhotin. It is pitiful and humiliating. For seventy years my opinion of women has done nothing but sink steadily, and yet it must go lower still. . . ."

At the celebration for Tolstoy's seventieth birthday in 1898, Sonya commented, "One may not drink to the health of Leo Nikolayevich because he belongs to a temperance league." As his views against smoking and for chastity strengthened, so did other anti-Establishment attitudes. In 1900, he wrote: "I cannot rejoice at the birth of a child into the wealthy class; it is the proliferation of parasites." Then in 1901, the Church, aggravated by Tolstoy's attacks in *Resurrection*, posted the announcement of his official excommunication on all the church doors of the city. Yet his followers hailed him as the second czar of Russia, with a moral and spiritual power far greater than the military force of Nicholas II.

Second to left is Alexandra, Tolstoy's daughter. At the head of the table is Sofya Andreevna, Tolstoy's wife. Seated to her right is Tolstoy.

By the last year of Tolstoy's life, any indication of his earlier life of luxury and excess had vanished from his immediate personal habits. His secretary, Valentin Bulgakov, a young student in the historical-philosophical department at the University of Moscow, recorded Tolstoy's comments during that year. Not only did Tolstoy refuse to hunt, but he regarded it as a moral evil. Moderation and simplicity were the key principles in his life. His new secretary followed his example. (N. N. Gusev, Tolstoy's previous assistant, had been arrested a few months earlier and exiled for sending through the mails certain of Tolstoy's writings that had been banned.)

Tolstoy enjoyed discussing vegetarianism with the endless stream of equals and worshippers who flocked to Yasnaya Polyana. Sometimes he would quote Plutarch, whom he felt most forcefully expressed the arguments against meat-eating. Bulgakov records in his diary for June 22, 1909, a delightful exchange about the rights of insects between his master and some guests who were Skopets—members of an ascetic religious sect that practiced castration.

Someone inquired what one should do in order to get rid of flies or insects without exterminating them.

"Chase them out of the house, or keep things clean," Tolstoy replied.

Then he added: "This was very well expressed by the Buddhists. They say one must not kill consciously."

Tolstoy explained that he saw a natural progression from killing insects to slaughtering animals to fighting other men. Another visitor, Vladimir Grigorevich, delighted in reminding Tolstoy that his current views had once been radically different; now Tolstoy sincerely expressed compassion for all.

"I myself used to be a hunter," Tolstoy agreed, "and I would kill a hare with my own hands. You know, you have to clutch it between your knees and cut its throat with a knife. And I did this and felt no pity whatever."

Two vegetarians entered his life that year. One arrived in the form of a letter—from the rising literary genius, Bernard Shaw. On the envelope that the letter came in, Tolstoy scribbled: "Clever-foolish."

The other vegetarian was the eccentric sculptor Prince Paolo Trubetskoy, who had visited Tolstoy before, accompanied by his wife Amelia Reeves, a novelist. In 1898 he made a lifesize bust of Tolstoy and another statue of him on his favorite horse.

Tolstoy was enchanted and intrigued by Trubetskoy.

"Have you read *War and Peace?*" he once asked him.

"I don't read anything," the sculptor replied candidly. Trubetskoy explained that his anti-reading policy helped him to preserve his freedom and creative individuality.

Tolstoy was impressed with Trubetskoy's thoughts about animals. Bulgakov entered in his diary Tolstoy's comments:

> . . . He's a terrific vegetarian and animal lover. According to him, animals are much more moral than humans, and people should

try to be more like them. I argued with him about this, and said that man cannot take an animal as his ideal. He can fall lower than an animal, but he can never go higher. Man has an innate shame which an animal lacks. And it is true that he covers with clothing everything that is unnecessary and leaves exposed only that which reflects the spiritual—his face. I have always had this feeling of shame; for instance, the sight of a woman with her breast bared was always disgusting to me, even in my youth. At that time there was another feeling mingled with it, but it was nonetheless shame.

Tolstoy's surviving daughter, Alexandra, is a vegetarian like her father. At the Tolstoy home in Russia, both vegetarian and mixed-diet foods were served. "He liked what he called 'almond milk' made with crushed almonds, sugar, and water," Alexandra writes from Valley Cottage, New York, where she established the Tolstoy Foundation after she left the Soviet Union in 1929.

In those later years, Tolstoy would have coffee and dry bread for breakfast; supper was starchy, consisting of borscht, rice or potato dumplings, and dessert. Tolstoy said during the last tumultuous year of his life: "To eat when one is hungry, drink water when one is thirsty; those are great pleasures of the body; but to refuse food and drink and everything the body desires is more than a pleasure, it is the joy of the soul! . . ."

10

Nutritional Controversies

Basic Issues

*T*he debate whether it is morally right or wrong to slaughter a living creature for food has been expounded for so many thousands of years that it often fails to appeal to "modern man" on either a practical or a philosophical level. For the past hundred years, the emphasis has continued to shift toward "How can I better *my* life?", so that now the key issues connected with a meatless diet are seen as the nutritional and economic ones.

The fear that surrounds a vegetarian diet is generated by the meager information available to the layman. Yet both a vegetarian diet—which lacks meat, fish, and poultry but includes milk, milk products, and eggs—and a vegan diet—which omits all animal foods but includes a mixture of unrefined cereal products, legumes, nuts, vegetables, and fruits supplemented with vitamin B_{12}—can meet the nutritional requirements of all age groups. However, either diet will be inadequate if it is low in energy or contains a high percentage of refined cereals and starchy foods.

The economic and nutritional factors overlap, since in spite of efforts to control or decrease human population, it continues to increase as available land continues to decline. Out of necessity, land *must* be cultivated to produce food as efficiently as possible. Some figures will illustrate whether meat is the most economical way to provide protein. A steer begins life as a calf weighing about 100 pounds. By the time it is sent to slaughter, about fourteen months later, it will weigh about 1,100 pounds. To accomplish that weight gain it will consume: 1,400 pounds of corn grain, 2,500 pounds of hay, 2,500 pounds of corn silage, and 6,000 pounds of pasture for a total of 5,544 pounds of Total Digestible Nutrients (TDN). The steer will gain 1 pound for every 5.54 pounds of TDN that it is fed.

What results from this 1,100-pound steer? Only about 460 pounds of retail meat for consumption, since 30 per cent of the carcass is inedible. Therefore, a ratio of 12:1 plant food is necessary to produce 1 actual pound of available human protein.

Milk is a far more efficient source of protein, since a dairy cow is usually able to produce milk for six years and only has two or three months of non-productivity each year when she is not lactating. It takes about 1.5 pounds of TDN for a dairy cow to produce 1 pound of milk, as compared to 10 pounds of corn to produce 1 pound of retail steer.*

An acre of cereal crops, on the other hand, provides five times more protein than if the same acre was devoted to meat production. There is ten times more available protein when an acre is used to cultivate legumes, such as lentils, peas, and beans, and fifteen times more protein per acre yield if leafy vegetables are raised.

So much of the confusion about a vegetarian diet is based on the dearth of public exposure to contemporary research on this subject. Numerous studies are conducted and described, but usually in the technical journals. Furthermore, the extremists who live only on rice or vegetables are lumped together with more careful vegans and vegetarians who consider nutritional requirements in planning their diets. The twelve nutritionists who answered my queries about the safety of a lacto- or lacto-ovo vegetarian diet *all* concurred that it is a nutritionally acceptable régime. However, each one was careful also to point out that it is necessary, from a nutritional standpoint, to distinguish between a lactarian and a strict vegan diet. "The critical point about vegetarianism," writes Dr. Jean Mayer of Harvard University, "is whether it merely excludes the eating of meat and fish, or whether it also rules out all animal by-products such as milk and eggs. The former practice can be nutritionally quite adequate, while the latter is fraught with risks."

The three key nutritional problems connected with a vegan régime are:

---

* Stuart F. Smith, of the Department of Agricultural Economics of Cornell University, supplied these figures—January 10, 1974.

- Protein sources must be derived from *several plants in combination,* as opposed to a single animal-based protein, such as fish, eggs, or cheese.
- Where does a vegan obtain *vitamin B_{12}* since the foods that contain that essential vitamin have traditionally been derived from animal sources?
- How is calcium ingested if milk is omitted from the diet?

In considering any diet, energy requirements have to be met before all others. Each person will have a varying energy demand, depending on such factors as weight, sex, age, and activity. Cereals, starches, sugar, fats, and oils are major foods that supply energy. The calorie is the unit used to measure the amount of energy in a specific foodstuff. Fats, a very concentrated energy source, contain twice as many calories per ounce as starches. The World Health Organization of the United Nations recommends the following amounts of calories each day for moderately active adults:

Men	2,800 calories per day
Women	2,400 calories per day

These requirements are merely guidelines since people's figures vary, especially during pregnancy, lactation, and child growth periods when additional amounts of energy are imperative.

Protein

Next to energy, protein is the nutrient need that must be fulfilled. Even the word "protein" means "of first importance" in its Greek derivative. Protein is a fundamental structural element of all body tissues for every man, woman, child, and animal. In order to form new tissues and to replace old and damaged ones, protein is a necessary part of any diet. As in energy requirements, growing children and pregnant women need far more protein to enable new tissue to be laid down. Lactating mothers also need increased protein in order to produce milk.

Therefore we *do* need protein, but how much? Are the requirements of all persons the same? In 1887, a Professor Rank found that without any muscular labor, his body neither gained nor lost weight when consuming 100 grams of protein or about 3.5 ounces. The requirements were higher for someone engaged in more active efforts—about 118 grams of protein or 4.2 ounces.

Unfortunately, many persons still think of protein requirements in terms of these outdated nineteenth-century guidelines. As a general rule, one-tenth of the diet should be protein. The World Health Organization recommends that the average man should consume 40 grams of good-quality protein each day. Of course, more protein is necessary in the diet of pregnant and lactating women.

The single most important source of protein in the world is the *cereals,* such as wheat, barley, maize, rice, rye, and millet. Next in significance are legumes and nuts. Meat, fish, and dairy products are much less abundant and generally available only to the wealthy; economically developed countries are usually the ones that consume them in appreciable quantities. Fortunately, most staple foods meet the requirements for protein, except for sago, cassavam potatoes, and plantains.

All foods *do not* have equal protein quality. For example, meat, fish, soybeans, and dairy products contain high-quality proteins whereas cereals, legumes, and nuts contain lower-quality proteins. However, foods are rarely eaten in isolation. Therefore, the protein quality of a diet will differ from its individual constituents. It is quite possible to create a high-quality protein by mixing low-quality cereals, legumes, and nuts.

It is well known that Americans currently eat about *twice* their recommended daily allowance of protein. Since protein is not stored in the body, and only a limited amount may be used to replace the small percentage that is broken down, the surplus is simply wasted by being excreted in the urine.

Proteins are comprised of amino acids, eight of which are called "essential" because they must be supplied in the diet. A "complete" protein is one that has an adequate combination of essential and non-essential amino acids to meet the requirements of the body for maintenance and growth when isolated from all other proteins and digested as the only protein in the diet.

The digestion process breaks down proteins into their component amino acids; they are then absorbed into the bloodstream, to be rebuilt by the body into its own proteins. The adequacy of the protein intake therefore depends, not on the completeness of any single protein, but on the composition of the mixture of amino acids that results from the breakdown of all the protein of a meal.

The eight essential amino acids are:

tryptophane	lysine
methionine	phenylalanine
threonine	valine
leucine	isoleucine

Everyone is taught in public school about these animal-derived protein sources: meat, fish, eggs, milk, and cheese. Less widely known are those obtained from plants, such as soybeans and other legumes, nuts, the germ of certain cereals, and cereals themselves. In addition, there are "borderline" proteins, such as peanuts, which can support growth and maintenance; but reproduction activities will suffer if they are the *only* protein source. Food-combining elevates a protein, inadequate in isolation, to a complete state. For instance, corn lacks lysine and threonine; baked beans supply these amino acids, but are devoid of methionine. Therefore, to obtain "one" complete protein, it would be necessary to eat baked beans and corn bread at the same meal. Obviously, food-combining is a new concept for most persons, who find it so much easier to have a piece of steak and feel content that all protein needs are met by just one food. But even the steak, an animal protein, has its protein derived originally from a plant source since that is how the steer grows and thrives.

Years ago proteins were divided sharply by "first-class," or animal protein, and "second-class," or plant proteins. These arbitrary distinctions have been largely discarded by nutritionists since it is generally accepted that one protein source in isolation need not be considered superior to various protein combinations.

Unfortunately, too many meat eaters visualize an "average vegetarian" as someone who is emaciated and existing on a boring, monotonous diet. There *are* some extremists, but they are rare. For instance, in Bombay I met an energetic eighty-year-old vegetarian who for the past thirty years had drunk only milk, ate no solid food, and chewed betel nuts. Yet he was vigorous, thin, healthy, and outspoken on animal rights. The combination of betel nuts and mother's milk was quite curious. Carefully he removed from his dark-red metal box the numerous ingredients for preparing the morsels for chewing betel nuts, a very stimulating and addictive drug.

The following table illustrates the high-protein concentration in plant-derived foods. It is important to note, however, that when comparing ounce-per-ounce servings, the calorie consumption for plant-derived sources is generally higher. That is why a vegetarian, and especially a vegan, diet requires a complete re-education in nutrition. The size of a portion may not be the criterion for adequate nourishment; there are other factors to be considered. If someone carelessly consumes vast amounts of soybeans or peanuts, he will notice a weight gain in spite of the high-protein content of these plant foods.

The fundamental importance of plant–protein–combining is summarized in the attempts to prevent *kwashiorkor*, a protein-calorie disease of

Protein, Fat, and Calorie Content of Protein Foods per 4 Oz. Serving*

Protein	Source	Protein Grams	Fat Grams	Calories
Beef (hamburger)	Animal	27	23	320
Beef (porterhouse)	Animal	22	47	530
Beef (standard)	Animal	23	12	200
Eggs (2 boiled)	Animal-derived	12	12	160
Wheat Germ (5 tb)	Plant	20	5	275
Cashew Nuts	Plant	20	42	670
Soybean Flour	Plant	41	23	505
Soybeans, mature	Plant	25	'I'	180
Ham, Virginia	Animal	23	25	315
Flounder	Fish	18	'I'	90
Cheese, Swiss	Animal-derived	32	32	420
Cheddar Cheese	Animal-derived	32	40	480
Peanuts	Plant	28	50	600
Lentils (whole seed)	Plant	28	1	380
Leg of Lamb	Animal	27	28	365
Bread (white)	Plant	9	1.6	270
Maize (wholemeal)	Plant	11	5	405
Rice (polished, raw)	Plant	7	1	410
Wheat Flour (100%)	Plant	15.6	2	385
Haricot Beans	Plant	25.5	–	290

* Figures are generally rounded off to the nearest unit of five. Compiled by the author from various sources with the assistance of Dr. Frey Ellis, Kingston and Long Grove Hospital, England.

malnutrition that afflicts the impoverished young of Africa, India, Central and South America, the West Indies, Mexico, and Southeast Asia. A mixture of plant proteins has been developed by the Institute of Nutrition of Central America and Panama which contains 29 per cent whole-ground maize, 29 per cent whole-ground sorghum grain, 38 per cent cottonseed flour, 3 per cent torula yeast, 1 per cent calcium carbonate, and 4,500 units of added vitamin A for each 100 grams. The total protein content of the mixture is 27.5 per cent and its quality resembles milk. The success of this mixture in treating and preventing *kwashiorkor* is further emphasized by the low cost of the food, enabling those who really need it the most to afford it.

The value of plant proteins has been known for decades; but the application of this knowledge to the relief of the unimaginable sufferings caused by protein deficiencies and malnutrition lags far behind scientific knowledge. In view of the desperate situation in many areas of the world, this reluctance to rely on plant protein is tantamount to criminal negligence. Twenty-five years ago Norman Pirie, a British biochemist, pioneered a method of pulping lush vegetation in bulk and extracting protein concentrate. Yet not until late in 1973 was a forthcoming two-year trial study announced for South India—three hundred children between the ages of two and five will be observed for the effect of protein extracted from the leaves of locally grown alfalfa. The protein is dried to a powder and mixed with various foods, such as legumes, peanuts, sugar, and corn. It is disconcerting that several decades had to pass before conscientious experiments started in a nation where an estimated 50 per cent of those 100 million children under five years of age are malnourished.

Soybeans

Most meat eaters rarely encounter soybeans or think of them as a main dish. Yet to the lactarian, and especially the strict vegan, soybeans are essential since they have the protein equivalent of animal sources— even the amino acid analyses of soybean protein is remarkably similar. Historically, the soybean is an ancient food: many records of soybean culture in China, some dating as far back as 2207 B.P., provide advice on soil preference, planting time, and varieties for each of the numerous uses of the early crop. Soybeans were considered one of the five sacred grains, the others being rice, wheat, barley, and millet.

Engelbert Kaempfer, a German botanist who lived in Japan from 1690 until 1693, introduced the bean to Europe. However, there was little interest in his "discovery" until the experiments of Friedrich Haberlandt, in 1875, demonstrated the soybean's nutritional value. In 1898, the United States Department of Agriculture began introducing large numbers of soybean varieties, mostly from Asian countries with a few from Europe and other parts of the world. Since that time, the number of varieties of soybeans has escalated to about 10,000.

Although persons on a mixed diet may not eat soybeans in their visible form, soybean derivatives are being increasingly incorporated into meats. The first edible vegetable-protein fiber, using a new process which rendered it commerically useful in food production, was invented by Robert Boyer, a chemical engineer who worked for Henry Ford during the Depression, although he did not patent his discovery until 1949. These foods derived from vegetable sources are low in saturated fat and have virtually no cholesterol—two major concerns with animal protein. From humble beginnings, the sale of meat extenders and analogues now runs to about $55 million a year—a five-fold increase from 1968.

Religious and ethical vegetarians were the first ones to utilize these similated proteins, but now they are being approved for school lunch programs and necessity is forcing their appearance on even the most traditional dinner plates.

Dr. Aaron M. Altschul, head of the nutrition program at the Georgetown University School of Medicine, is enthusiastic about the ability to produce texture out of soy flour. He says it "will probably rank with the invention of bread as one of the truly great inventions of food. It is possible to allow people the enjoyment they expect from meat-like components and yet avoid the excesses in calories, fat, and a high proportion of saturated fat that ordinarily come from such consumption."

Along similar lines are the results of a *New York Times* survey of soy-beef burgers that indicated they contain as much protein as all-beef burgers. The only difference was in taste, but skepticism was the main reason for those reactions; soy-beef burgers are thought to occupy the same position in the minds of consumers as oleomargarine held a few years ago when it first began to replace butter as the main cooking and baking ingredient where the animal-derived fat had been traditionally used.

What are the most important protein foods in a strict vegan diet? *Nuts*, such as pine kernels, almonds, cashews, walnuts, Brazil nuts, hazel nuts, pecans, chestnuts, and coconuts; *seeds*, such as sunflowers, sesame, and cottonseeds; *pulses*, like soybeans, peanuts, lentils, beans of all kinds, and peas; *cereals*, such as wheat germ, corn germ, whole wheat, millet, rice, buckwheat, barley, maize, sorghu, whole oats, whole rye; and *vegetables*, including green leaves and potatoes. *The key in a vegan diet is combination and variety.* For example, cereals tend to be low in lysine while soya is deficient in methionine. Some typical plant protein combinations would be:

wheat flour and soya flour
wheat flour and peanut flour
cottonseed flour and maize
sesame, maize, and peanut meals

wheat and rye
whole cereals and green leaves
wheat and buckwheat
potato flour, sunflower meal, and malt

Vitamin B$_{12}$

Next to amino acids and protein, the problem of how a vegan gets his vitamin B_{12} is the most controversial issue. Vitamin B_{12} is a crucial vitamin; a deficiency affects every cell in the body and may give rise to such symptoms as tiredness, sore tongue, breathlessness, and dyspepsia or indigestion. Some conditions associated with B_{12} deficiencies are nervous lesions, megaloblastic anemia, and mental disorders. Vitamin B_{12} is unique as it is the only vitamin almost exclusively synthesized by bacteria. All animals obtain their B_{12} from bacterial synthesis. They cannot make it themselves.

Is it true that the only sources for vitamin B_{12} are derived from animals in the form of liver, milk, eggs, and cheese? Traditionally that was so; now vitamin B_{12} may be produced synthetically by a fermentation process inside large aerated vats, similar to the ones used in manufacturing baker's yeast and antibiotics. Although Streptomyces were originally used to make synthetic vitamin B_{12}, they have been replaced by Propionibacteria and other microorganisms that produce high yields. Thus commercially available vitamin B_{12} is *not* extracted from liver and such a supplement would not therefore be a violation of the ethical grounds for avoiding traditional animal sources.

Adelle Davis has pointed out that for years it has been known that "vegetarians could keep healthy by taking a 50-microgram tablet of vitamin B_{12} once a week." Therefore, any deficiencies are unnecessary since the addition of vitamin B_{12}, either through fortified food, tablets, or injections, will prevent such a condition. The danger is that vitamin B_{12} may be stored for about five years without symptoms of deficiency appearing. Thus if a vegan begins his régime and does not supplement his diet, there may not be any signs for several years. It is therefore necessary to begin supplementation *immediately* after eliminating animal-derived sources in a diet and so avoid any future difficulties. Often those deficiencies are irreversible. British researchers have also discovered that a small percentage of vegans who were studied and who had never digested vitamin B_{12} through dietary sources did not develop deficiencies. This phenomenon is still unexplained and is certainly an important avenue for large-scale investigation.

What About a Lactarian Diet?

Even the 1968 edition of the conservative *Encyclopaedia Britannica* points out: "What is clear is that flesh-eating is not necessary to health." Many nutritionists, without an ethical stake in advocating a vegetarian diet, are in agreement. "The ordinary lacto-vegetarian (or ovo-lacto-vegetarian)," writes Dr. John Yudkin, professor of Nutrition at the University of London, "has as good a source of nutrients as has an ordinary meat eater." Dr. D. A. T. Southgate, nutritionist at the University of Cambridge, writes: "The lacto-ovo vegetarians should have no difficulty in eating a diet which contains sufficient protein with a good biological value." ". . . It is obviously easy to reach the optimal protein range (if not the peak, which isn't necessary)," says Dr. D. S. Kronfeld, professor of Nutrition at the University of Pennsylvania, "with ovo and lacto additions."

But more research is necessary to verify these enlightened opinions. Until now, only small studies have been financially feasible; for instance, Dr. Frederick Stare of Harvard University and Dr. Mervyn Hardinge of Loma Linda University conducted a survey of 112 vegetarians and 88 non-vegetarian adult men and women, pregnant women, and adolescent boys and girls. Their results demonstrated that there were no significant differences in the nutritional, physical, or laboratory findings of the vegetarian and non-vegetarian groups. A later analysis of the amino acid content of the protein intake of the subjects showed that *all* groups, including vegans, met and even exceeded twice their minimum requirements of essential amino acids. The major difference was that the pure vegetarians averaged 20 pounds less in weight than the others, who averaged about 12–15 pounds above their specific ideal weights.

It is to be hoped that the nutritional study of 100,000 lacto-ovo-vegetarians of the Seventh Day Adventist denomination that has begun in California will shed more conclusive information on the nutritional advantages and disadvantages of that type of diet. However, the future of the world lies in the *vegan* diet, so that land may be used to a maximum and plant production go directly to starving peoples, rather than to the animals that serve as intermediaries.

Experiments in the effectiveness of soybean-derived milk are essential, as is a re-education in the awareness that palatability need not be based only on conventional foods. Numerous persons have benefitted by a change from whole milk to skim milk, which necessitated adjusting to its thin texture and blander taste. A similar switch to a soybean-based milk would have economic as well as nutritional advantages, and would make available a milk-like drink to poor countries and to persons who, for unexplained reasons, have a lactose intolerance to cow milk. Thus, soy milk may be the answer for preventing calcium deficiencies, a particular problem for nursing mothers. Milk is a food designed for feeding the infant; it should be noted that man is the only species that uses it as an adult food.

Most vegans avoid cheese because the production of most milk byproducts is actually an ethical violation that involves killing: milk is transformed into cheese through the use of an enzyme known as rennin, or chymase. Rennin is present in the fourth stomach of a young milk-fed calf. In order to get the rennin in either liquid or dry form, the fourth stomachs of freshly slaughtered young calves are separated from the intestines. Then the contents of the stomachs are squeezed out and thrown away. Next, the fourth stomachs are either blown up and dried, or split open and stretched out flat between heavy layers of salt and cured for a few days. The extra salt is then discarded; the stomachs are packed in flat layers and shipped to the processor, who dries them at about 100°F. The rennin enzyme is carefully extracted from the cut-up stomachs. Thus the art of cheese-making is far removed from the gentle image maintained by most of us. Indeed, what was once a treasured skill has now become just another tried-and-true scientific process.

However, technology is on the side of the vegetarians and vegans. Vegetable rennets *are* available, although not yet universally commercially applied. Kosher and vegan cheeses can be found, though with effort and inconvenience. The Pfizer Company in New York has also produced a product called Sure-Curd that is made from the parasitic fungus *Endothia parasitica*, a crystalline enzyme that functions like rennet but even cuts in half the maturation time for cheddar cheese. When these products become readily available to the consumer, they will enable strict ethical and religious vegetarians to include protein-rich cheese in their diets.

In an automated farm in Virginia, dairy cows are kept busy eating during the milking process. This one obviously became distracted and later even tried to break out of the blocked area.

Other objections to drinking milk are that they deceive the dairy cow by allowing her to provide nourishment for thousands of persons comfortably, but once she is no longer useful she is whisked off to the slaughterhouse to become hamburger meat. Dairy cows actually provide about 18 per cent of all the beef that Americans consume annually. Therefore, drinking milk indirectly sanctions dairy cow slaughter. In addition, the condition under which cows live while they provide milk are a far cry from the idyllic pastoral setting associated with the earlier small family farms when cows were milked by hand. The dairy industry is increasingly automated and detached from human contact. Cows are milked by machines on a regular twice-a-day schedule. They graze in confined areas not for food, which is provided in confined feedlots, but to obtain a minimum of exercise. Since dairy cows are most productive during the two months following a calf's birth, their offspring are often immediately removed to automated nurseries so they never even know the sensation of a real udder. Land is simply too expensive to be constantly replanted with plants that animals trample as well as chew. However, milk products may be ethically maintained in a diet by letting dairy cows die naturally after they have performed their "human" duty for six to eight years; by using vegetable-derived rennin in cheese-making; and by improving dairy farm conditions.

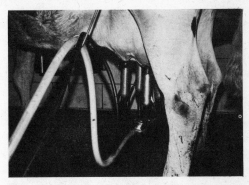

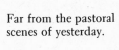

Far from the pastoral scenes of yesterday.

One study comparing vegans to vegetarians was a sociological one by John McKenzie of the Office of Economics in London, based upon the responses of 229 persons to a questionnaire sent in 1966 to members of the London Vegan Society. Within that sampling, 117 were vegans and 112 were vegetarians. Although a note of caution is necessary before generalizing from such a small study, it did point out some thought-provoking trends. For example, 92 per cent of the vegans were vegetarians before giving up all dairy products; of that percentage, 35 per cent were vegan for more than fifteen years. Of those vegetarians who hoped someday to become vegans—often seen within vegetarian circles as the élite and most ethical group—97 per cent did not eat meat *or* fish but most ate four or more eggs per week and 36 per cent had three or more pints of milk each week. Both groups supplemented their diets with vitamin pills; two-thirds of the vegans and 40 per cent of the vegetarians took vitamin B_{12} tablets. Within both groups, there was a preference for natural foods such as brown bread and brown sugar. Although smoking was drastically less common among vegans and vegetarians than the statistics for the whole population (respectively, 7%, 14%, and 57%), the figures for drinking alcoholic beverages were less distinctive: vegans, 40 per cent, vegetarians 50 per cent, and 70 per cent for the whole population.

Meat

A sirloin steak each night is still a dietary sign of prosperity. In spite of increasing prices, meat consumption in the United States has continued to rise: the average beef intake per person for 1940 was 55 pounds as compared to 117 pounds for 1972. But is meat-eating harmful? Most nutritionists point out that there is no evidence that meat should be avoided because of nutritional hazards. Furthermore, there are degrees of meat-eating found among all three communities in the world noted for their longevity: the Andean village of Vilcabamba in Ecuador, the land of Hunza in the Karakoram Range in Kashmir, and Abkhasia in the Soviet Union. However, the part meat plays in each of these diets is minimal. In Hunza, meat and dairy products account for only 1½ per cent of the total protein intake; in Vilcabamba, only 12 grams of protein daily are from animal sources. Yet in Abkhasia, where the people live longest of all three exceptional societies, 30 per cent of the diet comes from meat and dairy products.

The meatpacking industry is as much a part of our American heritage as slavery. A comic book distributed by the American Meat Institute begins *The Story of Meat* with a question:

"Why couldn't the North American Indians living in a land teeming with natural resources lift themselves above their primitive stone age culture?"

An answer is provided in the booklet: ". . . The answer is simple. . . . They didn't have time! They knew how to farm in a very primitive way, but except for the few cliff dwellers, who raised turkeys, North American Indians never domesticated livestock for their principle food necessity. . . ."

Meat . . ." William Pynchon, who founded Springfield, Massachusetts, is usually considered the father of the meatpacking industry in America, because he was the first person to devote all his energies to preparing and preserving meat; by 1830, Cincinnati, Ohio, was known as "Porkopolis"; Chicago soon became the country's leading meatpacking center after the opening of the Illinois-Michigan Canal in 1848. The booklet goes on to point out that meat is not the only product animals provide:

. . . Surprisingly, Only About Half of a meat animal is usable for food. But in the meat packing operations virtually nothing is wasted.

Valuable by-products are made from the inedible parts such as: leather, fats, tallow, wool for clothing, soap, bristles for brushes, bones for knife handles, pipestems, buttons, combs, chessmen, fertilizer, gelatin, decorative objects . . . the list is long!

Meat consumption in the United States is increasing: in 1960, an average American ate 190 pounds of meat as compared to 236 pounds in 1970. In addition, the time it takes for a steer to reach market weight has been cut in half over the past forty years: in 1929 it took thirty-six months; in 1969, only fifteen months. How are these decreases in raising time accomplished? The widespread use of antibiotics in animal feed and medical treatments is the answer; a reality that is causing considerable concern for the consumer, although the cattle raiser is quite pleased with the results.

The Animal Health Institute, a Washington, D.C.,-based organization that provides information and research into pharmaceuticals for the animal industry, proudly reports that "According to Food and Drug Administration statistics, 'about 80% of the meat, milk and eggs consumed in the United States comes from animals fed on medicated feed during part or all of their life.'" They also report in their booklet *The Meat on Your Table* that they are trying to develop physiological agents to foster multiple births in livestock.

Certainly allergic reactions are known to various meats, but this is also true of milk (or of the additives in it), nuts, and fruits, such as strawberries. Conditions in meat markets have been constantly criticized, from Upton Sinclair in *The Jungle* to Jon A. McClure, a former meat-cutter, in *Meat Eaters Are Threatened*. McClure mentions some of the clichés exchanged in the small cutting rooms; for example, if a piece of meat is dropped in the sawdust, someone would say, "'Charge extra for this one, it's breaded.'"

Yet depending on the dairy farm you visit, conditions range from sanitary and progressive to filthy and old-fashioned. The same is true of fruit and vegetable farms, which have not escaped the chemical-additive aspect of a previously "natural" industry.

It is known, however, that pesticides tend to accumulate in animals and fish far more than in vegetables. The process of accumulation results from organochlorine pesticides, such as DDT and Dieldrin, being retained in fat of the animals and fish and not easily broken down. Therefore, dairy products are also a source of pesticide residue but exposure is decreased by using low-fat dairy foods, such as skim milk or low-fat cottage cheese.

Proof is still lacking, but there is talk of a relationship between meat and certain types of cancer. Dr. H. Marvin Pollard, gastroenterologist from the University of Michigan, points out that the latest statistics show that cancer of the stomach continues to decline among Americans, but there is an increase in cancer of the colon and rectum, which already affects 76,000 persons a year. To try to explain the rise of bowel cancer among Japanese immigrants, Dr. John W. Berg led a study that traced the effect of 119 different foods. He reported that "six different meat items were found to be associated with a high bowel cancer risk." Dr. Berg had expected only one or two such associations at the most. There is also a high incidence of bowel cancer in Scotland and Argentina, two above-average meat-eating nations.

Studies in England have pointed to a definite effect of a strict vegetarian diet on faeces—50 per cent less of the enzyme 7-dehydroxylase was found in the faeces of vegetarians than in the control group on a mixed diet. Enzyme 7-dehydroxylase produces bile acids, and some have been shown to be carcinogenic. The report citing these findings is extremely technical and difficult for anyone but a nutritionist to understand, but it certainly pinpoints significant areas for further research.

Plant Hazards

Health problems are not confined to meat. In fact, in certain tropical countries good hygienic practices help to avoid any meat-related diseases. On the other hand, some diseases, such as aflatoxin from the *Aspergillus flavus* infection of traditionally harvested groundnuts, still need more research to find methods of avoiding outbreaks.

The hazardous situations that can befall foods of plant origin or cheeses is best pointed out by indicating a few sample entries on the Commercial Import Detention list issued regularly by the Department of Health, Education and Welfare of the Food and Drug Administration. The repetition of products and the reasons for their detention is considerable, but some samples are:

Food	From	Reason
Coffee	Colombia	"contains insect bored beans"
	Indonesia	"contained in oil contaminated bags"
Romano Cheese	Italy	"contains unsafe food additive . . ."
Grans Cheese	Italy	"contains unsafe food additive . . ."
Cocoa Beans	Ivory Coast	"unfit for food, contains filth and mold"
	Nigeria	"insect-infested with beetles"

Economics

Few persons will disagree that a lacto-ovo-vegetarian or a strict vegan diet is less expensive to sustain than a mixed diet, often amounting to as little as one-fifth the cost. Of course, many vegetarians also prefer organic foods or special products available only in health food stores and therefore the cost of even their fleshless diets has sharply increased.

Many people fail to consider the ramifications of the exploding livestock population throughout the world. Today the largest consumers of grain and soybeans are the *livestock*. For example, of the 5.4 billion bushels of corn produced in 1972 in the United States, 80 per cent was fed directly to livestock. During that fourteen- to sixteen-month lifetime of the American steer, it will eat approximately 560 pounds of corn, sorghums, oats, and wheat, as well as about 30 pounds of soybean meal *each month*.

Statistics of livestock populations are somewhat startling: in India there are 200 million; the United States ranks second, with 127.5 million;* the Soviet Union has about 104 million; and perhaps 100 million livestock thrive in Brazil. The effect of rechanneling plant foods from the steers directly to the consumers would also be startling and could give a direct impetus to focus on the problems of food availability, prices, and attitudes generally.

In a mixed diet, variety is usually provided in the preparation of the meat or fish. Most families develop a reliance on certain particular flesh foods and rarely experiment with such exotic varieties as venison, calf's brains, tongue, or pig's feet. Instead, the traditional steer meat is served in an assortment of ways: broiled, boiled, barbecued, stewed, or roasted. Most Americans rarely eat more than the following flesh foods during an average year: beef (steak or hamburger), flounder, sole, tuna, salmon, ham, lamb, chicken, or turkey. However, the taste of these protein sources require few culinary resources to render them palatable. The juices are succulent in themselves and only one vegetable and perhaps dessert is necessary to provide a completely satisfying and nutritious meal.

A vegetarian diet is quite different. For the lacto-vegetarian, there are hundreds of unique-tasting cheeses to utilize as a main course, but a chunk of cheese sitting on a plate fails to excite most persons as a slice of steak would. Therefore, a greater facility in the kitchen is necessary to

---

* As of January 1, 1974, up 5% from last year according to the Crop Reporting Board. (Release from Statistical Reporting Service of the U.S. Dept. of Agriculture, February 1, 1974.)

avoid boredom with a lacto- or lacto-ovo-vegetarian diet. Eggs may be prepared in numerous ways, but eating them boiled or scrambled week after week would become monotonous.

The vegan undertakes a completely unique culinary experience that ranges from utter simplicity of just nuts, vegetables, and fruits in their natural states to food combinations that elevate the cuisine to rival any other. Variety *need* not be a problem. For example, of the 10,000 varieties of apples that are grown, only 100 are grown commercially in America today. How many persons have tasted all these dominant possibilities: Rhode Island Greening, Stayman, York, Rome Beauty, Northern Spy, Newton Pippins, Winesap, Jonathan, Delicious, Grimes Golden, McIntosh, Cortland, Golden Delicious?

The nutritional controversies surrounding a lacto-ovo-vegetarian diet are minimized by distinguishing it from a strict vegan diet. If dairy products and eggs are added to vegetables, fruits, and grains, good health is virtually guaranteed. Ethical issues are avoided by clean, humane dairy and chicken farms.

In a strict vegan diet, there are distinct hazards, such as amino acid deficiencies, long-range vitamin B_{12} inadequacies, and possible calcium insufficiencies. Though more risky, these possible dangers may be avoided by proper plant-protein combinations, synthetic vitamin B_{12} sources, and calcium-enriched soy milk. Then the ethical violation of causing one's own body nutritional harm is satisfied along with the complete elimination of the slave labor of cows.

The adoption of both types of vegetarian diets involves a re-education toward portions and food preparation, although it is far harder to get used to a strict vegan diet than a lacto-ovo-vegetarian régime. Economically, and idealistically, a purely vegan diet could be the impetus to eliminating mass problems of malnutrition by placing protein-rich foods within the financial reach of those impoverished persons who need it the most.

The Abkhasians

In the quest for the secret to longevity, attention has focused on the Soviet Republic of Abkhasia, comprised of Abkhasians, Greeks, Georgians, and Russians. One-fifth, or about 100,000 persons, are Abkhasians. They live to well over one hundred and are largely vegetarian, not because of an ethical belief but simply as a result of a nutritional bias.

Agriculture is the primary occupation—tea and tobacco dot the valleys in the land stretching from the Black Sea to the Caucasus Mountains. They are a healthy, vigorous, and slim people. Obesity is viewed as a disease. A study conducted by the Ethnographic Institute in Sukhumi revealed that arteriosclerosis is rare there except in extreme old age—after one hundred. A nine-year study of 123 people over one hundred years old revealed no reported cases of mental illness or cancer.

There are several factors that may explain the prolonged lives of the Abkhasians: sexual practices, work, and diet. Virginity is an absolute prerequisite for a bride, and men wait to have intercourse until their marrying age, about thirty years old. But their sexual prowess usually continues into very advanced years. Retirement is unknown in Abkhasia —old people past ninety simply slow down or perform less demanding tasks; but they continue to feel useful by accomplishing farming and cultivating jobs such as pulling weeds.

A rehearsal of "The Long Living Peoples Ensemble" in Sukhumi, the capital of Abkhasia. They are a unique group because you must be at least 90 years old to join. Skill in dancing, singing, and playing musical instruments is also necessary; they perform native folk dances and songs throughout Abkhasia and on tour.

The older people eat even less meat than the younger ones, who consume meager amounts, since they are attuned to the needs of their bodies and know that they should avoid heavy foods. Every part of the edible blade of plants is used either for food or for medicine. When they do eat meat, it is freshly killed and cooked for the minimum amount of time. Leftover food is unknown—everything is fresh; remains are considered unhealthy. Cheese is consumed daily, along with at least two glasses of buttermilk. In addition, most fruits and vegetables are organically grown, picked freshly, and eaten raw with the meals. Honey is the only sweetener.

The longevity of the Abkhasians demonstrates that generalized statements about the inclusion of meat in a diet are unacceptable: how much meat and the method of preparation are of major significance.

11

Summing Up

lthough there are endless complexities that cause people to give up fish, flesh, and fowl, it is possible to group all the conscious explanations under seven general categories:

- *ethical* objections to killing animals for food
- *nutritional* disapproval of flesh foods
- *economic* limitations
- *religious* or *philosophical* conformity
- *aesthetic* repulsion at the taste of flesh or the sight of blood
- *ascetic* means to self-discipline
- *mystical* belief in the power of animal foods

Vegetarianism may also be viewed anthropologically as the third step from early primitive cannibalistic habits; meat-eating thus becomes the intermediate stage between two extremes. Some postulate that anthropophagy was a common practice during man's initial appearance on earth. For example, we noted earlier that evidence exists of cannibalism among Pekin man.

Similarly, devouring one's own is common within the lowest and the highest members of the animal kingdom, including amoeba, invertebrates, pike, trout, cod, sharks, amphibia, reptiles, snakes, beetles, termites, spiders, and birds, and mammals, such as cats, pigs, mice, and rabbits. All these are known either occasionally or habitually to eat their young, so that the phenomenon is quite within the scheme of nature.

But man gradually grew away from cannibalism with a change and sophistication in social values and the availability of other types of food. Of course, the practice persisted in isolated instances, even up through contemporary times: the word "cannibal" is derived from a man-eating tribe of Indians, the Carib, discovered in the "New" World by the Spaniards. Certainly man returns to cannibalism when there is no alternative.

At the trials of Nuremberg, contemporary documentation was provided of instances of human flesh-eating in the concentration camps of Belsen, Buchenwald, and Auschwitz. Now of course we are shocked, and horrified, but at the same time intrigued, by evidences of cannibalism. If such horror takes place among "civilized" persons, it may well become the subject of a bestseller. Even if the survivors of a plane crash are trapped in isolated territory and forced to eat the flesh of another dead victim, such a story is still sensationalized.

Once an alternative diet is acceptable and available, meat-, fish-, and poultry-eating will be universally viewed with the same horror that is now attached to cannibalism. They will be accepted only as ritualistic practices for "savages." Indeed, the typical responses if people are asked why they eat meat often recall the motivations that lay behind tribal anthropophagy: "I feel stronger if I eat meat." Human flesh has similarly been consumed because of the magical idea that the qualities—both physical and spiritual— of the dead person would pass on to the cannibal by the simple act of dietary assimilation. In parts of Australia, they ate the cheeks and eyes of foes to acquire bravery; in some African villages, the hearts of human victims were dried, pulverized, mixed with rum, and sold to those desiring courage. Numerous other examples are offered throughout anthropological literature, since anthropophagy holds an endless fascination for man, who may subconsciously wish to return to that amoral state. Thus, the anthropological view of vegetarianism is that a meatless diet stands as a third stage in the evolution of dietary selection in the sequence of cannibalism, meat-eating, and vegetarianism.

But there are also *unconscious* factors which cause a person to adopt a diet that is inconsistent with the food habits of his immediate family and peers. Deep behavioral motivations explain an inconsistent Hitler. This is not to say that being a vegetarian indicates pathology; rather, it shows that certain emotional and intellectual reactions synchronize to provide the same end result: a vegetarian diet. Of course, the dynamics of each person are unique, just as the psychological background of every meat eater is vastly different. But this dietary act of defiance may have common causations.*

---

* These unconscious factors are discussed only in reference to those vegetari-

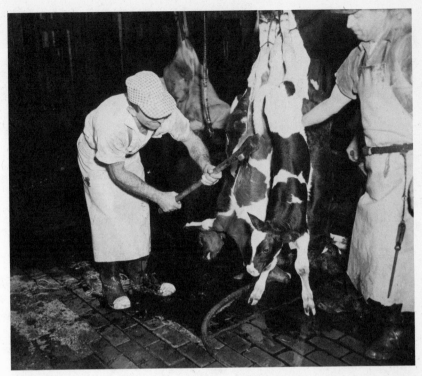

In this slaughter method used in many smaller plants not under Federal Inspection, calves are rendered unconscious before their throats are cut. The calf on the left has already been bled and the one on the right is just about to be hit on the head.

The adoption of a vegetarian diet quite often occurs during adolescence, as in the cases of Franklin, St. Francis, Shelley, Shaw, and most contemporary high-school and college students. Puberty is an intense and tumultuous period, for the earliest childhood experiences are revived. Adolescence may also be viewed sociologically as the span when goals and virtues are re-evaluated and there is, hopefully, a breaking away from "the family." Traditionally, adolescence occurs in the teen years, but it may be delayed or there may be a revivification of the same awakening patterns, as in Tolstoy's complete menopausal reversal.

Despite the dates of dietary change, whether during the teens or later, the roots lie in the very earliest mother-child relationship. It is

ans who do not belong to a religious sect from birth, such as the Seventh Day Adventists or Hinduism, since that is part of the dynamics of group conformity rather than of individual psychosexual development.

during the sucking and biting phases of the oral stage, or the first stage of development which Freud referred to as "cannibalistic," that the infant perceives the breast or bottle nipple as not just an extension of the mother but his actual mother. During those first twelve to eighteen months of infancy, the mouth is central for nutritional functions; it is also the basis for all later ego and psychosexual growth.

Many historical figures who were vegetarians, for example, Tolstoy, Gandhi, and Hitler, showed an over-reliance on their mothers. It is possible that meat is symbolically connected with motherhood: to consume the flesh is to eat the mother. No psychological studies of "average" vegetarians are available that might provide comprehensive conclusions. I made a small effort toward assembling some data on this point by sending around questionnaires to random names on lists of vegetarians and meat eaters. Of the eighty-five replies to the question: "Are you closer to your father or your mother?" 90 per cent of male and female vegetarians and female meat-eaters indicated that they were closer to their mother. However, only 33 per cent of the male meat-eaters were closer to their mother.

Anthropomorphism is a significant concept in considering vegetarianism from a psychological point of view. We tend to *adultmorphize* the child or non-verbal infant in the same way that the child tends to *anthropomorphize* the dog or stuffed Teddy bear. All children pass through this stage at about two years of age: the dog can communicate with the child and the stuffed lion really growls and feels. They appear to be *real*, rather than inanimate or divergent creatures. However, most persons grow to realize and accept the differences and to order their lives accordingly.

Vegetarianism may be seen as an adult extension of anthropomorphism. The dog or cat experiences the same pains and sensitivities as the human being; the cow is a friend being sent to slaughter, rather than an animal who is distinct and quite different from man. Therefore, the adult identifies with those sufferings and chooses to avoid eating meat or fish since it is as if one were to eat a fellow friend. Anna Kingsford's remark that she *felt* like the fox that she had killed during the hunt is similar to this adult anthropomorphic state of over-identification with non-human creatures.

Why do some people develop in this way while others remain completely devoid of intense compassion for and association with animals? Part of the answer lies in personality differences that are present even at birth. Each person may be born with equal rights, but we are far from equal.

The other factor is the sensitivity caused by even the most subtle disruption in an infantile relationship. The primary mother-child relationship is so vulnerable and fragile that a mother may unwittingly cause anxiety during the all-important oral stage and leave indelible scars. If there are any unpleasant disruptions in this love-hate relationship, the infant who is unable to express those frustrations may repress his hateful feelings until a point in his or her development when all these emotions come bursting forth to frighten and confuse. For example, if a mother without conscious awareness disturbs the highly important feeding period by either withholding or overwhelming with nourishment, the child may be assaulted by a specific need; but underdeveloped communication systems permit only a generalized reaction, such as crying. Thus a scream for milk may be misinterpreted as a wish to be held or cuddled. At this early stage, food is quite literally love and the two are completely interchangeable. Without either, the child will die. Therefore, any withdrawal of love, or nourishment, will result in a form of psychological death—repressed anger.

Later, when the underlying feelings of anger which may seem almost uncontrollable are revived, this blind rage must somehow be contained. One way to control it is through the process of *reaction formation*— doing exactly the opposite of what is unconsciously desired. Thus, an unconscious desire to kill becomes a conscious zeal for sparing life or even vegetarianism. This battle between rage and vegetarianism is seen most noticeably in the behavior of some schizophrenics who during certain periods of their "breaks" with reality will suddenly develop an inability to eat meat, even if previously they lived by a normal mixed diet. Historically, both Hitler and Leonardo da Vinci point to the ambivalence in these two diametrically opposed feelings, for both men had the hostility and anger to break through in spite of their vegetarian defenses.

There is often an unconscious association of meat with a fear of being "poisoned"—sometimes verbalized as the belief that meat-eating or flesh foods are bad for one's health. But it is the close association of meat with the mother that strengthens this belief, since controlled amounts of meat in the diet have not been proven harmful. In addition, many vegetarians do eat cheeses made with animal rennet, which indicates a symbolic association of meat with death rather than the processing of foods that incorporate dead animals.

Abstinence from certain foods as a means of self-punishment for hateful wishes is another psychological "gain" from a vegetarian diet. And the tendency of vegetarians to isolate themselves from the larger strata of society is a symptom of a further masochistic device. The approval of society at large is rationalized as unnecessary because of a deep, long-held loyalty to the larger, more compassionate animal world. In addition, the vegetarian is often an idealist who sees the world as an unfair place where killing should be unknown. Since he can do little about changing the larger order of events, he at least avoids its consequences psychically by nourishing his own palate in a moral and altruistic manner. He controls the world from his dinner plate and unconsciously restores it to that infantile time when it was far simpler and justifiable. By personally avoiding a participation in killing, the vegetarian unconsciously returns to his symbiotic, maternal state. Thus he can more readily cope with the injustices of everyday living because he does not personally participate in them. It is as if he is saying, "If I control myself, I can somehow control the world."

Inwardly the vegetarian often feels persecuted. He suffers mentally as he imagines how an animal feels that is being led to slaughter or a fish that is being hooked after following the inviting, yet deceptive, bait. His virtuous diet permits him to keep the lid on those aggressive feelings that are so frightening to him. This is *usually* an affective means, so that most vegetarians are also pacifists or committed to humane causes. However, many former vegetarians eventually abandon their diet because it creates a new "war" with their contemporaries; ostracized at parties and alienated from their meat-eating families, their moral actions create unnecessary conflicts between the people they value even more than animals.

The type of vegetarianism that is most easily traced to psychological motives is one that is based upon a trauma in later years so that it can be documented by description. For instance, a radio commentator who I interviewed explained that she was asked to visit a slaughterhouse since her meat advertisers wanted her to have a better idea of the product she was selling. The effect was the direct opposite of what anyone anticipated: the shock of what actually happened behind those secretive doors was the impetus to the adoption of a vegetarian diet from which she never wavered.

One of the most unusual stories of traumatic causation for vegetarianism is provided by Bolesław T. Milch, a retired captain of the Ulanow Regiment of the Cavalry, 14th Hussars, of Pland. Captain Milch on February 9, 1971 answered my *New York Times* query for personal testimonials with the following letter, which he has kindly permitted me to reprint:

> I am by profession the retired officer of the Army of Poland with rank of *Kapitan rotmistrz* and have served in such capacity many years in my native Poland prior to outset of war of 1939 with

Germany. In that period so well remembered to me, I was author of the volume *Nowoczesne taktyki kawalerii,* or *Modern Cavalry Tactics,* published in Krakow in 1936. I had also served during the war after leaving Poland with forces of Polish London Government at Tobruk, Narvik, Monte Cassino, and Rance with honour and was awarded Virtutis militari decoration.

Prior to the war of 1939, my diet, to the best of my memory, was in all ways completely normal and included meats and fishes of all kinds that had been in Poland available to one of my limited means as a military officer. The thought to abolish meats from my diet had never entered into my thinking. When war began on September 1, that year my Regiment immediately mobilized and moved to the front, which already then was, as we say in the Army, fluid. Many frustrations met us due to disorganization and poor material as well as betrayal and superior weaponry of the adversary. On September 14th, our regiment already decimated met on the field of Kutno west of Warsaw aircraft and heavy artillery. Despite heroic efforts, most of our number were destroyed and remaining members of our force retreated to a wooded area where for some time before we made our escape we were besieged by Nazi troops without supplies. At that time, having already exhausted our field rations, we were forced to eat whatever was at hand and in this instance found ourselves driven to slaughter our remaining horses as a source of meat.

You may well imagine how to us as Cavalrymen this was indeed a moment of shame and dishonour. None would have been able to lift sabre or knife to throat of a beast had not an example been set for us by our devoted Colonel of Regiment, the Count Władysław de B. Potocki, now and long since deceased. With tears in the eyes he did this shameful thing, still sharp in our memories, to induce in us the willingness to make the sacrifices that we might live on to fight for our Beloved Poland once more. For this act I render him honour even still. The meat in our mouths was like ashes or you might be imagining as we were all Calvalrymen but, as Soldiers of Poland we did our duty.

Rarely in the weeks that were following this event had I much opportunity to be eating meat yet always this tasted to me peculiar even when it might not be horse but pork and though health was involved I could not stomach it. Some months later, by way of Roumania, I made my way to Britain to join the forces of the Free Polish Army yet even there I was unable though supplies were ample to eat or even to endure the aroma of cooked meat. This aversion has continued to the present day though in years past upon coming to America to join my family I had tried often at their behest to force myself to be eating flesh. I cannot do it. Each attempt was painful as I was recalling the dishonour of Kutno and our treachery to our faithful beasts that had fought with us for Poland.

This Vegetarianism is to me no Principle or Ideological decision or act of Religion but the result somehow of this experience of mine which I am yet unable to comprehend yet I wish I could. Never have I tried to convert others to my peculiar taste nor have I sought the company of Vegetarians, with the exception of one person, a British officer whom I met in 1943 in London, who tried to teach me his principles which I have rejected though my practice has not varied from that which was his own. . . .

A further complication that sometimes motivates individuals to adopt a meatless diet is the belief that plants may have souls. This is no new dilemma, for Porphyry was forced to pose a similar question in his treatise written centuries ago: "But, if as they say, plants also have a soul, what will become of our life if we neither destroy animals nor plants?" His subsequent answer is as vague, and at the same time as valid, today as then: "But someone may, perhaps, say it is not proper to destroy that which belongs to the same tribe with ourselves; if souls of animals are of the same essence with outselves. . . ."

Many vegetarians defend their consumption of plants by pointing to the Eastern philosophies, which for thousands of years considered the mineral, vegetable, and animal kingdom to exist in a state of ascending spiritual value. To a vegetarian, eating plants does involve a value judgment as to their importance and may well lead some to declare, as Samuel Butler did, that a community exists who will only eat "cabbages that died a natural death."

More recently, the experiments during the 1960's of Cleve Backster, a leading American lie-detector expert, have caused a new consciousness-raising to the feelings of plants. It is now being debated whether people should feel guilty about how they treat their green offspring, if plants have sensitive souls or are even more aware than human beings. Backster impulsively decided to attach a galvanometer (part of a polygraph lie detector that indicates change in emotions) to his recently acquired dracaena. He wanted to see his tropical plant's reaction to watering. Much to his amazement, the plant responded in a similar fashion to a human being who had experienced a short-lived emotional stimulus. More astounding was his conclusion, after numerous experiments, that plants could pick up his thought waves: the act of thinking about a negative action, such as burning the leaf to which the electrodes were attached, caused a dramatic change in the tracing pattern on the graph. The plant, miraculously able to distinguish between real and pretended intentions, would self-defensively "faint" when threatened by dangers. Backster then began a program of research and discussion about the "souls" or thought patterns of plants that ranges from the scientific to the occult.

But man cannot live by stones alone and must establish priorities for his diet. A vegetarian régime is basically an ethical, anthropological, sociological, and psychological phenomenon. At the highest level is the humane vegetarian, who supplements his ingratiating attitude toward animals with a comparable kindness toward his fellow men by avoiding their deaths as well. The lowest type of vegetarian is the psychologically motivated zealot, who simultaneously practices hatred and violence toward mankind.

To become a vegetarian involves both a psychological predisposition and a distinct philosophical outlook. The recruiting efforts of religious and dietary fanatics are therefore contradictory to their desired end, for unless vegetarianism comes from the soul, it will be just another passing fad. Of course the idea must be exposed, but it cannot be indoctrinated. The basic issues involved are much too intricate and far-reaching to be overlooked or brushed aside. Just as war has been debated for centuries, so will the fleshless diet. Its appearance in contemporary societies is an indication of a positive questioning of traditional and age-old habits—a microcosm of the ideological conflicts facing thinking people of today.

List of Illustrations

Selected Sources

The broad scope of this book prohibits a listing of every newspaper, magazine, or book consulted. Many sources are unfortunately not available to the reader because they were obtained through personal communications and interviews: these interchanges are listed in the acknowledgments that follow the Bibliography. However, the published sources below are those that are particularly helpful for each chapter: numerous background readings and secondary sources are omitted because of space limitations.

Chapter 1. Roots

Earnest Hooten's *Why Men Behave Like Apes and Vice Versa* (Princeton U. Press, 1940) is the wittiest and most thought-provoking discussion of the ape-man, man-ape question; Bjorn Kurten's *Not From the Apes* (NY: Random House, 1972) is also invaluable. The accounts of chimpanzees by Jane van Lawick-Goodall, *In the Shadow of Man* (Boston: Houghton Mifflin, 1971), and of gorillas by George Schaller, *The Mountain Gorilla* (U. of Chicago Press, 1963) are well-written and comprehensive studies of all habits of these primates.

Also helpful for man's evolutionary development are Victor Barnouw's two-volume *An Introduction to Anthropology* (Homewood, Ill.: Dorsey Press, 1971), Margaret Mead's *Anthropology: A Human Science* (Princeton, N.J.: Van Nostrand, 1954), and J. S. Weiner's *The Natural History of Man* (NY: Anchor Books, 1973).

Most useful on present-day hunting and gathering peoples are Richard B. Lee and Irven de Vore's edited volume of a symposium of prominent anthropologists entitled *Man the Hunter* (Chicago: Aldine, 1972), and Elman R. Service's *The Hunters* (Englewood Cliffs, N.J.: Prentice-Hall, 1966).

A wealth of articles on the origins of domestication is *Prehistoric Agriculture*, edited by Stuart Struever (NY: Natural History Press, 1971).

Clifford J. Jolly's article, though highly technical, is outstanding: "The Seed-Eaters: A New Model of Hominid Differentiation Based on a Baboon Analogy," in *Man*, 1970, new series 5.

Other pertinent sources are:

Bates, Marston, "Man, Food and Sex," in *American Scholar*. Vol. 27, Autumn 1958.

Brothwell, Don and Patricia, *Food in Antiquity*. NY: Praeger, 1969.

Clark, W. E. Le Gros, *The Fossil Evidence for Human Evolution*. U. of Chicago Press, 1955. Also *History of the Primates*. U. of Chicago Press, 1963. Also *Man-Apes or Ape-Men? The Story of Discoveries in Africa*. NY: Holt, Rinehart and Winston, 1967.

Coon, Carleton S., *The Hunting People*. Boston: Little Brown, 1971.

De Vore, Irven, ed., *Primate Behavior*. NY: Holt, Rinehart and Winston, 1965.

Dyson, Robert H., Jr., "Archaeology and the Domestication of Animals in the Old World," in *American Anthropologist*. Vol. 55, Dec. 1953.

Fossey, Dian, "Making Friends with Mountain Gorillas," in *National Geographic*. Vol. 137, Jan. 1970. Also, "More Years with Mountain Gorillas," in *National Geographic*. Vol. 140, Oct. 1971.

Graves, Robert, "Mushrooms, Food of the Gods," in *Atlantic Monthly*. Vol. 200, August 1957.

Hogg, Gary, *Cannibalism and Human Sacrifice*. London: Robert Hale, 1958.

Kardiner, Abram and Edward Preble, *They Studied Man*. Cleveland: World, 1965.

Klintz, Warren G., "Evolution of the Human Canine Tooth," in *American Anthropologist*. Vol. 73, June 1971.

Lewis, John and Bernard Towers, *Naked Ape or Homo Sapiens?* NY: New American Library, 1972.

Linton, Ralph, *The Tree of Culture*. NY: Vintage Books, 1958.

Montague, Ashley, *The Human Revolution*. NY: Bantam, 1967. Also *Man: His First Two Million Years*. NY: Dell, 1969.

Morris, Desmond, *The Human Zoo*. NY: McGraw Hill, 1969. Also *The Naked Ape*. NY: McGraw Hill, 1967.

Napier, John, *The Roots of Mankind*. NY: Harper & Row, 1970.

Oakley, Kenneth, *Man the Toolmaker*. U. of Chicago Press, 1961.

Russell, Claire and William, *Violence, Monkeys and Man*. London: Macmillan, 1968.

Scarf, Maggie, "Goodall and Chimpanzees at Yale," in *The New York Times Magazine*. Feb. 18, 1973.

Shepard, Paul, *The Tender Carnivore and the Sacred Game*. NY: Scribner's, 1973.

Stevens, Henry Bailey, *The Recovery of Culture*. NY: Harper & Bros., 1953.

Watson, Lyall, *The Omnivorous Ape*. NY: Coward, McCann & Geoghegan, 1971.

Chapter 2. Land of the Sacred Cow

Some good overviews of the evolution of vegetarianism in Hinduism may be gleaned from chapter 4 of Frederick J. Simoons's *Eat Not This Flesh: Food*

Avoidances in the Old World (U. of Wisconsin Press, 1967); Max Weber's *The Religion of India* (Glencoe, Ill.: Free Press, 1958); the entry for "Diet" in *The Hindu World*, ed. by B. Walker (NY: Praeger, 1968); Heinrich Zimmer's *Philosophies of India* (Cleveland: Meridian, 1951); Louis Renou's *The Nature of Hinduism* (NY: Walker, 1962); Thomas Hopkins's *The Hindu Religious Tradition* (Encino, Ca: Dickenson, 1971); and Michael Edwardes's *Everyday Life in Early India* (London: Batsford, 1969).

Pertinent primary sources are:

Abhedanda, Swami, "Why a Hindu Is a Vegetarian," a lecture before the New York Vegetarian Society, 1900.

Prabhupada, A. C. Bhaktivedanta, *Bhagavad-Gita As It Is*. NY: Macmillan, 1972.

Buhler, Georg (trans.), *The Laws of Manu*. NY: Dover, 1969.

On Jainism, see Jaini Jagmanderlal's *Outline of Jainism* (Cambridge U. Press, 1916), C. R. Jain's *What Is Jainism?* (Madras: Jaina Mission, 1950), and Balwant Nevaskar's *Capitalists Without Capitalism* (Westport, Conn: Greenwood, 1971).

Other excellent background references are:

Basham, A. L., *The Wonder That Was India*. NY: Grove Press, 1959.

Berry, Thomas, *Religions of India: Hinduism, Yoga, Buddhism*. Beverly Hills, Ca: Benzinger, 1971.

Burtt, E. A. (ed.), *The Teachings of the Compassionate Buddha*. NY: New American Library, 1955.

Harris, Marvin, "The Cultural Ecology of India's Sacred Cattle," in *Current Anthropology*. Vol. 7, Feb. 1966.

Ling, Trevor, *The Buddha*. NY: Scribner's, 1973.

Zinkin, Taya, *India*. NY: Walker, 1965.

Gandhi's writings are the best primary source for his struggles on dietetics (all of the following are published by Navajivan Publishing House, Ahmedabad, India): *An Autobiography* (1969), *The Moral Basis of Vegetarianism* (1959), *Satygraha* (1958), *Diet and Diet Reform* (1964), *Drink, Drugs and Gambling* (1961), *Women and Social Injustice* (1970), *Key to Health* (1972), *Fasting in Satygraha* (1965).

Of the multitude of biographies of Gandhi, I found the most useful to be Robert Payne's comprehensive *The Life and Death of Mahatma Gandhi* (NY: E. P. Dutton, 1969), Geoffrey Ashe's *Gandhi* (NY: Stein and Day, 1969), Joseph J. Doke's *M. K. Gandhi* (New Delhi: Gov't of India Press, 1919), George Woodcock's *Mohandas Gandhi* (NY: Viking Press, 1971), Vincent Sheean's *Mahatma Gandhi* (NY: Knopf, 1962) and *Lead, Kindly Light* (NY: Random House, 1949), and Erik Erikson's *Gandhi's Truth* (NY: Norton, 1969).

Other Gandhian sources of interest are:

Jack, Homer, *The Gandhi Reader*. NY: Grove Press, 1961.

Kripalani, J. B., *Gandhi*. New Delhi: Government of India Press, 1970.

Nag, Kalidas, *Tolstoy and Gandhi*. Calcutta: Sree Sarawaty Press, 1950.

Pyarelal, Nair, *The Epic Fast*. Ahmedabad: Navajivan Pub., 1932.

Sutterland, H. R., "Diversities of Mr. Gandhi," in *The Dalhousie Review*. Vol 13, April 1933.

Chapter 3. Orpheus Ascending

The original writings of the Greeks and Romans discussed in this chapter are indispensable:

Euripedes, *The Plays of Euripedes*. Trans. by Moses Hadas and J. H. McLean. NY: Dial, 1936.

Hesiod, *The Works and Days*. Trans. by Richard Lattimore. Ann Arbor: U. of Michigan Press, 1959.

Horace, *Selected Odes, Epodes, Satires, Epistles*. Trans. by Burton Raffel. NY: New American Library, 1973.

Ovid, *The Metamorphoses of Ovid*. Trans. by Mary Innes. Harmandsworth, Middlesex: Penguin, 1973.

Plato, *The Republic*. Trans. by B. Jowett. NY: Random House, 1941.

Plotinus, *The Essential Plotinus*. Trans. by Elmer O'Brien. NY: New American Library, 1964.

Plutarch, *Moralia*. Trans. by Harold Cherniss and William C. Helmbold. Vol. 12. Cambridge: Harvard U. Press, 1957.

Plutarch, *Moral Essays*. Trans. by Rex Warner. Harmondsworth, Middlesex: Penguin, 1971.

Porphyry, *On Abstinence from Animal Food*. Trans. by Thomas Taylor. Boston: Branden Press, 1965.

Seneca, *Epistulae Morales*. Trans. by Richard M. Gummere. Vol. III. Cambridge: Harvard U. Press, 1953.

Background reading for chapter 3 and other later sections is provided in Bertrand Russell's eloquent *A History of Philosophy* (NY: Simon and Schuster, 1945), Roy Walker's *The Golden Feast* (NY: Macmillan, 1952), Howard Williams's *The Ethics of Diet* (London: F. Pitman, 1882), and A. Albu's *Die Vegetarische Diat* (Leipzig: George Thieme, 1902).

Other useful books on Greece and Rome are:

Blumner, H., *The Home Life of the Ancient Greeks*. London: Cassell, 1895.

Burnet, John, *Greek Philosophy*. Part 1. *Thales to Plato*. London: Macmillan, 1914.

Carcopino, Jerome, *Daily Life in Ancient Rome: The People and the City at the Height of the Empire*. New Haven: Yale U. Press, 1940.

Dyson, G. W., "Orphism and Platonic Philosophy," in *Speculum Religionis*. Oxford: Oxford U. Press, 1929.

Jaspers, Karl, *The Greek Philosophers*. Ed. by H. Arendt. Trans. by R. Manheim. NY: Harcourt, Brace & World, 1962.

Jones, A. H. M., *Sparta*. Oxford: Blackwell, 1967.

Livingstone, R. W. (ed), *The Legacy of Greece*. NY: Oxford U. Press, 1921.

Mellersh, H. E. L., *Soldiers of Rome*. London: Robert Hale, 1964.

Preston, Harrier Waters and L. Dodge, *The Private Life of the Romans*. Boston: Bej. H. Sanborn, 1900.

Sedgwick, H. D., *Horace: A Biography*. Harvard U. Press, 1947.

Shapiro, Herman and Edwin M. Curley (eds.), *Hellenistic Philosophy*. NY: Random House, 1965.

Timayenis, T. T. *Greece in the Times of Homer*. NY: D. Appleton, 1885.

Warner, Rex, *The Greek Philosophers*. NY: New American Library, 1958.

Chapter 4. Judeo-Christian Ethics

Most relevant are The Bible (both Old and New Testaments); Dayan Grunfeld's two-volume study, *The Jewish Dietary Laws* (NY: Soncino Press, 1972); Josephus' *The Jewish Antiquities* (Vol. 8, trans. by Ralph Marcus, ed. by Allen Wikgren, Cambridge: Harvard U. Press, 1963); also Vol. 9 (trans. by Louis H. Feldman, Cambridge: Harvard U. Press, 1965); Edward Westermarck's *Christianity and Morals* (London: Kegan Paul, 1939); Rev. J. P. Arendzen's "Jewish Monks in the Days of Christ," in *The Irish Ecclesiastical Record* (Vol. 23, Dublin, 1928); back issues of *The Jewish Vegetarian* (London); *The Rule of St. Benedict* (London: Chatto & Windus, 1926); Rhigyfarch's *Life of St. David* (trans. by J. W. James, Cardiff: U. of Wales, 1967); and Thomas of Celano's *The Lives of St. Francis* (trans. by A. G. Ferrers Howell, NY: Dutton, 1908).
Other material that indirectly applies includes:

Alt, Albrecht, *Old Testament History and Religion*. Trans. by R. Wilson. NY: Doubleday, 1969.

Bernard, R. W., *The Dead Sea Scrolls and the Life of the Ancient Essenes*. Mokelumne Hill, Ca.: Health Research, 1956.

Bourke, Vernon J., *History of Ethics*. NY: Doubleday, 1968.

Chamberlin, Roy B. and H. Feldman, *The Dartmouth Bible*. Boston: Houghton Mifflin, 1965.

De Vaux, Roland, *The Bible and the Ancient Near East*. Trans. by D. McHugh. NY: Doubleday, 1971.

Dupont-Sommer, A., *The Jewish Sect of Qumran and the Essenes*. London: Vallentine, Mitchell, 1954.

Green, Joe, *The Jewish Vegetarian Tradition*. Johannesburg, S. Africa: Mimeographed printing, 1969.

Lloyd, J. E., *History of Wales to 1282*. London: Longmans, 1911.

Rosenthal, G. (ed. and trans.), *Maimonides*. NY: Funk and Wagnall, 1969.

Szekely, Edmond B. (trans.), *The Essene Gospel of Peace*. San Diego: Academy of Creative Living, 1971.

Chapter 5. Da Vinci and the Dietetic Renaissance

Original sources of primary importance are Edward MacCurdy's edited versions of da Vinci's *Notebooks* (NY: George Braziller, 1956); various British and American translations of Cornaro's essays; Cocchi's *The Pythagorean Diet, of Vegetables Only, Conducive to the Preservation of Health and the Cure of Disease*, (London: R. Dodsley, 1745); Jean Jacques Rousseau's *Emile* (London: Dent, 1972); and Montaigne's *The Complete Essays* (trans. by D. Frame. Stanford U. Press, 1971).
Background material is gleaned from:

Burkhardt, Jacob, *The Civilization of the Renaissance in Italy*. NY: Random House, 1954.

Chamberlin, E. R., *Everyday Life in Renaissance Times*. London: Batsford, 1967.

Christensen, Erwin, "Freud on Leonardo da Vinci," in *The Psychoanalytic Review*. Vol. XXXI, April 1944.

Clark, Kenneth, *Leonardo da Vinci*. Harmondsworth, Middlesex: Penguin, 1973.

Eissler, K. R., *Leonardo da Vinci: Psychoanalytic Notes on the Enigma*. NY: International Universities Press, 1961.

Elton, G. R. *Renaissance and Reformation 1300–1648*. NY: Macmillan, 1970.

Freud, Sigmund, *Leonardo da Vinci and a Memory of His Childhood*. NY: Norton, 1964.

Kristeller, Paul Oskar, *Renaissance Thought*. NY: Harper & Row, 1961.

Rousseau, Jean Jacques, *Confessions*. NY: Bibliophilist Society, 1923.

Sellery, G. C., *The Renaissance: Its Nature and Origins*. U. of Wisc. Press, 1950.

Simons, Madeline, "Rousseau's Natural Diet," in *The Romantic Review*. Vol. XLV, Feb. 1954.

Symonds, John Addington, *Renaissance in Italy*. NY: Random House, no date.

Van Dyke, Paul, *Renaissance Portraits*. NY: Books for Libraries, 1969.

Vasari, Giorgio, *Lives of the Artists*. Baltimore: Penguin, 1968.

Voltaire, *Philosophical Dictionary*. Trans. by P. Gay. Harcourt, Brace & World, 1962.

Zubov, V. P., *Leonardo da Vinci*. Trans. by D. Kraus. Harvard U. Press, 1968.

Chapter 6. British Advocates

Original writings of the major British figures in vegetarianism are: John Howard's *The State of the Prisons in England and Wales* (Warrington: W. Eyres, 1784); William Lambe's *Reports of the Effects of a Peculiar Regimen in Scirrhous Tumors and Cancerous Ulcers* (London: J. Mawman, 1809); John Frank Newton's *The Return to Nature: or A Defence of the Vegetable Regimen* (London: T. Cadell & W. Davies, 1811); Shelley's essays have been reprinted in *Shelley's Prose; or the Trumphet of a Prophecy* (ed. by David Clark, U. of New Mexico Press, 1954); his poetry is most accessible in the Random House edition, *John Keats and Percy Bysshe Shelley: Complete Poetical Works*, with notes by Mary Shelley.

Also used were: *The Works of Lord Byron*, Vol. VI (ed. by Ernest Hartley Coleridge, NY: Scribner's, 1903); Dr. Anna Kingsford's *Perfect Way in Diet* (London: 1881); Dr. Kingsford and Edward Maitland's *Addresses and Essays on Vegetarianism* (ed. by Samuel Hopgood Hart, London: John M. Watkins, 1912); Annie Besant's pamphlet, "Vegetarianism in the Light of Theosophy" (1932); Shaw's *On Vivisection* (Chicago: Alethea, 1950) and *Sixteen Self Sketches* (NY: Dodd Mead, 1949); and Archibald Henderson's *Table-Talk of G.B.S.* (NY: Harper & Bros., 1952).

Related references are:

Axon, William, *Shelley's Vegetarianism*. NY: Haskell House, 1971.

Chappelow, Allan (ed.), *Shaw The Villager: A Biographical Symposium*. London: Charles Skilton, 1961.

Clark, David Lee, "The Date and Source of Shelley's 'A Vindication of Natural Diet,'" in *Studies in Philology*. Vol. 36, 1939.

Ervine, St. John, *Bernard Shaw: His Life, Work and Friends*. London: Constable, 1956.

Forward, Charles W., *Fifty Years of Food Reform: A History of the Vegetarian Movement in England*. London: Ideal Publishing, 1908.

Grabo, Carl, *Shelley's Eccentricities*. U. of New Mexico Publications in Language and Literature. No. 5, 1950.

Henderson, Archibald, *George Bernard Shaw: Man of the Century*. NY: Appleton-Century-Crofts, 1956.

Henslowe, Leonardo, "Just What Mr. Bernard Shaw Eats and Drinks," in *Health and Strength*, Sept. 28, 1907.

Jones, Frederick, *The Letters of Percy Bysshe Shelley*. Vol. 1, *Shelley in England*. Oxford: Clarendon Press, 1964.

Kronenberger, Louis (ed.), *George Bernard Shaw: A Critical Survey*. Cleveland: World, 1953.

Laden, Alice and R. J. Minney, *The George Bernard Shaw Vegetarian Cook Book*. NY: Taplinger, 1972.

Maurois, André, *Ariel: A Life of Shelley*. NY: Frederick Ungar, 1924.

Rossetti, William M., *A Memoir of Shelley*. London: Richard Clay, 1886.

Shaw, Bernard, "Letter to Cyril Clemens," in *Dalhousie Review*. Vol. 19. Jan. 1940.

Southward, Martin, *John Howard: Prison Reformer*. London: Independent Press, 1958.

Winsten, Stephen, *Jesting Apostle: The Private Life of Bernard Shaw*. NY: Dutton, 1957.

Woodberry, George (ed.), *The Complete Poetical Works of Shelley*. Boston: Houghton Mifflin, 1901.

Vyvyan, John, *In Pity and In Anger*. London: Michael Joseph, 1969. Also *The Dark Face of Science*, 1971.

Chapter 7. Wagner, Hitler, and Germany

Correspondence and interviews were invaluable for this chapter, but there are some published primary sources available, such as Richard Wagner's essays, reprinted in *Prose Works* (Trans. by W. A. Ellis, Vol. 6. NY: Broude Brothers, 1966) and *Parsifal* (Trans. by Stewart Robb. NY: G. Schirmer, Inc., 1962). Also Adolf Hitler's *Mein Kampf* (Trans. by Ralph Manheim, Boston: Houghton Mifflin, 1943), and *Hitler's Secret Conversations. 1941–1944.* (NY: Farrar, Straus, 1953); and Albert Schweitzer's *Memoirs of Childhood and Youth* (NY: Macmillan, 1961).

Other references to Richard Wagner's vegetarian theories are in Janet Barkas's "Frau Wagner," in *Opera News* (July 1972), and in Nietzsche's writings, *The Case of Wagner* (Trans. by Walter Kaufmann. NY: Vintage, 1967).

Accounts of those who knew Hitler and wrote about his eating habits are found in Otto Dietrich's *Hitler* (Trans. by R. and C. Winston. Chicago: Henry Regnery, 1955); Joseph P. Goebbels's *Diaries 1942–1943* (NY: Doubleday, 1948); Kurt Kreuger's *Inside Hitler* (NY: Avalon, 1941); August Kubizek's *Young Hitler: The Story of Our Friendship* (London: Allan Wingate, 1954); Kurt Ludecke's *I Knew Hitler* (NY: Scribner's, 1937); Herman Rauschning's *The Voice of Destruction* (NY: G. P. Putnams, 1940); Dr. Paul Schmidt's *Hitler's Interpreter* (NY: Macmillan, 1951); Albert Speer's *Inside the Third Reich* (NY: Macmillan, 1970); and Otto Strasser's *Hitler and I* (Boston: Houghton Mifflin, 1940).

Additional useful references for the German aspects are:

Altpeter, Werner, "War Hitler Vegetarier?", in *Der Vegetarier*. Nov. 1960.

Binion, Rudolph, *Hitler and Germany: A Psychoanalytic Approach*. Unpublished paper read at the American Historical Association, Dec. 1971.

Brockhuas, Wilhelm, *Von der Ehrfurcht vor dem Leben und dem Recht der Tiere*. Ludenscheid: Verlag Rudolf Beucker, 1953.

Bromberg, Norbert, "The Psychotic Character as Political Leader: I and II. A Psychoanalytic Study of Adolf Hitler." Unpublished papers read at the Annual Meeting of the American Psychoanalytic Association. Chicago May 1961 and Toronto, 1962. Also "Further Observations on Hitler's Character and Its Development." New York City, 1970.

Bullock, Alan, *Hitler: A Study in Tyranny*. Rev. ed. NY: Harper and Row, 1962.

Chamberlain, Houston Stewart, *Richard Wagner*. Trans. by G. A. Right. London: J. M. Dent, 1900.

Champigneulle, Jean Vinchon et Bernard, "Hitler et le Wagnerisme," in *Mercure de France*, 15–VI, 1935.

Fest, Joachim, *The Face of the Third Reich*. Trans. by M. Bullock. NY: Pantheon, 1970. Also *Hitler*. NY: Harcourt Brace Jovanovich, 1974.

Gunther, John, *Inside Europe*. NY: Harper & Bros., 1938.

Gutman, Robert W., *Richard Wagner: The Man, His Mind, and His Music*. NY: Harcourt, Brace and World, 1968.

Härtel, Gerhard, "Dr. Lahmann und Seine Lehren" in *Der Vegetarier*. Aug. 1971.

Hitler, Brigid, *My Brother-in-Law*. Unpublished manuscript in New York Public Library, no date.

Jenks, William, *Vienna and the Young Hitler*. NY: Columbia U. Press, 1960.

Kelley, Douglas, *Twenty-two Cells in Nuremberg*. NY: Greenberg, 1947.

Koenigsberg, Richard, "Culture and Unconscious Phantasy: Observations on Nazi Germany," in *The Psychoanalytic Review*. Vol. 55, 1968–69.

Kurth, Gertrud, "The Jew and Adolf Hitler," in *The Psychoanalytic Quarterly*. Vol. 16, 1947.

Langer, Walter, *The Mind of Adolf Hitler*. NY: Basic Books, 1972.

Marshall, George and David Poling. *Schweitzer*. NY: Doubleday, 1971.

Mauer, Hedwig Simpson, "Herr Hitler At Home in the Clouds," in *The New York Times Magazine*. Section VII, Aug. 20, 1939.

McGranahan, Donald and M. Janowitz, "Studies of German Youth," in *The Journal of Abnormal and Social Psychology*. Vol. 41, Jan. 1946.

Newman, Ernest, *Fact and Fiction About Wagner*. NY: Knopf, 1931. Also *The Life of Richard Wagner*. NY: Knopf, 1946, and *Wagner as Man and Artist*. NY: Vintage Books, 1952.

Nietzsche, Friedrich, *The Gay Science*. Trans. by Walter Kaufmann. NY: Vintage Books, 1974. Also *Genealogy of Morals*. NY: Vintage Books, 1969.

Panofsky, Walter, *Wagner: A Pictorial Biography*. London: Thames and Hudson, 1963.

Schopenhauer, Arthur, *The Philosophy of Schopenahuer*. Trans. by Irwin Edman. NY: Random House, 1928.

Shaw, George B., *The Perfect Wagnerite*. NY: Dover, 1967.

Shelton, Herbert, "A Picture of a Mad Man," in *Dr. Shelton's Hygienic Review*. May 1947.

Shirer, William L., *The Rise and Fall of the Third Reich*. NY: Simon and Schuster, 1960.

Trevor-Roper, H. R., *The Last Days of Hitler*. 3rd. ed. NY: Collier Books, 1962.

W.W.C., "Early Recollections of Adolf Hitler," in *The New Statesman and Nation*. July 29, 1933.

Waite, Robert (ed.), *Hitler and Nazi Germany*. NY: Holt, Rinehart and Winston, 1965.

Chapter 8. Back—and Forth—to Nature

Some general background books of this period are Gerald Carson's *Cornflake Crusade* (NY: Holt, Rinehart, 1957), and Ronald M. Deutsch's *Nuts Among the Berries* (NY: Ballantine, 1962).
However, the original writings are the most useful:

Alcott, Bronson, *The Journals of Bronson Alcott*. Boston: Little Brown, 1938.

Alcott, William, *Vegetable Diet As Sanctioned By Medical Men, and By Experience in All Ages*. Boston: Marsh, Capen & Lyon, 1838. Also *Tea and Coffee*. Boston: Light, 1839, *Confessions of a School Master*. Andover: Gould, Newman, 1839; and *Ways of Living on Small Means*. Boston: Light, 1837.

Franklin, Benjamin, *The Autobiography of Benjamin Franklin*. NY: Heritage Press, 1951. Also *Poor Richard's Almanack*. Mt. Vernon, NY: Peter Pauper Press, 1967.

Graham, Sylvester, *Science of Human Life*. Boston: Marsh, Capen, Lyon & Webb, 1858.

Greeley, Horace, *Recollections of a Busy Life*. NY: J. B. Ford, 1868.

Kellogg, Ella Eaton, *Science in the Kitchen: Principles of Healthful Cookery*. Battle Creek, Michigan: Good Health Publishing, 1910.

Kellogg, Dr. John Harvey, *The Battle Creek Sanitarium System*. Battle Creek: 1908. Also *The Miracle of Diet*. Battle Creek: 1904.

Robertson, Constance Noyes, *Oneida Community: An Autobiography 1851–1876*. NY: Syracuse U. Press, 1970.

Sinclair, Upton, *American Outposts*. Port Washington, NY: Kennikat Press, 1969. Also "The Diet Problem in Durope," in *Physical Culture*. Vol. 28. Dec. 1912; *The Fasting Cure*. London: Heinemann, 1911; "Fasting Experiments and Experiences," in *Physical Culture*. Vol. 29. March 1913; and *The Jungle*. NY: New American Library, 1960.

Thoreau, Henry David, *Walden Or Life in The Wood*. NY: Dodd, Mead, 1956. Also *The Portable Thoreau*. Ed. by Carl Bode. NY: Viking, 1964.

White, Ellen G, *Counsels on Diet and Foods*. Washington, D.C.: Review and Herald, 1938.
Related secondary sources of interest are:
Canright, Dudley, *Life of Mrs. E. B. White*. Cincinnati: Standard, 1902.

Clark, Annie Marie, *The Alcotts in Harvard*. Lancaster, Mass: Clark, 1902.

Davis, Max, *The Case for the Vegetarian Conscientious Objector*. Brooklyn: Tolstoy Peace Group, 1945.

Derleth, August, *Concord Rebel: A Life of Henry David Thoreau*. Philadelphia: Chilton, 1962.

Ford, Paul Leicester, *The Many-Sided Franklin.* NY: Century, 1899.

Jones, Joseph, "Transcendental Grocery Bills: Thoreau's *Walden* and Some Aspects of American Vegetarianism," in *Texan Studies in English.* Vol. 36. U. of Texas Press, 1957.

Macdonald, A. J., "Utopian Communities," unpublished 19th century manuscript in Yale U. Library.

Muncy, Raymond Lee, *Sex and Marriage in Utopian Communities: 19th Century America.* Bloomington, Ind.: Indiana U. Press, 1973.

Sanborn, Franklin, *Bronson Alcott.* Cedar Rapids, Iowa: Torch, 1908.

Schwarz, Richard, *John Harvey Kellogg, M.D.* Nashville, Tenn.: Southern Publ. Assoc., 1970.

Shepard, Odell, *Pedlar's Progress: The Life of Bronson Alcott.* Boston: Little, Brown, 1938.

Chapter 9. Tolstoy and the Doukhobors

Two volumes in the *Collected Works* of Tolstoy are essential references: *The Kingdom of God and Peace Essays.* Trans. by Aylmer Maude. London: Oxford U. Press, 1935. (Vol. 20) and *Recollections and Essays* (Vol. 21).

Maude's biography of Tolstoy's later years (Vol. 2) is useful on this period. Henri Troyat's biography of Tolstoy (trans. by Nancy Amphoux, NY: Dell, 1969) is a good starting point for an account of his life.

Other diary accounts and visits to Tolstoy are:

Bulgakov, Valentin, *The Last Year of Leo Tolstoy.* Trans. by Ann Dunnigan. NY: Dial, 1971.

Kennan, George, "A Visit to Count Tolstoy," in *The Century Magazine.* Vol. 24. No. 2., June 1887.

Stockham, Alice, *Tolstoi: Man of Peace.* Chicago: Alice B. Stockham, 1900.

Sukhotin-Tolstoy, Tatiana, *The Tolstoy Home: Diaries.* Trans. by Alex Brown. London: Harvill, 1950.

Tolstoy, Alexandra, *Tolstoy: A Life of My Father.* Trans. by E. R. Hapood. NY: Harper & Row, 1953.

Sources on the Doukhobors and Abkhasians include:

Benet, Sula, "Why They Live to Be 100, Or Even Older, in Abkhasia," in *The New York Times Magazine.* Dec. 26, 1971.

Hindus, Maurice, *A Traveler in Two Worlds.* NY: Doubleday, 1971.

Leaf, Dr. Alexander, "Every Day Is a Gift When You Are Over 100," in *National Geographic.* Jan. 1973.

Woodcock, George and Ivan Avakumovic, *The Doukhobors.* London: Faber, 1968.

Chapter 10. Nutritional Controversies

The best overview up to the present is to be found in two articles of a three-part series by Dr. Mervyn G. Hardinge and Hulda Crooks: "Non-Flesh Dietaries," in *Journal of the American Dietetic Association.* Vol. 43, Dec. 1963, and Vol. 45, Dec. 1964. Though rather technical, a series of volumes devoted expressly to vegetarianism and veganism is *Plant Foods for Human Nutrition.* London: Pergamon Press. Vol. 1 (May 1968, Feb. 1969, June 1969, Nov. 1969) and Vol. 2 (June 1970, Jan. 1971, March 1972).

Other pertinent articles and books are:

Aries, Vivienne C., *et al.*, "The Effect of a Strict Vegetarian Diet on the Faecal Flora and Faecal Steroid Concentration," in *The Journal of Pathology*. Vol. 103, 1971.

Burton, Benjamin T., *The Heinz Handbook of Nutrition*. NY: McGraw-Hill, 1965.

Cotes, J.E., *et al.*, "Possible Effect of a Vegan Diet upon Lung Function and the Cardiorespiratory Response to Submaximal Exercise in Healthy Women," in *The Journal of Physiology*, April 1970.

Davis, Adelle, *Let's Eat Right to Keep Fit*. NY: New American Library, 1970.

Dovring, Folke, "Soybeans," in *Scientific American*. Vol. 230, Feb. 1974.

Dwyer, Johanna T., *et al.*, "The New Vegetarians," in *Journal of the American Dietetic Association*, Vol. 62, May 1973.

Ellis, Frey R. and Pamela Mumford, "The Nutritional Status of Vegans and Vegetarians," in *Proceedings of the Nutrition Society*. London, Vol. 26, 1967.

Fernstrom, John D. and Richard J. Wurtman, "Nutrition and the Brain," in *Scientific American*. Vol. 230, Feb. 1974.

Greenberg, Daniel S., "Slaughterhouse Zero: How Soybean Sellers Plan to Take the Animal Out of Meat," in *Harper's*. Nov. 1973.

Hellman, Hal, "The Story Behind Those Meatless 'Meats,' " in *Popular Science*. Oct. 1972.

Lappe, Frances Moore, *Diet for a Small Planet*. NY: Ballantine, 1971.

Margolius, Sidney, *Health Foods: Facts and Fakes*. NY: Walker, 1973.

O'Neil, Paul, "How Now World's Greatest Cow?", in *The Atlantic*. Sept. 1973.

Van Houweling, C.D., "Use of Antibiotics in Food Animals," in *FDA Papers*. May 1969.

West, Eric D. and Frey R. Ellis, "The Electroencephalogram in Veganism, Vegetarianism, Vitamin B$_{12}$ Deficiency, and in Controls," in *J. Neurol. Neurosurg. Psychiatr.*, No. 29, 1966.

Westoff, Leslie Aldridge, "Eat Your Nice Yogurt," in *Esquire*. June 1973.

Zwerdling, Daniel, "Food Polution," in *Ramparts*. Aug. 1971.

Chapter 11. Summing Up

General points of departure are possible from the following readings:

Abraham, Karl. *On Character and Libido Development*. Ed. by B. Lewin. NY: Norton, 1966.

Barahal, Major Hyman, "The Cruel Vegetarian," in *The Psychiatric Quarterly Supplement*. Vol. 20, 1946.

Bates, Marston, *Gluttons and Libertines: Human Problems of Being Natural*, NY: Random House, 1958.

Bergler, Edmund, *The Basic Neurosis: Oral Regression and Psychic Masochism*. NY: Grune and Stratton, 1949.

Besdine, Matthew, "Mrs. Oedipus Has Daughters, Too," in *Psychology Today*. March 1971.

Erikson, Erik, *Childhood and Society*. NY: Norton, 1950.

Fritz, Martin. "Diet and Racial Temperament," in *Journal of Social Psychology*. Vol. 7, 1936.

Freud, Sigmund. *Totem and Taboo*. Trans. by James Strachey. NY: Norton, 1950.

Henry, Jules. *Pathways to Madness*. NY: Vintage, 1973.

Hoffs, Joshua. "Anthropophagy (Cannibalism): Its Relation to the Oral Stage of Development," in *Psychoanalytic Review*. Vol. 50, Summer 1963.

Lewin, Bertram. *The Psychoanalysis of Elation*. NY: The Psychoanalytic Quarterly, Inc., 1961.

Stekel, Wilhelm, *Patterns of Psychosexual Infantilism*. NY: Grove Press, 1959.

Tompkins, Peter and Christopher Bird, *The Secret Life of Plants*. NY: Harper and Row, 1973.

Acknowledgments

To compile the research for this study, I needed the cooperation of hundreds of specialists in varying fields from anthropology to literature, philosophy to religion, nutrition to psychology. I thank all those who gave generously of their knowledge and time, especially Dan H. Laurence, Irving Wallace, Hayes B. Jacobs, Sidney Offit, James Masterson, Jr., Associate Dean Reuben Abel and my students at The New School for Social Research. Frederick, Daisy and Linda Stein, and Hildegard Altoff provided German translations. Sections of the manuscript were read by Victor Barnouw, James McRandle, Gertrud Kurth, K. R. Eissler, Victor Navasky, Reuben Fine, Phyllis Greenacre, Edwin Burrows, John Ware, Lawrence Grauman, Jr., Frey Ellis, Mervyn G. Hardinge, and Gail Schiller. I am appreciative of all comments and suggestions from all sources, but credit or blame for the final book is my own.

My research trips throughout the United States, Canada, Europe, and India were enhanced by the cooperation and hospitality I found and everlasting friendships that I formed. A note of thanks to *The New York Times* for printing my author's query in their book review section and also to numerous libraries around the world, especially The New York Public Library for the use of the Frederick Lewis Allen Room.

Certainly the efforts of my editor, Patricia Cristol, may not be minimized nor may her friendship and enthusiasm. Shirley Sulat conscientiously typed the final manuscript.

Correspondence and Interviews

My numerous correspondents are listed by chapters where their comments were most pertinent. Those names followed by an asterisk indicate persons interviewed more extensively. To avoid repetitions, published works or affiliations have been listed only when there was no reference in either the text or the Bibliography.

Chapter 1. Roots

Jane van Lawick-Goodall, Desmond Morris, Ashley Montagu, George Schaller, Dian Fossey, Clifford J. Jolly, W. W. Howells (*The Heathens*), Alexander Alland, Jr. (*Evolution and Human Behavior*), Ian Tattersall (Am. Museum of Natural History), Robert A. Hinde (University of Cambridge), Sol Tax and Barbara Metzger (*Current Anthropology*), J. S. Weiner, H. R. Hays (*From Ape to Angel*), Robert L. Carneiro (Am. Museum of Natural History), Malcolm Collier (Dir. Am. Anthropological Asso.), Wendy Ranan, George Crossette (National Geographic Research), Robert W. Goy (Regional Primate Research Center), and Geoffrey H. Bourne (Yerkes Regional Primate Research Center).

Chapter 2. Land of the Sacred Cow

My trip to India proved productive and enlightening because of the extraordinary kindness and generosity, which obliterated any preconceived notions I might have had of how a total stranger would be treated: *T. K. Mahadevan (editor of *Gandi Marg*) corresponded with me for two years and arranged for my stay at the Gandhi Peace Foundation in New Delhi; *Dr. Radha Karnad (nutritional adviser); *Seguna and Djalma Desai (who with Dr. Karnad head a Meals for Millions program on a completely volunteer basis; Radha and Seguna's father was a freedom fighter with Gandhi); *Manubha Koya, who lives in America but arranged for me to live with his friends; the wonderful *Kalmalchant Joshi family in Bombay; *J. N. Mankar (director of the Bombay Humanitarian League, who treated me as a daughter during my stay); *Anand Prakash; *R. K. Sharma; *Pramila and *Konti Poddar, whose friendship and help still continue.

Others were: *V. V. Giri (president of India), John Blofeld (U.N. Ecafe Secretariat, Thailand), *Morarji Desai (ex-finance minister and secretary to Gandhi), *Kakasaheb Kalelkar (former secretary to Gandhi), *Vinoba Bhave, *Pyarelal, Horace Alexander (who knew Gandhi for twenty years), Vincent and Diana Sheean, Yehudi Menuhin, Thomas Berry, Robert Payne, D. R. Saggar ("Friends of Gandhi"), P. G. S. Mani (Hon. Sec. Indian Veg. Congress), Krishna Chandra (Nature Cure Ashram), Shriman Narayan (governor of Gujerat), Kisanbhai Trivedd (director Gandhi Smark), J. M. Jussawalla (Natural Therapy Clinic), M. M. Bhamgara, the late C. Rajagopalachari, Jayaprakash Narayan, Mary Claycomb, P. C. Gupta (Santiniketan), S. M. Mehta, Umashankar Joshi (Gujarat University), V. N. Jai (nutritionist), Rajiu Budh-Raja, V. S. Chinnaswamy, V. Raghavaiah, S. M. Mehta, Kyojo Vergara, Parvarajika Yogaprana, and Renee Taylor (*Hunza Health Secrets*).

Chapter 3. Orpheus Ascending

Rex Warner, D. A. Russell, Richard Lattimore, Burton Raffel, H. E. L.

Mellersh, Reynold Z. Burrows (Sweet Briar College), Gregory Vlastos, Edwin Curley, Dorothea Wender, Mary M. Innes, James K. Feibleman (*Understanding Philosophy*), and J. W. Binns (U. of Birmingham).

Chapter 4. Judeo-Christian Ethics

Rev. M. Basil Pennington, Rev. Noel Wall, J. W. James (*Saint David*), Rabbi Irwin Isaacson, *Javier Teixidor (Columbia U.), Simona Friedman (Lib. of Jewish Theological Seminary), Harold Whaley (Unity School of Christianity), William P. Roberts, Raphael Brown (50 *Animal Stories of St. Francis*), Mary Maccoby (Kamenitzer Maggid Fund), Claude Peifer (St. Bede Abbey), Philip L. Pick (Jewish Veg. Soc.), Joe Green, Judah Goldin, Solomon Grayzel (*History of the Jews*), Alex Hary, J. Everette Pleyer (Nazarene Publishing), and Jacob I. Dienstag (Yeshiva U.).

Chapter 5. Da Vinci and the Dietetic Renaissance

Sir Kenneth Clark, Theodore Besterman (Voltaire Foundation), Donald Frame, Cornelia Otis Skinner (*Madame Sarah*), Christopher Thacker (U. of Reading), John Carey (*Milton*), Paul Oskar Kristeller, and Opal Macrae (*Paganini*).

Chapter 6. British Advocates

*Dan H. Laurence (*The Collected Letters of George Bernard Shaw*), *Vera Scabiane (New York Shavians), Honors Young, *Mort Weisinger (*The Contest*), Grace Hegger Lewis, Dame Sybil Thorndike, Leslie Marchand (*Byron*), John Vyvyan, Carolyn Keefe (*C. S. Lewis*), Aaron B. Lerner (Yale U.), Leslie D. Wheeldon, Mike Storm (*The Vegetarian*), Major W. Angus-Jones, Geoffrey Rudd (*Why Kill for Food?*), Ann M. E. Jackson, Anne Pedersen, Arthur H. Nethercot (*The Five Lives of Annie Besant*), G. E. Bentley, Jr. (*Blake Records*), David L. Hull (*Darwin*), Dr. Philip Cauthery (University of Aston), Brigid Brophy (*Black and White*), and Nora Barlow (Darwin's granddaughter).

Chapter 7. Wagner, Hitler, and Germany

*Albert Speer, *Gerda Christian (former secretary to Hitler), *Frau Winifred Wagner, *Werner Zabel, *Joachim Fest, *Rudolph Binion, *Werner Altpeter, H. R. Trevor-Roper, A. J. P. Taylor, L. Jedlicka, *Wilfred Daim, R. G. L. Waite, Karen Kuykendall, *Roland V. Layton, Jr. (Hiram College), Walter Kaufmann, Heinz Linge, Adolf Pollitz, Otto John (*Twice Through the Lines*), Johanna Wolf (former secretary to Hitler), Nicolaus von Below (member of Hitler staff from 1937 on), Georg Hiller (pres. of German Veg. Soc.), Gerhard Hartel, Ebba Waerland, Ilse & Ernst Becker-Burks, Reinhard Bollmus, Wilhelm Borckhaus, Meinrad Nagele, Arno Breker (former artist to the Reich), Robert Neumann, Dietmar Leupolz, Peter Hoffman (McGill University), Nancy Creshkoff, Carl Anders-Skriver, Norbert Bromberg, Joachim Remak and William Ebenstein (U. of Cal., Santa Barbara), Martin Bernstein (N. Y. University), Else Gruno, Ronald

W. Clark (*Einstein*), Anita Daniel (*The Story of Albert Schweitzer*), Henry Boessl, Edwin Burrows (Columbia U.), and Erika Anderson (A. Schweitzer Friendship House and Library).

Chapter 8. Back—and Forth—to Nature

*Helen and Scott Nearing (*Living the Good Life*), *Pegeen Fitzgerald, *Robert Heckert, Efrem Zimbalist, Jr., Isaac Bashevis Singer (*The Seance*), Ray Muncy, Gloria Swanson, Ethel Fairmont Beebe, Ethel Young and Ella May Stoneburner (General Conference of Seventh Day Adventists), Richard N. Schwarz, *Nellie Shriver (Vegetarian Collective), *Dudley Giehl (Animal Liberation), Hope Sawyer Buyukmihci (Beaver Defenders), Ronald Gotessman (University of Wisconsin) Glyndon G. Van Deusen, Jules Archer (*Fighting Journalist*), Hannah-Josephson, Will Durant, Norman D. Ford, Jesse Mercer Gehman (Am. Veg. Union), Harry L. Gage, Jay and Freya Dinshah (Am. Vegan Society), James Coburn, Walter Matthau, Leon A. Harris, Jr. (*Upton Sinclair*), *Bob Cummings, and Mary McCarthy (*The Birds of America*).

Chapter 9. Leo Tolstoy and the Doukhobors

Alexandra L. Tolstoy through her secretary Catherine Wolkonsky (Prof. Emeritus Vassar College), *Sula Benet (*Abkhasians: Long Living People of the Caucauses*), *Ann Dunnigan, Henry Bailey Stevens (*Tolstoi*), George Woodcock, and David Magarshack (*Gogol*).

Chapter 10. Nutritional Controversies

R. W. Bray and Norman F. Olson (U. of Wisconsin-Madison), Grace A. Goldsmith (dir. Grad. Program in Nutrition, Tulane U.), Stuart Smith (Dept. of Agri. Economics, Cornell U.), John C. Caygill, Victor H. Campbell, D. A. T. Southgate, John Yudkin, D. S. Kronfeld, Frank Wokes, Frey R. Ellis, Michael Jacobson (*Nutrition Scoreboard*), Derik B. Jelliffe (Caribbean Food and Nutrition Institute), Gerald Dryer (National Milk Producers Federation), Edwin S. Rubenstein (Columbia U.), Robyn C. Baugham (Nat. Agricultural Library), Pamela Mumford, Jean Steckle (International Development Research Centre, Senegal), and O. L. Oke (U. of Ife).

Chapter 11. Summing Up

Anna Freud, *Phyllis Greenacre (*Emotional Growth*), Lyall Watson, *Reuben Fine (*Freud: A Critical Re-evaluation of His Theories*), John Gunn (*Violence*), *William and Clare Russell (*Social Biology*), *Cleve Backster, William H. Smith (The Menninger Clinic), Erich Fromm, and Edward A. Dreyfus (*Youth: Search for Meaning*).

Index

Q

R

S

W

Y

Z